DEEP TRAILS IN THE OLD WEST

DEEP TRAILS
IN THE
Old West
A Frontier Memoir

by
FRANK CLIFFORD

Edited by
FREDERICK NOLAN

UNIVERSITY OF OKLAHOMA PRESS : NORMAN

Also by Frederick Nolan

The Lincoln County War: A Documentary History (Norman, 1992)

Bad Blood: The Life and Times of the Horrell Brothers (Stillwater, 1994)

The West of Billy the Kid (Norman, 1998)

(Ed.) *Pat F. Garrett's "The Authentic Life of Billy, the Kid"* (Norman, 2000)

Tascosa: Its Life and Gaudy Times (Lubbock, 2007)

(Ed.) *The Billy the Kid Reader* (Norman, 2007)

LIBRARY OF CONGRESS CATALOGING-IN-PUBLICATION DATA

Clifford, Frank, 1860–1946.
  Deep trails in the old West : a frontier memoir / by Frank Clifford ; edited by Frederick Nolan.
    p. cm.
  Includes bibliographical references and index.
  ISBN 978-0-8061-4186-2 (cloth)
  ISBN 978-0-8061-6506-6 (paper)
  1. Clifford, Frank, 1860–1946. 2. Southwest, New—History—1848—
Biography. 3. Billy, the Kid—Friends and associates. 4. Frontier and pioneer
life—Southwest, New. 5. Southwest, New—History—1848– 6. Cowboys—
Southwestern States—Biography. 7. Frontier and pioneer life—Southwestern
States. 8. Emporia (Kan.)—Biography. I. Nolan, Frederick W., 1931– II. Title.
  F786.C584 2011
  978.1′02—dc22

                                                    2011004070

The paper in this book meets the guidelines for permanence and durability of the Committee on Production Guidelines for Book Longevity of the Council on Library Resources, Inc. ∞

Copyright © 2011 by the University of Oklahoma Press, Norman, Publishing Division of the University. Manufactured in the U.S.A. Paperback published 2020. All rights reserved.

CONTENTS

ILLUSTRATIONS

EDITOR'S INTRODUCTION

Once upon a yesterday, there were any number of autobiographical memoirs by one-time cowboys, lawmen, and the like, each telling the "I was there" story of their life on the frontier. Many of them featured the life and career of Billy the Kid, written by men who "knew" him—beginning with Pat Garrett and his "authentic life" and going on to include George Coe, Miguel A. Otero, Charles A. Siringo, John W. Poe, Henry Hoyt, and R. B. Townshend, to name but a few. But as the world turned, and the old-timers died off one by one, it did not seem likely that there could ever be any more. Then some years ago I found myself in correspondence with Michael Winter in Arkansas, who told me that his family owned an unpublished memoir written by his great-grandfather that described his involvement (as "Frank Wightman") in the Colfax County War with Clay Allison, his experiences (as "Frank Clifford") with Billy the Kid and Charlie Siringo, and his cowboying on the Bell Ranch, gold-mining, Indian fighting, and engaging in quite a few other exploits before he quit the frontier life, changed his name yet again—this time to John Francis (or J. Frank or Frank) Wallace—and moved to Emporia, Kansas.

The family's possessing such a treasure seemed impossible, and yet it was true. There was plenty of evidence that a Frank Clifford had indeed been one of the Panhandle cowboys sent into New Mexico in 1880 to recover cattle stolen by Billy the Kid and his compañeros, references to him in books by Siringo and in other accounts of the events of that time, and more than enough corroboration of his life in Emporia as John Francis Wallace.

Reading the memoir, I was struck (and still am) most strongly by how, back then, by doing no more than ride a hundred miles or so in any direction, a man could completely reinvent himself, no questions asked. Whatever name he gave, whatever his backstory or lack of it, he was accepted at face value. In that America, if he was willing to work hard and make good, he could put down roots and become a respected member of that community.

And that was precisely what Frank Clifford did. Why he chose to settle in Emporia, Kansas, he never revealed. But as John Francis Wallace, he found work, a wife, and a way up from nothing to a responsible position on the council of his adopted city. And somehow, for more than forty years, he kept most of the truth about his birth, his background, and his adventures in New Mexico and elsewhere concealed from his family and everyone else. It was only in the very last years of his life that he decided to set down his story—or at least as much of the story as he wanted them to know.

In 1940, on a train journey from Little Rock, Arkansas, to Wichita, Kansas, the eighty-one-year-old retired railroader J. Frank Wallace struck up a conversation with Mrs. H. B. (Genevieve) Frickel, an amateur portrait painter with a studio on Main Street in Wichita. So interesting were the old man's stories about his life in the early West that Mrs. Frickel asked him to sit for a portrait, and a few months later her oil painting of this "typical American pioneer" won first prize in a contest for Wichita women artists. She persuaded Wallace to tell her the story of his life on the frontier as she painted, with his granddaughter, Mary Frances, recording it in shorthand. If any questions arose, Mary simply checked with her grandfather and amended accordingly. It seems more than likely that the family intended it for publication, but it never happened.

The manuscript remained in possession of the Wallace family, "lost" but intact, for more than fifty years, and it was not until Wallace's great-grandson Michael Winter retired from the army and, aided by his father, Elmer Winter, determined to see what he could find out about the old man's life and origins. In Colfax County, New Mexico, and in Monmouthshire, Wales, they found records indicating that his name had actually been John Menham Wightman. Further research conducted into English census records, in South Wales, and at the school where both John Wightman and his brother Sinclair were educated, confirmed the Winters' findings.

John Menham Wightman was born March 18, 1860, at Panteg, a small village near the coal-mining and ironworking town of Pontypool in southeastern Wales. His father, James Temple (sometimes Templar) Wightman, born in Newcastle-on-Tyne around 1821, was at various times in his life a coal merchant, colliery owner, mineral agent, and mining engineer who married Sarah Walker, daughter of a Worcestershire-born farmer. There were six children. The first two, James, born in 1850, and Jane Anne, born the following year, died within ten days of each other in October 1853. Another daughter, Marianne Isabella, was born in 1855; another daughter Kate in 1858; a son, Sinclair (sometimes given as St. Clair) Walker, was born in 1859; and John Menham was born two years later. All were baptized at St. Cadoc's Church in Trevethin (Trefddyn in Welsh).

James Wightman prospered; by 1861, he owned his own colliery business and employed a live-in governess for his children and two local young women as servants at his Blaendare farm. In addition, he provided a home for his seventy-five-year-old father-in-law, Richard

Walker. The family soon moved to the Wern House that Wallace remembered so vividly, where Sarah Wightman died on October 25, 1866. Two years later Wightman sent his two sons to board at St. Saviour's School in Shoreham, a small seaside town on the south coast of England. Founded by Canon Nathaniel Woodard in 1858, the school's aim was "to provide education based on sound principle and sound knowledge, firmly grounded in the Christian faith." By 1868, when eleven-year-old Sinclair and seven-year-old John enrolled, the school had moved from its original location to a 196-acre estate south of the village of Ardingly.

The boys remained there—indeed, Sinclair became a prefect—until 1871, when their father was employed by the Maxwell Land Grant & Railway Company and the family emigrated to Cimarron, New Mexico. For some reason, Kate Wightman stayed behind; it is possible that she suffered from mental illness and needed care, because when she died in 1910, she was living in an asylum.

James Temple Wightman died in September of 1874. Where or with whom his children went to live then is not recorded, but the following year, the family seems to have broken up. On June 2, 1875, Marianne, now nineteen, married John Walters at Cimarron; the officiating pastor was Rev. Franklin J. Tolby. Their five-month-old son, John Frederick Walters, died at Cimarron on August 6, 1876. Some time before 1881 the couple returned to Wales. John Walters died at Usk, near Pontypool, on April 24, 1931; his wife, Marianne, died November 20, 1948. Altogether there were nine children; a son, Henry, was killed in 1915 during World War I at the age of twenty-six.

On May 10, 1875, just a month before his sister's wedding, nineteen-year-old Sinclair Walker Wightman filed on a 160-acre homestead in Colfax County. The 1880 census shows him as a twenty-four-year-old unmarried farmer employing a thirty-six-year-old Scottish-born farmhand named David Y. Bradford. What became of him thereafter neither history nor his brother record; even his grave in the Cimarron cemetery is gone.

Behind these bare facts lie several mysteries. Why did John Menham Wightman sever all connection with his brother and sisters (or they with him)? What did he do, what sins did he commit, that made it necessary for him to become a cowboy drifter using a succession of false names? Why did he never tell his wife, his children, or his grandchildren the whole truth about his early life and upbringing? We will probably never know; like a lot of men who had lived the kind of life he had lived, John Francis Wallace chose to take his secrets with him to the grave.

"For secrets are edged tools
And must be kept from children and from fools."
John Dryden (1631–1700)

FREDERICK NOLAN
Chalfont St. Giles, England

ACKNOWLEDGMENTS

It is thanks to the determination and persistence of Michael Winter and his father, Elmer, great grandson and grandson of its author, that this unique addition to the eyewitness history of the American frontier finally sees the light of day. The hard work they did to establish something of the truth behind the story of John Francis Wallace made it very easy for me to put the rest of the story together. Others whose invaluable contributions helped to fill in some of the gaps include Kenneth R. Bailey, West Virginia Historical Society; the late Alice Blakestad, Hondo, New Mexico; Harold "Lee" Edwards, Bakersfield, California; Michelle Enke, Wichita Public Library, Wichita, Kansas; Elvis E. Fleming, Historical Society of Southeastern New Mexico, Roswell; Roberta Haldane, Tijeras, New Mexico; the late Duane Hale, Roswell, New Mexico; Robert A. Hodge, Lyon County Historical Society, Emporia, Kansas; Chuck Hornung, Odessa, Texas; Andrea King, Archivist, Ardingly College, Haywards Heath, West Sussex, England; Gene Lamm, Cimarron, New Mexico; Nancy Brown Martinez, Center for Southwest Research, University of New Mexico, Albuquerque; Jim McKinney Vallejo, California; Ivy Naude, West of the Pecos Museum, Pecos, Texas; Chuck Parsons, Luling, Texas; Charles Riggs, Wells Fargo Historical Services, San Francisco, California; Nancy Robertson, Raton, New Mexico; Richard Roynon, Talywain, Monmouthshire, Wales;

Gregory Scott Smith, Jemez, New Mexico; Nancy Sherbert, Curator of Photographs and Special Collections Acquisitions, State Archives and Library, Kansas State Historical Society, Topeka; Russ Taylor, Supervisor of Reference Services, Perry Special Collections, Harold B. Lee Library, Brigham Young University, Provo, Utah; Frances Younson, Archivist, Gwent Record Office, Cwmbran, South Wales; and last and most especially Robert G. McCubbin, Santa Fe, New Mexico, without whose enthusiasm for it this memoir might still be waiting to be published.

EDITORIAL NOTE

While I have tried hard not to impose myself too frequently upon the narrative that follows, I have, in order to distance them slightly from the story itself, italicized the introductions to each chapter contributed by Genevieve Frickel and/or Mary Wallace. I have also added bracketed corrections of incorrect facts or misguided observations made by the narrator and have standardized inconsistencies in those places where he—or they—have been careless or cavalier with capitalization or inconsistent with quotation marks. Other than this very minor fine-tuning, nothing has been changed or omitted from the original text.

DEEP TRAILS IN THE OLD WEST

Preface

If you expect to get a hair raising account of the ways and customs of the Old West, you will probably be disappointed in this book. I have a few sorta thrilling experiences which I have related, but mostly it is just a simple account of the ways of the Old West. I have read three of Charles A. Siringo's books of his life, and I was mentioned in each, but in his second book he, having lost all track of me, disposed of me by saying that I had "turned outlaw" and been killed in Old Mexico. In his book "Riata and Spurs," [*A Lone Star Cowboy*] he had me jump into the Pecos River with all my cloths [*sic*] on, and yell, "Hurrah for Billy the Kid!" Now neither of these stories are true, as I am still alive and kicking sixty years after I was supposed to be killed and, while I do not claim that I was wise in the old days, I never was a big enough fool to jump into any river with my cloths on.

Charlie Siringo and I were close friends in those days, and would have fought for one another at the drop of a hat! But, he made a great many errors in his last book. Another mistake he made was in saying that we went to the "Kid's" hideout on our way back to Texas. I never saw that old stone shanty, although I should have liked to. He was inaccurate in other things, such as certain details of his story of my mix-up with the school-master at White Oaks, which I have told in this book.

I am giving you the high spots and the low spots of my life just as it happened—even giving you the names of folks I met in both lives, for I have lived two different kinds of lives here in my time.

I have tried to be as truthful as possible. If I was in doubt about something, I have said so. I have had to go back a long ways for some of these memories, but they are as clear to me today as they were sixty years ago in the Old West.

John Francis Wallace, April 21, 1942.

CHAPTER ONE

Early Days in Cimarron

EDITOR'S NOTE

When New Mexico became part of the United States in 1848, something like 150 private land grants lay within its borders; by 1865, the largest of them all—indeed, the largest ever— was the Maxwell Land Grant, owned by Lucien Bonaparte Maxwell. He lived like a feudal baron in a twenty-room mansion beside the Cimarron River, where often thirty and more guests dined at his lavish table. He raced fine horses and gambled heavily; thousands of dollars could change hands in his gaming rooms in a single evening. He owned a thousand horses, ten thousand cattle, and thirty thousand sheep, and he employed five hundred men.

In 1867, when gold was discovered on the slopes of Mount Baldy in the heart of his domain, Maxwell profited from the gold rush both as entrepreneur and investor. By 1870, his rough-hewn empire was making so much money—his majority stake in the Aztec quartz mine was contributing nearly $50,000 a year, his sawmill at Ute Creek another $20,000, not to mention further substantial sums from the sale of farms, mining claims, and land—that the huge potential of the Maxwell Land Grant attracted the attention of capitalists both at home and abroad.

That same year, Maxwell entered into a series of complex negotiations that, in spite of uncertainties about the actual size of his holdings and the validity of his title, resulted a year later in the sale of the grant to an English company for $1,350,000. Shortly thereafter, the Maxwell Land Grant & Railway Company was organized under American trusteeship, the stocks and bonds being held by American, English, and Dutch investors.

The new owners, understandably eager to secure clear title to, and profit from, the grant's land, water, and mineral rights, proceeded as though there was no uncertainty about their claim to the vast acreage involved. They soon discovered that many of the settlers living on the grant refused to recognize the company's title or to surrender the mining claims, farms, or ranches the company had established.

Disinclined to negotiate, the company, backed by the notorious Santa Fe Ring, embarked upon a vigorous campaign of legal expulsions to get rid of the settlers, but when eviction notices were served rebellion flared. On October 27, 1870, rioting Elizabethtown miners set fire to the homes of their foes; troops had to be sent in to restore peace. The following April, an armed mob took possession of the Maxwell Company's property; this time, the governor of New Mexico hurried to the scene to restore order. The miners agreed to stand down but made it clear that they would not quit their claims until the company proved its title was valid. More violence lay ahead.

It was at this juncture that former coal colliery owner and mining engineer James Temple Wightman arrived in

New Mexico with his daughter Marianne Isabella, sixteen, and two young sons, Sinclair, fifteen, and John, eleven. Given the company's energetic mining activities, it is not too difficult to guess what duties his "high position" might have involved.

Wightman would have doubtless soon become aware of the difficulties that his employers were facing as they zealously pursued their policy of forced evictions. The incident described below, in which two men came to kill Wightman, must have happened quite soon after his arrival; the men involved would almost certainly have been anti-grant, so could it perhaps have been an attempt to scare him off? It is important to keep in mind also that at the time it happened, the narrator would have been only eleven years old.

"Some time," said Mr. Wallace, settling himself more comfortably in the old wing chair, "I should like to see a hand-carved ivory fan, such as my mother used to carry. I hadn't thought of it for years, but lately, sitting and thinking about this and that, it came to my mind—the memory of mother's hand-carved ivory fan."

"Did she carry it on the plains with her?" I [Mrs. Frickel] asked, wondering at the connection of a former cow-hand with a hand-carved ivory fan. I was at that time completely ignorant of his story, and, I must confess, of that part of the country which [had been] the setting of his life in New Mexico and Texas.

"Oh, no," he answered, "she was never in America. She died when I was about six years old [on October 25, 1866]."

We lived then in England, on a handsome country estate. I remember [a] butler, maids, footmen, gardeners, and grooms. I remember a fine large house, beautifully furnished. I remember my grandfather, a white-haired old man, holding me on his knee when I was a little chap of three or four, telling me with great pride that we were descended from Sir William Wallace, the famous Scottish hero. He always seemed to be proud of our lineage. He had a genealogy of our family tree, and used to read to me from it.

Our home in England was called "The Wern," and it was located in Monmouthshire [in Wales, not England]. I remember this because I had to address my letters that way when I was off at school. The house was large and very beautiful, and there was a terraced garden beside the driveway. The garden was really lovely. The first terrace was devoted to flowers and shrubs and lawn, the second was a vegetable garden.

The driveway curved into the estate beside a high stone wall. Broken glass was sunk into the top of the wall along its entire length—just huge broken chunks of sharp glass which would have seriously injured anyone trying to climb the wall. I have often wondered why it was there, for my father's brother lived on the other estate located beyond the wall. I finally decided that it must have been placed there because of a quarrel, and it wouldn't surprise me to learn that my father did it! He was a very proud and stubborn man. If he thought he was right, nothing could move him.

I am certain that the wall and garden were located beside the driveway, because I remember standing there one day and watching one of the grooms riding a horse down this driveway. He was having trouble, for the horse had bolted and the groom couldn't stop him. Just as they reached [the] stables, the horse suddenly halted, and threw his rider over his head. It didn't hurt the groom and I was highly amused. I have often wished that I had a picture of the old place. I can still see it in my memory, but it would be a pleasure to know that it is still there, and still the same.

When I was eleven years of age, my father brought me across the ocean and out to New Mexico. I remember crossing Kansas in a train, and seeing my first herd of buffalo through the train windows. The train had to stop to let them pass over the tracks, for you know, the buffalo will not turn. When their heads are set to go a certain way, they will keep on that way and nothing can change their direction. It was a marvelous sight to a young boy to see that great herd of shaggy beasts, several miles wide and reaching all the way back to the horizon, coming along in waves the way they do—wave after wave like the waves of the ocean.

We took the stage [probably from Kit Carson] over the Raton Pass, and eventually we arrived in Cimarron. There my father had a very high position with the Maxwell Land Grant and Railway Company. I suppose you know what that is, and the place the Maxwell family played in the early days of old [New] Mexico?

At my confession of ignorance [Mrs. Frickel said,] he shook his head in mock reproof, and settled himself back to talk and smoke.

"My father and I," he told me, "lived in the old Maxwell house, which at that time was a sort of hotel for the officials of the company."[1]

It stood in the little town of Cimarron, then county seat of Colfax county, New Mexico, [Cimarron became the county seat in 1872] which is built on the Cimarron River a couple of miles down from the mouth of the canyon at the edge of the foothills of the Rockies, where the topography changes abruptly from mountain to prairie. On crossing the river from the east by way of the old stage road, you were at once in the main square of the town. [Henry M.] Porter and [Asa] Middaugh's general store was on the east side of the square. The printing office of the local newspaper, the Cimarron News and Press [founded in January 1875] was situated between that store and the bridge which crossed the Cimarron River. On the north [*sic*, west] side of the square stood the old Lucien B. Maxwell house. To the west and northwest [*sic*, southwest] of the square were the smaller stores, saloons, and so forth, of the business section. This was table-land, or rather second-bottom-land, flat and smooth for about a quarter mile from the river. There a long mesa stood. I remember an amusing incident concerning this mesa.

A couple of Englishmen went up on the mesa one day to practice rifle shooting. They had their target between them and the town below. After firing they found themselves surrounded by a hastily-gathered-up posse from town. Their bullets had gone whining over the town, and the "cits" [citizens] thought it was Indians attacking.* A few drinks all around and a big laugh closed the incident.

Over towards the southeast there was a double mountain about three [ten] miles from the foothills. These twin hills were called the "Cedar Hills," as they were covered with cedars. I have ridden to the top many times to enjoy the view, which could be seen for miles in any direction. To the [south-]west of Cimarron about three [*sic*, ten] miles, the Cimarroncito Creek ran. The sheriff, Joe Holbrook, lived

---

*At the time, Cimarron was the agency headquarters for the Mohuache Ute and Jicarilla Apache reservation; it was relocated in 1875.

on that creek.² There was fine rainbow trout fishing up in the foothills on the Cimarroncito, and no fish and game laws existed. I soon found that out, and availed myself of the knowledge. This creek was so narrow that I could jump across it almost anywhere in the upper canyon, but it was nevertheless alive with rainbow trout. I used to catch a hundred-pound flour sack full some days, using a sapling pole and a piece of line, with grasshoppers for bait.

A lot of choke-cherries were growing not far from the mouth of the Cimarroncito canyon, and it was not uncommon for me to disturb a black bear feeding on the fruit when it was ripe. Down below Cimarron there was a large patch of wild yellow plums, small trees but full of fruit. They could be raked off by the handfuls, and were very sweet. I would usually manage to strip these trees as soon as they got ripe. It was the only patch of wild yellow plums I ever saw, although there were many patches of wild red plums along the creeks outside of the mountains.

I was treated like a young prince in those days. I always had a horse to ride whenever I wanted him, and I wanted him often, for I rode constantly, which explains my familiarity with that country. Even after my father's death, the folks thereabouts treated me royally, and I never wanted for a place to stay, nor for grub and provisions.

The old Maxwell house, in which Father and I lived, was really a palace for that country in those days. It had a wide porch about five feet above the level of the square. From this porch the front door opened into a large living room. A great fireplace with a beautifully decorated mantel-place added glamour to this room, which was filled with costly furniture. Below that floor was a full basement, as the ground on the east [*sic,* north] dropped sharply to the river. This made the Maxwell house in effect a two story house [with 22 rooms].* The basement was also divided into several rooms, which were completely furnished. Lucien B. Maxwell himself I never met, as he had moved away from Cimarron before I got there. Old Lucien went to New Mexico as a young man, and married the daughter of the old Spanish Don, Beaubien y Quintana, or Beaubien, as they usually called him thereabouts. You know, the Spanish names are compounded from the two names of the parents. In this case, "Beaubien" was the father's name, and "Quintana" the mother's; "y" of course means "and." The land constituting the Beaubien y Quintana ranch was the original Spanish land grant. It spread out for sixty-six square leagues, which was quite a lot of country even in those days. Old Lucien Maxwell—young Maxwell then—married the ranch and they threw in the girl, so folks said in Cimarron.[3] However that may be, he owned the whole three hundred [and] eighty thousand some odd [1,714,764.93] acres, until the English company bought it from him.

I was told that Lucien Maxwell was at one time a frontier scout and a sort of side kick to Kit Carson, and was himself a picturesque character. I heard at the time several stories concerning him which entertained me highly. One such incident concerned a rather pompous Englishman who was making an exploring trip over New Mexico. One evening he reached Cimarron and asked at Maxwell's house if he could put up there for the night. Maxwell made him welcome and next morning when the Englishman was ready to leave, he asked for his bill. Maxwell laughed at him good-naturedly and explained that there was never any charge at his house for a night's lodging. The Englishman protested, not being used to the ways of the West.

---

*Maxwell's enclave was actually two large houses facing each other; between the houses and enclosed by a high adobe wall was a large, open courtyard.

He said he wanted to pay for his lodging. Maxwell again refused—it was unheard-of then to accept money for hospitality—but the Englishman insisted, and even stated heatedly that he wasn't begging his way! So Maxwell, who was standing with his back to the fireplace which had a fire burning in it, coolly told his guest, "All right then, it's twenty dollars." The Englishman was game, and he handed Maxwell a twenty-dollar bill. Maxwell turned around, stooped over, and deliberately laid the bill on the burning logs. That ended the dispute.

Another story I heard about Maxwell had to do with old man [Henry] Pascoe. When Pascoe first came to New Mexico, he looked around for a location, and found what he wanted in what was then called the Merino valley, between Cimarron and Taos. As this piece of land was on the Maxwell Land Grant, Pascoe went to see Maxwell about it. Pascoe had a sort of whine in his speech which made him seem to be half-crying when he talked, especially if he was at all excited. Maxwell asked him what he wanted, and he answered in that peculiar way, "Why, Mistah Maxwell," he quavered, "I want to settle in the Merino valley!"

"Well," Maxwell boomed out at him. "What do you expect to do there, and how are you fixed to do it?"

"Well, Mistah Maxwell," answered Pascoe, "I got quite a family, sah. I hain't got no boys, just the old woman and ten gyurls, and sixteen head of cows, and they are all fresh, and I thought I would start a dairy," he finished, all in that half-crying voice of his. Maxwell looked him straight in the eye without a smile, and said, "Well! If you are in that kind of a shape, I think it's the best business you can get into. Go on! Go on and settle there!" Pascoe did settle there, and was living there when I was in Cimarron. I met several of his girls later, after they were married. They were a fine capable lot of women. I remember that [Deputy] Sheriff Joe Holbrook's wife was one of them. I am not sure of the exact number of girls in the family, but it was close enough to ten for me to feel justified in putting it that way.[4]

While we are on the subject of Pascoe, I may as well tell of a personal experience I had with him. I found out early that, in spite of his white hair and querulous voice, he was not a man to be fooled with. I was about fourteen years old at the time, and one day when I was riding in the Cimarron canyon above Ute Creek, I met the old man. He stopped me and asked if I had seen anything of a stray horse around anywhere. "I lost mine las' night," he whispered in that half-crying voice. This struck me funny, and as I was pretty sassy in those days, I answered drawlingly, "Waa-al, Mistah Pascoe, I wouldn't worry about that, you'll find him all right. I wouldn't cry about it if I were you." Now the old man had one of those bull-whips hanging from the horn of his saddle. It was about fifteen feet long, with a short handle, and could be used very effectively by him.

"Why, you so-and-so, blankety-blank-blank-blank!" he yelped, loosening his whip. "I'll show you who's doin' the cryin' around here." I thought it was time to get out of the way, and started down the canyon, the old man right behind me, and it seemed as if that whip was popping within a few inches of my back, but my pony outran his, and I turned up Ute Creek, and the first chance I got, when I was far enough ahead of him, I wheeled into some timber and kept mighty still, letting him ride ahead of me. Soon as he had passed my hiding-place, I hopped out again and streaked it down the canyon for Cimarron. I never fooled with that old man again.

Pascoe was still in Cimarron when I lived there, but Maxwell had left after he sold the land grant to a company of Englishmen called "the English Company." They gave their concern the imposing name of the "Maxwell Land Grant and English Company," and stocked the land with cattle, sheep, and horses at what seemed to them favorable locations. It was the formation of this company that brought my father to New Mexico as a high official.

There was quite a controversy between the men who wanted to settle up the country and the members of "the English Company" as to the size of the original land grant. The old Don had always claimed it was sixty-six leagues square, but the settlers claimed it was sixty-six square leagues! If they were right, it would leave much of the originally claimed grants public domain, open for settlement. Also, it would locate some very valuable coal deposits outside the grant as originally claimed. This controversy dragged through the courts for several years. I am not sure which side won in the end, but I think the settlers did.[5]

I never knew exactly where the boundary lines of the land grant ran, as accepted in those days, but they went fairly close to where the town of Raton, New Mexico, now is. There was no town there then. There was only the Red River stage station.[6] It was on the Red River, which changed its name to the North Fork of the Canadian River when it came out of the lower end of the canyon at Fort Bascom.

In another direction the land grant took in Old Baldy mountain, said at the time to be the tallest mountain in New Mexico. On the side of this mountain was the Aztec gold mine, and maybe a mile or so across the gulch was another mine, the Montezuma. These mines were at the head of Ute creek. There was a stamp mill at the Aztec mine, and water for the use of the mill was brought around the mountain from Ponil Creek in a ditch. Water from the ditch was also used to wash out placer gold near the log house at Aztec. I don't know how rich these mines were, as I was too young then to be interested in that angle. But, as I never read anything about them later in the papers, I suppose they were not bonanzas.* The peak of Old Baldy towered hundreds of feet above timber line. I was [so] intrigued by it that I couldn't be satisfied until I had climbed to the top. At that time they claimed the altitude was over fourteen thousand feet, but I notice now the maps call it close to thirteen thousand [12,441 feet]. Be that as it may, I had never seen anything so imposing. One day two of us started out to climb it. We took our lunch with us, and when we had got to the top and rested, we ate it and looked around a bit. I noticed particularly that there was water-washed gravel at the very top of the peak. Pebbles, round and smoothed by the action of running water, where no water had been for ages. At one place, we had to run across a gravel bed which sloped toward a sheer, steep cliff. When we walked on it, the gravel would commence to flow down towards the cliff, so we had to run to keep from sliding over.

From the top of the peak, we could see for miles around. I don't know how far, but it was an impressive view. I do know that we could see for long distances in that country. Long afterwards, I saw the reflection of the sun on the windows in the house located on the side of Old Baldy when I was below Cimarron, at a point which was at least thirty miles away from the house.

This house was a two-story log building, a very fine dwelling except that it was built of logs. It was well-made and roomy, and well-furnished. My father and I lived there when he went up to manage the two mines. The side of the mountain had been dug out so that the floor could be leveled off, and a passage to the kitchen was dug

---

*In fact, these mines were some of the richest in the Elizabethtown mining district.

right out through the ground. One day while we were there, lightning struck a pine tree nearby and threw kindling slabs over into the entrance passage. We had to clear away the slabs before we could use the passage, but we were grateful for the kindling as well as for the escape from more serious consequences.

While we were living in that house, an incident occurred that has always stuck in my memory. We were lounging in the sitting-room one evening shortly after dark. A knock came at the door. When I opened it, two men walked in. They were fully armed, their guns strapped to their hips. After a few minutes of talking, they told my father they had come up on purpose to kill him. He had no weapon on him. His six-shooter was on a shelf near where the men were seated. He argued with them about it, and read them a lecture on their way of living. He really told them about it, and actually made them ashamed of themselves.

My father was not afraid of anything. He sat and talked to those two killers calmly and coolly, without raising his voice, as if it didn't matter much anyhow. Apparently he really showed them the error of their ways, for they got to talking like human beings and finally gave up entirely the idea of shooting my father, and bade us good night. Later we found out that they had been companions of Tom Taylor and "Coal Oil Jimmy [Buckley]," who had been killed for the reward offered by "the English Company." The two outlaws had come up that night with the intention of getting even by wiping out my father, who was one of the head officers of the company.

There was a lot of stock rustling as a matter of course from "the English Company," and Tom Taylor and "Coal Oil Jimmy," (whose real name I never heard) were two of the worst of the rustlers. They got so bold that the company put up a reward of $1000 [$600] apiece for them, dead or alive. This reward tempted a couple of fellows [Joe McCurdy or McIntyre and John or Frank Stewart] who had previously been in cahoots with them, to go to their hideout, and when they were caught off guard, to shoot them down. It was of course pure treachery. Taylor even had on his gauntlet gloves when he died. The last time I ever saw Tom Taylor and "Coal Oil Jimmy" was when the fellows who killed them brought their bodies into Cimarron in a lumber wagon, and collected the two thousand dollars reward.[7]

I had seen Taylor several times before. I was appointed as mail carrier for the mines, a job which paid me two dollars a week. I'd have been glad to do it for nothing for the rambling around I got out of it. I used to pack mail for everybody between the mines and Ute Creek post office. The creek runs straight on up the canyon between Elizabethtown and Taos, and this was a little branch route turning off from the main one.

There were about fifty Cornish miners that the English Company had transported to work the mines. Most of them had left their families back in Cornwall, England. They were always glad to get mail from home, and of course I was always welcome at their camp. I got along well with them, and they always seemed glad to have me stop and eat with them. They were a very religious group of men, and as near as I can remember resembled the Quakers in their ways. One Sunday (of course none of them worked on Sunday) they had a peculiar experience. They all ate in a large mess hall, which was close beside a little branch of a creek. They had excavated a place in the bank, and let the water run through to make a little cooling house, walled up with rough, fairly large, rocks. On the Sunday mentioned, one of the miners went down to get the milk, or butter, and bring it back to the cook who had everything on the table ready for them to eat. When the miner came back he was carrying a small striped animal by the tail. He explained that he had seen this tail sticking out through the rocks and had pulled on the tail till the animal came out. Carrying the little creature, he walked back through the hall and in his broad Cornish brogue said, "Eh, lads! See what a bloody purty kitty I found!" and lowered it to the floor. The "kitty" immediately advertised the fact that it wasn't a kitty! Indeed it seemed to resent being called a kitty! The Cornishman had never seen a skunk before. His mates ran him out, and none of them ate in the mess hall that day.

To return to Tom Taylor, whom I saw several times while I was carrying mail on this route, there was a log house which had probably been built by some old miner who had abandoned it and was now occupied by a band of outlaws; all on the dodge. Philo Weaver was one of them, and Tom Taylor was another. I frequently ate a meal with them, and got along with them all right. I have often wondered if this had any bearing on my father's escape from the two desperados who were going to shoot him, as they were among this band and acquainted with me through my office as mail carrier.

My father was not quite so tall nor large as I am, but he was built like me. He was a very dominating man, in that he expected his word to be final in affairs that concerned him. He was too ignorant of conditions in that country to be afraid, as the following incident shows. There was a fellow [called Francis Clutton, formerly manager of the Grant-owned Maxwell Cattle Company, or Long H outfit] living in a rude cabin on the Cimarroncito (the little Cimarron) creek, where outlaws were always welcome. Although he sold whiskey, the place couldn't correctly be called a saloon. It was mostly just a hangout for outlaws. One day my father got word that an outlaw who had been preying on the company's stock and was wanted badly, was at the place. So my father immediately got the [Deputy] Sheriff (Joe Holbrook) to go with him and they rode out to capture the outlaw. Now there was a piece of open prairie perhaps a hundred and fifty yards wide in front of this hut. No one should have been expected to ride up and arrest an outlaw unless the outlaw wanted to be arrested. He would have all the opportunity he needed to shoot them down before they had crossed the clearing. Joe Holbrook should have known this, but I suppose he didn't want to seem afraid in front of my father. So he ignored the danger and when they saw a horse hitched to the rail in front of the hut, and my father cried "He's there! Come on, let's go get him!" Holbrook went with him, and they rode together to the door of the hangout.

Well, it wasn't the rustler's horse. He had left a little while before, and the horse which was tied to the hitching-rail belonged to some other fellow. I heard much laughing about this incident during the next few days in Cimarron. Nobody laughed at my father's courage, for he had plenty of that; but everybody was highly entertained by his ignorance. They had a high respect for bravery, and that he would have shot it out with any of them. Yet, any of those fellows could have hit him three times before he could have got out his gun.

Along these lines, I am reminded of a duel which took place about that time between two Englishmen, employees of the English Company. One night while "under the influence" they quarreled, and one of them challenged the other to a duel. The next day, everything having been arranged in advance, they faced one another at twenty paces, got their instructions from their seconds, and at the word to fire one of them emptied his six-shooter as fast as he could, the other standing motionless, seemingly too surprised to shoot. When the first one had emptied his gun, he cussed and threw it on the ground and started to walk away. The other, who had not had his turn, called him back and reminded him of it. So number one turned back and faced his adversary to receive his bullets. Number two took deliberate aim at his rival, held his revolver steady for a few seconds, then raised his hand and shot into the air. The crowd then broke loose, yelling and whooping. The fact that [Deputy] Sheriff Joe Holbrook was one of the seconds ought to have told the duelists that the affair was a farce, as indeed it was. Both pistols had been loaded with blank cartridges! Everyone knew it except the principals. At first they were angry about the trick, but they finally got into a good humor, and didn't have another quarrel while they were in Cimarron.

While we lived on the side of Old Baldy, I used to gather wild red raspberries in season. There was a place where the timber was burnt off, lying between the head of Ute creek and the head of the Ponil, and this place was full of raspberry bushes that I visited regularly when they were ripe. I would bring back a bucketful every trip. They were the finest flavored raspberries I ever ate in my life. Wild gooseberry bushes also grew in the mountains. I found quite a lot of those thickets as I rambled around, and the fruit was really fine eating when ripe. Something else that I remember vividly was a beautiful wild lily growing in a shady draw running down the side of the mountain. It had a brownish center, and streaks of red ran up the white petals. These lilies were very scarce and I never found out the name of them [probably scarlet gaura, *Gaura coccinea*]. I would just look at them and ride on.

In the deep gullies around Old Baldy, snow would pile up in the winter and could be found as late as July, in the shady places where the sun seldom shone. Even if it did strike the slopes where the snow remained, the sun would reach them only a short time during the day, so that the old snow remained most of the summer in those spots.

I was always out with my rifle hunting squirrels and chipmunks, and in my ramblings around I found myself one day on top of one of the smaller mountain peaks near the head of the Ponil creek on one side [east side] of Old Baldy. I happened to let out a yell just for fun. I heard it echo and re-echo from different directions. It beat anything in the line of echoes that I had ever heard, or have heard since. First, after about five seconds, the first echo came back, then at intervals of a few seconds each, other echoes would come from different directions until seven or eight had sounded. Then, after a longer silence of ten or twelve seconds, I would hear the last echo sounding—faintly, yes, but still clear. Sound carries far in those mountains, and I found that if I could get there very early in the morning, I got clearer echoes. I have been there by sunrise, and then it was at its best.

As I recall, it would take a rather tough climb on foot from any point that a motor could reach, but it would be worth the time and trouble, and should be an attraction to many people. I think it would be reached easiest by going over from Ute Creek valley and walking around the mountain. I cannot now tell anyone just how to find the exact spot from which to holler, but it is there and well worth looking for. This echo may be an established attraction now; if not, it should be.

In the fall of 1874, my father took sick with a kind of intestinal disease, and died. He is buried in Cimarron.[8] I stayed on there, and grew up in New Mexico, as I liked the life. A carpenter, a fatherly old fellow who took and interest in me, spoke of my going back to relatives. I must have had rich relatives in England, for my father had at one time been wealthy. The carpenter did speak of receiving letters from some of them, but I wouldn't think of going back, and he didn't press the matter. I stayed in Cimarron until I was about seventeen years old, working on the ranches thereabouts, and in general, having a good time. Clay Allison was a good friend of mine, and I rode with him in some of the stirring incidents of the Colfax county "war." I have often wished that I might go back to Cimarron and nose about the town, and perhaps find some old fellow who lived there when I did, and get him started, talking over old times.

Once, on the way to California, I went through that part of New Mexico. It was not possible for me to stop at Cimarron, but I looked through the window of the train, trying to locate the Cedar Hills. I never caught a glimpse of them, and don't know if they were bare of trees after all of these years, or if it was only that they could not be seen from the train.*

Perhaps it is just as well that I haven't gone back, for time must have worked many changes in the place, and I doubt if there is a soul there who was there when I was. As it is, I can keep clear in my mind the memory of the old frontier town, unconfused by the changes the years have wrought.

---

*The Cedar Hills, located on the plains between the Cimarron and Vermejo rivers about ten miles west of the Santa Fe track, would be hard to see from a fast-moving train.

CHAPTER TWO

The Colfax County War

The new owners of the Maxwell Land Grant soon realized that their dream of fast profits was not going to come true. The Aztec mine that had made Maxwell rich had to be closed down in the face of declining ore values; continuing problems with the Ute and Jicarilla Apache Indians deterred potential settlers from coming in. To add to the company's woes, the panic of 1873, a collapse of the financial sector as catastrophic as that of 2009, rendered the Maxwell Land Grant & Railway Company unable to pay its employees' wages or even its local taxes, and it went bankrupt. This encouraged the beleaguered settlers to believe that they had won and that they could take what they liked and do what they liked, but it was not to be so. The owners of the grant company and their Santa Fe Ring backers had no intention of letting themselves be harassed into surrendering.

The violence that flared up in Colfax County during the 1870s was in no way the lark that the narrator's version of it suggests, but rather the beginning of a long and bitter battle for land rights played out against a background of civil insurrection. Only a few attempts have been made to catalog the numerous killings that happened during the period described here, but it can safely be said that Cimarron was as desperately dangerous a place to live as anywhere in the frontier West. During the years Clifford covers, law and order in Colfax County was virtually nonexistent; for extended periods the town of Cimarron was completely in the hands of and at the mercy of badmen and killers who defied anyone to challenge their right to dispense the rough sort of justice that removed Coal Oil Jimmy and his sidekick Tom Taylor permanently from the annals of Colfax County.

However, despite the fact that Colfax County's records and the files of local newspapers are at best skimpy, some details have been preserved. A hint of how poor an inventory this may be can be found in the fact that in 1901, when Henry Lambert's sons replaced the roof of the St. James Hotel, they found more than four hundred bullet holes in the ceiling above the bar. Today, the ceiling displays only a token twenty-two bullet holes to remind visitors that during the hotel's lifetime twenty-six men died violently there.

Legend has it that in 1870 Clay Allison, recently arrived in Colfax County, led a party that lynched one Charles Kennedy, who had robbed and murdered a number of travelers who had the misfortune to choose his roadside hotel for an overnight stop. Having hanged Kennedy, Allison then decapitated the corpse and impaled the bloody head on a spike outside the St. James Hotel. But legend, as always, is only that: the facts of the matter seem to be that Kennedy was lynched by unknown persons at Elizabethtown on October 7, 1870, and buried there. His head could not have been displayed outside Lambert's hotel for the simple reason that the hotel was not there until 1872.

However, Clay Allison certainly was there, and so was Davy Crockett (not to be confused with the legendary hero of the Alamo although there was a family connection); they would figure largely in the events described—albeit using his own somewhat erratic chronology—by John M. (or, as he seems to have called himself, "Frank") Wightman.

"Did I ever tell you?" asked Mr. Wallace, "about the time we threw the newspaper into the river? Not exactly the paper itself, but the printing press that produced it. It was during the Colfax County 'war,' and perhaps I should start at the beginning of that story, and bring in the printing press at the right place."

Colfax County commenced to be settled up with cowmen.* There were no farms. The only agriculture was being carried on in a few scattered spots under irrigation ditches along the streams, with mostly Mexicans raising small crops of corn, and a little green truck. I remember when corn sold by the barrel.

Dick Steele (he was blind in one eye, and had a fine hay meadow at the junction of the Cimarron and Ponil creeks). [M. M.] Chase and [John B.] Dawson (they had a ranch on the Ponil), Pete Burlison [Burleson], [Irvin W. and Lewis G.] Lacy and [James A.] Coleman, Tony Maloche [Meloche], (his wife [Mary Isbull] weighed a good

---

*The region was first settled by miners in the late summer gold rush of 1866; cattlemen began coming in around 1870–71.

part of a ton), the Noyes brothers, Clay Allison, and several others ran their cattle on open range, and in two or three years' time there were quite a lot of white families scattered around the town. H. N. [Henry M.] Porter and Asa Middaugh had a well-stocked all-around store at Cimarron and did a banking business there. Holbrook was sheriff when I first went there.[1] He was a good man and a good officer. But later, during the Colfax County "war," Jack Rhinehart [sic, Isaiah "Ike" Rinehart] was sheriff, and that was a different story.[2]

The Colfax County "war" was really a revolt by the cowmen and settlers against a political "ring" which was in power in the county [and throughout the Territory]. This "ring" had things fixed up to suit the notion of its members, and it really worked a hardship on the ranchers and settlers. Many people did not approve of the way things were being handled, and among them was a preacher, the Reverend Mr. [Franklin J.] Tolby.[3] This was in the summer of 1875, and the preacher was exposing the "ring" in a St. Louis paper [The New York Sun], as the home paper at Cimarron was under the ring's control. Mr. Tolby preached alternate Sundays at Cimarron and Elizabethtown, and made the trips back and forth on horseback. He started to Elizabethtown one week-end; as usual, but never reached there. His body was found hidden in the brush a couple of days later [September 14, 1875]. He had been shot from ambush.

Of course, the ring was suspected, and the "Law and Order League," which was formed of the cattlemen and the white settlers, got busy. In the course of a week or so, a Mexican [Cruz Vega],[4] who seemed to have a more than usual amount of money and was spending it freely, confessed, after considerable questioning, that he and another Mexican had been hired to kill Mr. Tolby. The Mexican was taken out and lynched [on October 30, 1875], but before he was lynched, he made a full confession.

Just as he was strung up, a rider came up with the news that Sheriff Rhinehart was taking the other Mexican [Manuel Cardinas, who had been arrested on November 5][5] to the Cimarron jail for protection.

Clay Allison,[6] an absolutely fearless man who [had been a strong supporter of the Grant Company but now] was by common consent the leader of the "Law and Order League," shouted, "Come on, boys! We'll see about that." He started his horse on the run, and a few of the men went with him at once. After a short time, the rest followed. The Cimarron jail was built on a flat at the [southern] edge of town, and was surrounded by an adobe [flat stone] wall about eight feet high. The gate by which the enclosure was entered was about half-way between two corners of the [east] wall. There was a young moon, not quite a half-moon yet, but quite bright. Clay, with three of four men, reached the jail before Rhinehart did, and waited at one corner of the wall for the sheriff to come.

When Rhinehart reached there, accompanied by one of his deputies and the Mexican murderer, they dismounted. The deputy held the Mexican by one arm and Rhinehart held the other. Rhinehart started to unlock the gate when Clay stepped out alone and said, "Just a minute, Jack." The three, startled, turned and faced him. Clay shot once, then said, "That's all, boys!" He and his men then rode into town and everybody celebrated in Henry Lambert's saloon. The Reverend Mr. Tolby's death was avenged, for both of his murderers were also dead, and the "ring" had learned its first lesson.

That night several prominent citizens of Cimarron left that part of the country, and as far as I know, they stayed away. One man, however, did not go that night, and the next day a watch of two men was put on him. I remember the name of this man well, but I dislike to put it into a published account.[7] After dinner he sent a Mexican boy to the livery stable for his team and buggy. When the boy brought it to his house, he came out very deliberately with his wife on his arm, helped her into the buggy, and started off leisurely. The two men were following and watching him closely, but they thought he really was taking his wife out for a ride, and they didn't expect what actually happened. As soon as the buggy rounded the bluff and [was] thus out of sight of town, the driver whipped up his team into a run and was really off. The two guards raced back to town and reported what had happened, and a bunch of "Leaguers" followed fast, but could not catch up. He dropped his wife at the home of an old Spanish [Mexican] Don at Ocate [Rayado, where the family still lives], it was Don Jesus Abreu, and managed to get to Fort Union about twenty minutes ahead of the "Leaguers," so he saved his life, but he did not return to Cimarron. I presume he did not consider it a healthy place anymore.

After the more obnoxious of the "ring" leaders had been persuaded to leave, or had been otherwise disposed of, it was decided by the "Law and Order League" that something had to be done to gag the "Cimarron News and Press." This was the town paper, and it had always favored the political ring [it was originally owned by the grant company]. After considerable discussion, it was decided that the only sure way to take care of the matter was to wreck the printing office completely. So one [Wednesday] night [January 19, 1876] we rode into town and did just that very thoroughly. Breaking up the press, we carried the pieces a few steps to the bridge and dumped them into the river. I distinctly remember white-headed "Old Man" Pascoe, who still lived in the Marino valley, squealing in his half-crying voice, "Here goes the last issue of the *News and Press!*" As we usually did, we dispersed quietly when it was pronounced to be a thorough job.[8]

That was the last time I rode with the boys. I was just a kid myself, and it was all very exciting to me, of course. My memory on the whole thing is very clear and positive. There seems to be a good deal of confusion and ignorance concerning this incident, but I was there, and I know what happened!

Of course, there was plenty of excitement around Cimarron then. The "politicos" had Colfax County placed under martial law. They took our courts away and indicted everybody who was suspected of being implicated in the recent occurrences, and we had to go to Taos for trial.[9]

At least a hundred Colfax County men were in the Taos courtroom when court opened. All wore guns, but the officials did not seem to see the guns, and the county attorney "noll prossed" [slang for *nolle prosequi,* a formal legal term signifying the abandonment of all or part of a suit] the cases as fast as they were called up. So we left the court and put in the rest of the day celebrating at different saloons, and the next day rode back home.

Clay Allison, as I knew him, looked like a typical Texan. He was about five feet eleven inches tall, and carried no extra flesh on him. He had a full black beard, and black hair, and was somewhere around thirty years of age, probably twenty-eight or twenty-nine. Clay was very manly, very easy-going and even-tempered except when aroused. Rumor said he never *started* a fuss, but generally *ended* one if he was in danger. Certainly, this was true as long as I was around him. He was a very good friend to me and, in many of his talks to me, he advised me to try always to avoid a fight, but if attacked, to give a good account of myself. "Always keep cool," he told me, "and don't lose your head no matter what happens!"

Clay was naturally a dead shot with a six-shooter, and was accredited at that time with having killed around twenty men, all in self-defense. This naturally made him a target for "bad men" who wanted to enhance their reputations as such, and I recall a couple of such instances.

One time when a fellow by the name of "Chuck" Wilson [John "Chunk" Colbert] was under the influence of "red eye," he confided to a few companions that he was going to kill Clay Allison. Clay heard about it, and was on the alert. One day [January 7, 1874] when they met at the Red River stage station [Clifton House] and were going to eat dinner, they sat down at the same table facing one another. As "Chuck" sat down, he slipped his six-shooter onto his lap and watched for his chance. Clay saw this, and he did the same. The plates, cups, and saucers on the table were of the old boarding-house type which were commonly in use at that time, very thick and almost unbreakable. When "Chuck" saw what he thought was his chance, he slipped the muzzle of his gun above the edge of the table and shot, but the bullet was deflected. It glanced off the lower edge of the plate, and missed Clay entirely. The next instant "Chuck" was dead, shot in the temple. Clay *never* missed![10]

Shortly after "Chuck" was killed, another "bad man," a Mexican, tried it out on Clay in Lambert's saloon in Cimarron. I was present at this incident [on November 1, 1875, the day after Cruz Vega was lynched], so I can vouch for its accuracy. The Mexican's name was Poncho [Juan Francisco "Pancho"] Griego [who was Vega's uncle].[11] There were several men in the bar room, Mexican and white. Griego was drinking. He had his six-shooter in his right hand and a red handkerchief in his left hand. Clay's .45 was in its holster. The Mexican stepped in front of Clay and started to taunt him about being such a "bad man." He dared Clay to take hold of the other end of the handkerchief and shoot it out with him and see who was really the "bad man."

"Let me alone," said Clay. "I got no quarrel with you." However, the Mexican persisted, working up his nerve for the killing. Suddenly someone in the crowd called out sharply in Mexican, "Look out behind you, Poncho!" It was an old trick, but it fooled Poncho, who partly turned his head away. As he turned it back he took Clay's bullet between his eyes, and that was all for him. They never did find out who pulled the trick.[12]

A day or so after the shooting of Poncho Griego, Clay and I were riding towards his ranch on the Red River (his brother John's ranch was on the Vermejo). Presently Clay spoke to me seriously. "Kid," he said (he always called me "kid," although the term was not so commonly used as it is now). "Kid, you haven't told anybody who it was that spoke up and told Poncho Griego to look behind him, have you?" I told him no, and I hoped nobody else would.

"Do *you* know, Clay?" I asked.

"Why, of course I do! And you're right; we'll keep it to ourselves, for the feller who done it wouldn't live a week if them greasers found it out!" declared Clay. So, as I wasn't ready to die yet, I kept my counsel, and have continued to keep it until this day!

Clay had one short leg which came from a gun wound. He was shot in a scrape in Trinidad [Colorado]. I never knew the particulars, but the Wooten (*sic*, Wootton, pronounced *hooten*) boys, Dick and Bill, were mixed up in it some way.[13] He was still using a crutch when I first knew him. I remember just as well as if it were yesterday where I first saw him. It was over on the Red River just above where Springer now stands. He was carrying his crutch across his saddle and I thought it was a rifle until I got closer. There are probably different versions of how he was lamed, but this is what I know about it.

One evening shortly after that, Sheriff Jack Rhinehart got word that Clay Allison was stopping overnight at Chase and Dawson's ranch house at the mouth of Ponil Canyon about three miles east of Cimarron. Jack figured he could place a full-sized feather in his hat by arresting Clay and taking him to Taos for trial, so the Sheriff got the military C.O. to give him a company of colored soldiers (9th calvery [sic]) as a posse, and he went out and quietly surrounded the ranch-house with them. Then Jack knocked on the door and asked if Clay was there. They told him "yes," so he entered the house. Clay had hung his six-shooter on the wall and was unarmed. Jack told him he was under arrest for the murder of Griego, and Clay said indifferently, "All right, Jack, I'll go with you."

When they got outside, Clay discovered that Jack had the colored soldiers with him, and did he cuss Jack out! Clay was from southern Texas, and hated Negroes, but he had to go on anyway, and Jack put him in jail for the night. The next morning they set out for Taos without the soldiers. Jack wanted the glory of having brought Clay Allison in alone. After they had ridden a few miles up the canyon, they reached a small spring in the bank of a little cut on the side of the road.* This spring was about two and a half feet above the road level, and just below where the spring came out, a little basin had been built to form a pool. This made a very convenient place to get a drink beside the road. Clay said he was dry; and stopped and got off his horse and bent over to drink out of this basin. He got his drink, and smacked his lips and bragged about how good the water was. This made Jack

---

*The spring, which still runs, is a few hundred yards from where Ute Creek joins the Cimarron River.

thirsty and he concluded he would try it too, so he dismounted and stooped over for his drink. While Jack was drinking, Clay quietly took from its holster the six-shooter which was the only gun Jack was carrying. He then told Jack what kind of a man he considered him to be, and he subjected Jack to an indignity which made him the laughing-stock of the country thereabouts after it became known, but which I can not put into print. He told Jack that he would meet him in the Taos court room the next morning, but warned him not to show himself before then, or he would get filled full of lead. Then Clay rode on.

Clay did not hurt or abuse Jack in any way except with his tongue. I have wondered since why Clay did not go further in humiliating Jack. He could easily have done it without injuring anything except his pride. I guess Clay did not think of anything more at the time.[14]

Jack did as he was told, and met Clay at the court room in Taos. The case was "noll prossed" quickly when it was called up. Jack left that part of the country after a new sheriff [Peter Burleson] was elected. He was running a saloon in Tascosa, Texas, the last time I saw him. The last time I saw Clay Allison was in Roswell, New Mexico, about the time "Billy the Kid" escaped from the Lincoln County jail [April 1881]. Clay had moved his herd from Colfax County to down below Chisum's range [at Seven Rivers] on the lower Pecos River, and was then returning home from a trip back to Cimarron. He had gone there to marry a Colfax County girl. I forgot her name [Dora McCullough]; but she was very good-looking; and she and Clay had been acquainted for years. They camped near us for the night. When they pulled out the next morning; it was the last time I ever saw Clay Allison. It took men like him to straighten out the Old West; and he was one of the best.

During the time in which Colfax County was declared to be under martial law; there was a company of Negro soldiers stationed at Cimarron. They belonged to the 9th calvary [sic]; which had been sent to New Mexico to assist in maintaining order. These soldiers were camped in the old livery stable yards; which was quite a large plot of ground, surrounded by a high adobe wall. At one time, an incident occurred in connection with the presence of the colored soldiers in Cimarron, which I have remembered, and which had a peculiar sequel many years later in another part of the country.

Two riders, one of whom was Gus Heffron [Heffernon], and the other a fellow who called himself "Davy Crockett" after the old plains scout [Crockett was a great-nephew of the defender of the Alamo], were running wild and occasionally coming to Cimarron for a high old time. Both of them were former southern cow-punchers, and had a hatred for the Negro race in general, and for "nigger" soldiers in particular. One day [March 24, 1876] they were in Lambert's saloon drinking, and some of the soldiers came in for a drink. Gus and "Dave" would not allow them to be served while white men were at the bar. This resulted in a quarrel and one soldier was killed. The rest retired to their quarters, but after taps that night, three of them decided to slip uptown and avenge the death of their comrade. Two started to enter the saloon, the third one prudently standing outside the window looking in. "Dave" and Gus opened fire on the two who came in, and dropped them dead in the doorway. The third one got back to headquarters as fast as possible.[15]

Years after this, I was in a real estate man's office in Emporia, Kansas, when a Negro named Knox came in to talk over some business. While they were talking I noticed Knox's military bearing, and after he had concluded his business, I asked him if he was an ex-soldier. He said, "Yes, suh, I belonged to the old Ninth Cavalry."

"Were you ever stationed at Cimarron, in Colfax County, New Mexico?" I asked.

"Yes, suh, I was. What do you know about that town, suh, may I ask?"

"Did you ever hear of "Dave Crockett" or Gus Heffron?" I persisted. The man was getting excited. "Ah sure did!" he exclaimed. "How come you askin' me about them fellers?"

"Well, Knox," I explained, "I just got curious to know if you happened to be the third man that night when three soldiers went to Lambert's saloon to kill those fellows."

"Well, suh!" he cried, "Ah nevah thought I'd heah of that again, but Ah sure was, and Ah reckon Ah made the best time Ah evah made in my whole life, runnin' back to quarters! Ah sure was glad to get away from there alive!" We explained the incident to the real estate man, and we all three had a good laugh over it. Knox was then a good citizen of Emporia, and one of the few with whom I talked over the old days in the West.*

There is a little more to the story of Gus and Dave. The two desperadoes grew bolder, and after Pete Burlison was elected Sheriff, they came to town one day [September 30, 1876], got drunk as usual, and proceeded to shoot up the town, riding up and down the streets shooting and yelling. Now Pete was an old southern Texas man himself, and well acquainted with both of the fellows. He tried to get them to behave themselves, but only got cussed out for his pains, so he quietly got a few men posted where they could do the most good; then he walked out to Gus and Dave and told them quietly that they *had* to leave town. One of them started to "throw down" on

---

*None of the soldiers involved in the Cimarron incident was named Knox.

Pete with his gun; and the posse opened fire on them, killing Dave and badly wounding Gus.[16]

I attended Dave's funeral next day, and I remember noticing Pete Burlison's sorrow at the grave. He acted as if he were stricken with grief; and some time later I was told that "Dave" was Pete Burlison's younger brother. It may or may not have been true; I never knew whether it was or not.* Whatever the truth; whether relative or friend; the story simply illustrates the integrity of a man like Burlison. He had to enforce the law, and he did his duty to the people regardless of his own feelings in the matter.

Pete [who held office from 1877 to 1880] was an excellent Sheriff, and was highly respected as a man as well. There was little trouble during his term of office, as he enforced the law justly and indiscriminately. In fact, I do not remember there being any trouble at all after he had been in office for a short time. Pete Burlison brought peace to Colfax County.

---

*It was not true. The two men had been friends in Texas.

CHAPTER THREE

Gold Mines and Indians

EDITOR'S NOTE

The mining town of Hillsboro, New Mexico, sprang up in April, 1877, when two prospectors, Daniel Dugan and David Stizel, discovered gold along Percha Creek not far from Kingston. For its first three or four months it was a tent town, but by August the first log cabin had been erected. The place was not actually called Hillsboro until December; the story goes that because of his especially big gold strike, Silver City pioneer Joe Yankie got the honor of naming the town and chose "Hillsborough" for his home town in Ohio.

By 1879, although plagued with frequent Apache raids, Hillsboro had a post office, and rich new placer diggings brought in a further influx of gold seekers; perhaps it was at this point that John Wightman got there. On February 5, the *Las Cruces Thirty-Four* reported that Jose Alert, formerly of Las Cruces (could this have been Wightman's "Ackley"?) had two *arrastras* in operation "running day and night" netting him sixty-four dollars per ton of rock crushed. "The lode upon which most work has been done is the Snake mine of Dan Dugan," the report continued. "He has shafts sunk and a large body of ore on the dump. In some of the quartz the free gold is plainly visible."

The few clues the author gives us in this chapter are little help in accurately dating the events he recounts. He says later that he was eighteen when he worked at the Bell Ranch but also mentions the area newspaper, which did not begin publication until 1880, at which time Wightman would have been twenty or more. So other than establishing that the events related here must have taken place between April 1877, when the first strike was made at Hillsboro, and some time in 1880, it is impossible to say when he arrived, how long he stayed, and when he left.

For the same reason, it is not possible to pin down with any certainty the date of the fight in which his friend Tom Hughes was killed. It is tempting to conclude that it must have been during the fight "near Hillsboro" between "a party of citizens and about one hundred Apaches" that took place on September 17, 1879, in which ten members of the posse were killed and all their stock was captured. It may be that the narrator confused this event with the battle fought the following day by a "civilian militia" from Hillsboro and two troops of the Ninth Cavalry led by Captain Byron Dawson, following a particularly bloody attack on the McEvers ranch in Lake Valley. And it should be noted that the raiders were led by Victorio, not Geronimo.[1]

When Sierra County was formed in 1884, Hillsboro became its county seat, and by 1907 its population had grown to about 1,200, but after the county seat was moved to Hot Springs (now Truth or Consequences) the town went into decline. Today, perhaps a hundred and fifty people live there, and tourists come mainly to hear the legend of English-born

Sadie Orchard and to see the ruins of the courthouse, built in 1892, in which Oliver Lee, Jim Gililland, and Bill McNew, the alleged killers of Col. Albert J. Fountain, were tried for (and acquitted of) his 1896 murder.

⸻

"Once upon a time," said Mr. Wallace, "I almost owned a gold mine. That was the time there was a nest of gold nuggets buried under our doorstep, and we never knew it. Following the Colfax County War," he said, "things got pretty tame in Cimarron, and I, kid-like, grew restless. I started rambling around here and there over New Mexico, sowing wild oats in a wild way. I drifted from this to that, work a little here, fool around a little there, drink a little, dance a little, and in general have a fairly good time. I got into a few quarrels here and there, nothing serious as it happened at that time, but because I never knew when something serious would come up, I would use a different name in different localities. I wanted to keep my father's name out of any scrapes that I might fall into, and it was easy enough to fall into one, in that country at that time. A man could get into serious trouble through a chance remark, intended for a joke."

A hundred miles was a good long distance in those days, and a fellow could drift from one place to another and never be heard of again. I had an uncanny sense of direction, and could start out across the plains and ride straight from one point to another, whereas most men couldn't do so. They had to have signs to go by, but I didn't. If I got into a bit of devilment in one place, I could hustle out for another and ride across country, and even if they'd wanted to follow me, they couldn't. I was just young enough to think it was a lot of fun to stir up a little excitement and then disappear. Not that I ever shot up a town, or the like, for I didn't, but I liked to play pranks, and make joking remarks to people, and sometimes the consequences were such that I was better off somewhere else.

During my rambling around, I got a hankering to learn something of gold mining, so, being at Las Cruces, I struck out for Hillsboro, a mining community in the Black Range about thirty-five [ninety] miles or so away. When I arrived there, a man by the name of Ackley hired me at once as windlass man on a lode mine he had leased. Tom Hughes, a former sergeant in the Army, and Bill Bates, an old bull-whacker from Missouri, had been working for him for some time. They batched in a small shanty, a half-dug-out near the mine, and they asked me to go in with them. I did, and we were partners during the whole time I was there. Ackley extracted his gold with a device called an "arastra." The arastra [*sic, arrastra,* from the Spanish *arrastrar,* "to drag"] was a makeshift outfit taking the place of a stamp mill until capital could be secured with which to buy and install the mill. The arastra was used in California in the early days. It was a slow, tedious way of extracting the gold from the quartz, but in good ore, running expenses could be made by using it. The arastra was constructed by first digging a circular pit about twenty-five feet in diameter and sixteen inches deep. This pit was paved with large rocks with clay tamped firmly in the cracks between the rocks. In the center of the circle a good stout post was placed securely, yet so it could turn. To this center post, a cross-pole was firmly bolted. One side of this pole reached only to the edge of the pit, the other end extended about five feet over the outer edge. A horse or mule (or a burro, if nothing else was available) was hitched to the long end of the cross-pole, and on the shorter end two fairly heavy rocks were fastened by a chain so they would drag on the bottom of the pit. Quicksilver was placed above the hard-tamped clay in the cracks between the floor rocks. Ore from the lode was dumped into the pit, water was run in to facilitate the grinding of the ore, the horse was blindfolded so he could not see if anyone was close around, then the operator of the mill would start him to pulling the pole around. The man would have to stick around pretty close the first day or two and start the horse up with a whip, or toss a rock at him every time he stopped, but in the course of time, the horse learned that he had to keep moving, which he did as slowly as he could. The operator would have time then to run off the ground-up rock and add new ore in place of it. When the cracks seemed to be filled pretty well with the quicksilver and gold amalgam, the motor power got a rest, and the pit was thoroughly cleaned out, the amalgam placed in an iron gold-pan over a fire with a larger pan upside down over it so that the edges of the upper pan extended over the lower. The quicksilver would evaporate and gather on the upper pan, and run off into a pan placed below to catch it. Thus, the quicksilver could be used over again and again to gather more gold. I didn't learn the price of lode gold, but placer gold brought one dollar a pennyweight at that time.

Ackley had no regular pay. He paid up when he cleaned up his arastra and sold the gold. Therefore, for a long while his workers had to go without pay. I threw in with Tom and Bill and used my money for food until pay day should come. They ran out of cash before I did, so I used my money for us all, and by the time Mr. Ackley cleaned up, I was about out of money, too. I worked forty-two days for him before he cleaned up. When he did, he showed us in the evening a nice lot of gold, and told us he would sell it the next day in Hillsboro, and pay us all up in full.

When the next morning came, Mr. Ackley and the arastra horse were both gone, and so was the gold. We supposed he had gone to Hillsboro as he had said he intended to do, to sell the gold. Well, he went to Hillsboro all right, but he didn't stop there. He kept on going and took the gold with him, and we never got a cent for our work.

It was December and we three were flat broke, so what could we do? While we were still pondering this question, an old-time "burro, pick and shovel" prospector by the name of Hank Dorsey came by headed for town. He told us he had struck placer gold right in the grass roots a couple of miles away, and made us an offer.

"Boys, I'll tell you what," he said, "I'll keep this here a secret till after you all has a chance to pick ye up a claim, if so be ye'd like to." We decided to do it, and the next day Hank came back and the four of us went over to what was called Los Alamos [*sic*, Las Animas] Creek. It was a very feeble dribble of water, not over a mile or so long, with only enough water to pan or "rocker" out the gold. Hank staked his claim, we took the next claim to it and all went to work with a will.

It was coarse gold, and as soon as we took a few nuggets into Hillsboro to trade for grub, we had a miniature gold rush. Men poured into the place and began taking up claims, each yearning to make his pile. There was one man, however, who did not come to try his luck. That was Mr. Ackley. If he had, he would have had to settle in one way or another with Tom, Bill, and me. If he had come, and had not had enough money to pay us what we had earned working for him, we would have taken every stitch of clothes off his back and run him out of the country. We really wanted to meet that fellow!

Hank's claim soon petered out, but he found another just as good nearby, and washed out one hundred dollars a day for a while from it, until that one petered out, too. The gold in our claims, which we staked lengthwise of the little creek, was in pockets in the creek bed. Some days we took out twenty-five to thirty dollars' worth apiece, and then we would go a few days getting next to nothing. Five dollar nuggets we often found, and several from ten to twenty dollars, but we soon cleaned out the claim, and could not make a dollar a day apiece. We then abandoned the claim, and went to work for George Wells, [a Pennsylvanian] who had struck a rich claim not far off.

We had built us a kind of rough half-dugout, half-rock shanty just at the edge of the little creek. After we left the claim, an old prospector moved into the shanty. The second day he was there, he dug between the shanty "door" (which was really a blanket) and the creek bed, and took out over $100 before noon. One nugget he took out weighed fifty-three Pennyweight [one-twentieth of an ounce troy, i.e. 2½ ounces], and there were the usual five and ten dollar nuggets besides. We sure cussed ourselves for not having dug up our doorstep ourselves, but it was too late then.

George Wells arranged with some Mexicans to haul the dirt from his claim to a real creek about four miles distance and he sluiced it there. His claim was "in the grass roots," too, and the term means literally that. The gold is in the dirt which surrounds the roots of the grass, and it is dug out and sluiced the usual way.

George had a rich claim, which got richer as he followed it down a little. When he got further down into the draw, the gold was below the surface, and he had to "peel it" (that is, lift back the sod) to get to it. He cleared a thousand dollars a week for a while, but was making somewhat less when I left there. I myself panned three dollars and a half out of one pan of dirt from George's claim.

Tom, Bill and I used to draw our pay Saturday noon and clean ourselves up and hit for town, where we would play poker in the back of the saloon until Monday morning. We were all more than six feet tall, sparingly built and full of life, and I guess we thought we were hard to beat. We *were* for a *fact,* at poker.

One day when we were absorbed in a game, a queer thing happened. There was a young fellow at the bar who was "on the prod"— swaggering around half-drunk, making mean remarks to everyone, trying to pick a fight. He'd keep demeaning this one and that one, trying to start something, bragging himself up and running everybody else down. Presently an oldish gray-headed feller came into the saloon, and quietly ordered a drink, strictly minding his own business, and this young nitwit started getting personal and "blowing off" at him. Finally he took a swing at the older man, who promptly swung back. At that we three started to get up from our chairs and take care of the situation. It looked pretty bad, you know, a husky youngster like that picking on a gray-haired old man (for so we considered him, although he was probably no more than middle-aged). He was an Irishman, known to be a good, steady man, but completely unknown as to his past history. He motioned us to stay back.

"Lave 'im alone, bhoys!" says he, "Oi'll take keer of 'im!" And blessed if he didn't! He just trounced that young sprout right until it was pitiful to see. The Irishman really knew how to box, and the blowhard kid didn't have a chance. When he left that saloon, he didn't stop going. He would have been laughed out of the country if he had tried to stay. That was one experience that would ruin a reputation without fail, and it surely ruined him!

I wish that I might be able to call the Irishman by some name well-known in the annals of boxing history, but unfortunately his name meant nothing to me then, and I cannot now even recall it. It probably wasn't his own anyway. It was really true that a man's past was his own in that country at that time, and nobody inquired into it.

While I was on Los Alamos Creek, I had what was perhaps as close a call as I ever had in my life. The butcher there wanted a steer to kill for meat, and he knew I was a range rider, so he asked me to get one. He got me a horse and saddle, and I went for the steer he told me about. I ran that critter eight or ten miles, until both it and my horse were so tired they could hardly walk. Finally, I got it headed for the camp, where the rest of the bunch of boys were sitting around the fire. Instead of shooting the steer, they got out of the way and let it go on through, upsetting the coffee and grub and all. Well, it was so worn out it couldn't run, but my horse was in the same fix, so I thought, "Here's once I'll chance it afoot." I knew perfectly well that this was foolish, for a steer will chase a man afoot no matter how tired they are, whereas they would not hurt him as long as he was on a horse.

Well, I thought that this time it might be different, and I got off my horse to head him afoot. The minute that critter set eyes on me, he made for me full speed. The horse was too far away for me to jump on him, as I couldn't have reached him on time. There was nothing I could do to hide. I could only stand and wait, trusting to my first shot to lay him out. The situation wasn't helped by the other fellows shouting "Run, you fool, run!"

To run was the worst thing I could have done. Those steers always run faster than ever after you if you tried to run away from them. So I stood still and waited for him. On he came, one horn up and one horn down, and I stood there waiting. I was like the old fellow, a buffalo hunter, who told of a buffalo coming at him, and him out on the open, treeless prairie—no place to hide, no rock for shelter, no fence to put between 'em.

"What did you do?" they asked him.

"Well, sir," he said, "I climbed a tree!"

"But how could you? There wasn't any trees!" they said.

"Shucks," he answered. "There was nothing else I could do. There just *had* to be a tree!"

I couldn't invent a tree, so I stood my ground, with the boys screeching to me to run, and when the steer was about six feet away I shot, and luckily brought him down. Even so, his horn knocked me off my feet. The boys thought I was crazy, but I knew what I was doing. I had to stand still and wait till I could shoot to kill. I aimed at his head but I think the bullet struck just behind the ear. After that, as long as I worked there, the boys gave me the sign, one arm up and one arm down, to represent that old steer's horns. The fellows marveled at my narrow escape.

The Mexican who owned the steer appeared the next day, and the butcher left town, but I stayed put. If he had said anything to me, I would have told him that the butcher sent me after it, but he never came near me. I really think that was the hardest thing I ever had to do in my life—stand there waiting, while that old steer, boilin' mad, was making for me. If I had missed he'd have stuck a horn in me sure! Fortunately for me, I must have hit him close to where I aimed.

It was [during] this period of my wanderings that I ran into more Indian experiences than any other time. At that time old Geronimo [Victorio] and his braves went through Hillsboro on their way down to old Mexico. They weren't on the war-path, just going through the country stealing horses. They would get up a band of horses and drive them across the border and sell them down there. Hillsboro was about a hundred miles each way between Sacorro [sic] and Silver City, and lay right in their line of travel.

One day, I well remember, I was standing talking to a Mexican who had a sway-backed mare grazing in a little *vega* (meadow) nearby. Suddenly the Mexican gave a little "yip," and I whirled and saw an Indian come running up to the mare. He put his hands on her flanks, sprang upon her, and went on, all in one movement, or so it seemed. That was the slickest getaway on a horse I ever saw. Of course, I started right away for Hillsboro. By the time I got over the two miles or so to town, a posse of about fifty men were ready to follow the Indian's trail. There happened to be a horse handy, and they told me to take it and come along. That was about the middle of the afternoon. We followed their trail without seeing them until about sunset, when we sighted them and opened fire on them at once. They immediately scattered and melted away into the under-brush and rock, a few of them driving on ahead the herd of stolen horses they had gathered. We could not follow the horse herd without exposing ourselves to be ambushed by the Indians, so we had to scatter them first.

I don't know whether we killed any or not. I do know that one Indian was hit as he ran dodging up the mountain from cover to cover. It was a long shot, but we had one old buffalo hunter in the crowd who had his "Betsy" along with him. Those old buffalo guns were fine for long-range shooting. His first shot raised the dust ahead of the Indian. His second raised a puff of dust behind the red man. Then the old fellow chuckled, and said "I'll get him next time, boys. Got the range now!" Sure enough, the Indian dropped at his third shot, but was picked up and carried off by other Indians, so we didn't know if he was killed or not. They will always do that if it is at all possible. They do not leave one of their men behind if they can help it.

By that time it was getting dark, and of course we could do nothing after dark, so we returned to Hillsboro. That night eight of us agreed to take up the trail of the Indians the next morning, and try to take their stolen horses away from them. We had a good night's rest, and started before sun-up the next day.

We trailed those cussed Apaches through the Black Range nearly a week, but never caught sight of them again. Then we decided to ride into Fort Bayard and get the commanding officer to stake us to some grub. When he found out what we were doing, he laughed and told us we were wasting our time. "Those Indians are in Mexico by now," he declared. "They passed through here, headed for the Florida mountains, yesterday!"

We knew he was right, and we gave up the chase and went back to Hillsboro, planning to get a quicker start the next time, but there wasn't any next time. When old Geronimo [Victorio] returned the next Spring, he came killing instead of stealing, and that made the story entirely different.

At the Lake Valley ranch, some fifteen miles from Hillsboro, there were women and children, unprotected from the Apaches. So a posse of fifty or sixty men gathered at Hillsboro and started for that ranch, aiming to try to get there before Geronimo [Victorio], who was coming from the opposite direction. This party split, and fourteen or fifteen of them took a trail that cut through the mountains, while the rest took the easier route around the mountains. I was with the party that went around.

We reached the ranch too late, as the Indians had been there and gone after burning the buildings, killing, mutilating, and scalping all the whites they could find there. I tell you, it was a horrible sight that we saw as that ranch came into view, but that wasn't all the

Apaches had done. Tom Hughes, my old buddy, had led the bunch through the mountain trail. I don't know why I didn't go with him, for ordinarily we would have stuck together. It just happened that this time we separated. His party ran into an ambush in a pocket in the hills, from which only one man of the whole group escaped, and how he managed to do it, I could never understand. He told us all about it, and he said Tom was the first to die. If I had gone with Tom, as ninety-nine times out of a hundred I would have, I'd have almost certainly got mine, too.

Somehow, the life there did not suit me after that, so in the late Spring I pulled out again for the "wide open spaces."

CHAPTER FOUR

Mexicana

❧ Mr. Wallace tightened the screw in my easel and handed me the screwdriver. He set up the easel and shook it a little. "Theah you are," he said, "she'll hold for a while, now."

This was the second sitting, and I knew very little about him. I did, however, know that he had been a cowboy in his youth in New Mexico, and impulsively, I tried out my meager Spanish.

"Gracias, señor," I said airily, and immediately wished I hadn't, for he turned to me and smiled, and his deep old voice rolled out a liquid sentence which I recognized as Spanish, but of which I could translate only the final word, "Señora."

"Oh, yes," he explained at my questioning, "I learned to speak Mexican like a native in New Mexico. I had to, for there were so many of them, and so few whites, that often for days, they would be my only companions. My knowledge of their language came in handy more than once. For the most part," he continued, "the social part of our lives in the Old West consisted of visiting with the Mexican population."

MEXICANA: HOSPITALITY

The owners of the large land grants were of Spanish blood, rich and educated, and looked down on ordinary, poorer white folks as they did on the Mexican *peons*. The poorer Mexicans were by nature very hospitable and welcomed any guest, however poor, or however scanty their own possessions might be. There were very few of them that had anything better to live in than the old adobe huts (built of sun-dried bricks made of mud) with dirt floors tamped down hard, and dirt roofs. They mostly used blankets for windows.

Because of my ability to speak their language, I always found myself welcome at any Mexican house, and even the old Spanish Dons' families made me welcome. I have ridden all the way across New Mexico several times without having to spend a penny for food for myself or my horse. Of course, if it was summer, the horse could eat grass, but I could not! But I did not need to worry about food, for there was always a place for me at the table of some hospitable Mexican.

I enjoyed Mexican food, and often ate with them. The poorer class of Mexicans ate and slept on the floors of their little "dobe" shanties. They would cook up a stack of tortillas and have a big pot of coffee which they drank out of tin cups. It was not etiquette to take a whole tortilla at once. The proper way was to break off a third or so, placing the rest back on the stack. Then you would break off a smaller piece of the one you kept, and press it into a spoon shape with your thumb, and dip it into the pot for the meat and gravy. Then put it all at once into your mouth and eat it, and continue in the same manner.

The pot of food was a common pot, for they seldom had individual plates, and almost never table knives, forks, or spoons. But their food was tasty, and everyone seemed to like it, even the "tenderfeet" after they become accustomed to the chili pepper used in it. The tortillas they made out of whole corn, themselves. They boiled the corn until it was soft, and the grains were thoroughly cooked. They would then grind it with a *metate*, which was a primitive device made of two stones.

The bottom one was a smooth, flat, hard, close-grained rock about sixteen inches in diameter, roughly disc-shaped. The other rock, with which the actual grinding was done, was about a foot long and from two to three inches thick in the center. It was slightly rounded at the ends. Of course, I have no way of knowing the original shape, as these rocks were handed down from mother to daughter from generations back, and were highly prized by the ones who owned them. They used the long rock as modern housewives use a rolling pin to roll out dough. It was also hard and close grained, and very smooth.

A double handful of the well-cooked corn was placed on the flat rock, and then rolled out until pasty, gathered up and rolled again, and this process continued until the corn had been transformed into a smooth paste. Of course, the hull remained in, but they used it anyway. They could always pick their teeth after they had finished! Usually, they picked them with a knife.

Most of the corn raised by the Mexicans up to the late 70s was a blue-grained variety and this corn was preferred by them to any other for making tortillas. In native parlance, tortillas were called *tortillas pi n'esta mal*, the literal meaning of which would be "not bad." I have eaten and enjoyed very much many a meal of *tortillas pi n'esta mal, con carne y chile colorado.*

MEXICANA: FOOD AND COOKING

The Mexicans raised their own chile, and when the pods were thoroughly dried they would simply crush them up in their hands and put the crushed pods in with the dried meat, which was generally called buffalo meat, but which usually was somebody's beef, and seldom their own. Sometimes there were beans mixed in with the dried meat and chile, unless they had eaten up their yearly crop of beans. No matter how hard up they were, they would be insulted if you didn't eat with them. They were as a rule, very clean, considering what they had to cook with, and I for one never refused a chance to have a good meal with them.

As I grew up they got so they had regular corn meal such as we have now, and *stole* (corn meal mush) was a stand-by. Sometimes they would cook the *stole* well-done, and sometimes they would just scald it. In that case it was barely cooked, and gritty to the taste. If they had a cow they could milk, they would use milk with their mush. A milk cow was rare, but often they would have a couple of milk goats, which kept them well-supplied with goat's milk. Frequently they would have a few chickens, when there was anything for them to eat, and in that case they would have eggs to eat.

This was the way they lived when I was a boy in the 70s, rambling around amongst them, seeing the country and learning the Mexican language. By the 80s their standard of living had improved a great deal. From eating on the floor out of a common pot, with a piece of tortilla for a spoon, they came to use wooden boxes for tables, and perhaps they would have plates. From that they began using rough wooden tables, cheap knives and forks and spoons, and even china plates on occasions, but they used the tin cups as long as I was there.

I have been speaking, of course, of the very poorest people. The Spanish Dons had a high standard of living, and no matter what the cost, they kept it up. They lived in beautiful houses, luxuriously furnished, and used fine china and silver and crystal and linens for daily use. They had fine clothes, too, and sent their children to college. They could afford to do this, because they kept large herds of sheep which cost them very little to keep up. The system was very much the same as that of the old southern plantations on which cotton was raised, and the Southern plantation owners were no prouder than the Spanish Dons, who spoke pure Castillan [*sic*] Spanish and lived well, and held themselves superior to people who worked for a living, white and Mexican alike. But at that, I don't believe they enjoyed life any better than the carefree *peon* class.

MEXICANA: SHEEP RAISING

Sheep raising in the old days of free range was a money-making business. Herds of 2,500 to 5,000 each would be attended to by one Mexican man whose wages were from ten to twelve dollars a month, food, and one boy. He was paid eight dollars a month. They hired a few more men at lambing time. At shearing time, they paid so much a head for each sheep that was taken care of.

The sheep-herder and his boy had one burro that they used only when moving their camp to fresh pastures. The "camp" consisted of a frying pan, coffee pot, three or four tin plates, a pot to boil meat in, a spoon or two, and a couple of butcher knives, and of course, a little bedding. They had no tent or shelter of any kind. Their grub was corn meal for *stole* (mush), meat from the flock (or what they could shoot, such as antelope, rabbits, etc.), some chili pods, and that was about all.

They had to be very careful about getting on any range claimed for cattlemen, and if they did get too close they had to get away fast when the cattlemen ran onto them. Cattle would not eat grass that sheep had ranged over, until the rains had washed the scent of the sheep off. And it did not rain very frequently in New Mexico. The old Dons would each have four or five of these herds of sheep, each herd on a different range.

There was a *mayordomo* (foreman) whose duties were to select new camps for the separate herds, and keep them moving onto fresh grass as needed. Although his work was light, the *mayordomo's* life was not a happy one, for he had to stand between the sheep-herders and the cattlemen. He was much better paid than the herders. He usually got about fifty dollars a month salary, and in his camp there was better food. Also, he had a saddle horse to ride and a tent to sleep in.

I would frequently stop at these camps and eat when I made my rounds as a cowhand. One meal which I have always remembered occurred when I was riding for the Bell Ranch. I used to start out about daylight, and often wouldn't get in till supper. A fellow really got hungry doing that. One day, about the middle of the afternoon, I had to ride outside the circle (the border line between the ranges) and I chanced to ride upon a *mayordomo's* camp. I noticed they had the ashes of their fire raked up into a neat little heap, so I got off my horse, took a stick, and investigated. I raked out a sheep's head from those ashes, then I rummaged through the outfit until I found a few cold tortillas, and proceeded to make a good meal. I think I enjoyed it fully as well as any meal I ever ate in my life. The meat was white, clean, and tasty, and cooked to a turn. It was the sweetest meat I ever sampled. I often wondered what kind of language that *mayordomo* used when he got into supper that night and found his sheep's head picked clean. I never had any regrets that I had ate it for him.

Mexicana: Farming

Farming as done by the Mexicans in the early 70s was rather crude and primitive. Their team would be a yoke of oxen, their plow a forked stick. This was all right for scratching in the loose dirt of that country, for the little preparation they needed. They would make the plow by getting a forked branch from a *piñon*, and fastening a second stick to one end for a handle. Then they would secure the oxen to the other end for a tongue, and used the fork of the stick for a plowshare.

In the land thus prepared, they planted corn, and from then on, after the corn had come up, they tended it with a hoe. No wheat was raised by the Mexicans, who limited their crops to corn and a little garden truck. Wheat and oats were introduced by the white settlers.

They would put a little dam in a creek somewhere, where there was sufficient fall to bring the water down, then take out a ditch. There were no irrigating laws at that time to hinder a man's putting a ditch where he wanted it, and taking all the water he needed. Each man had his own ditch, and he would irrigate three times a year, once before plowing in the spring, and twice afterwards. I never knew positively how high the figures ran, but I was told that some of the wheat raised then ran up to fifty and sixty bushels an acre.

Alfalfa was unheard of in the early 70's. While I was there, it began to be talked of in Cimarron, and the first crop in that country was put on by me and another young fellow. We were trying our hands at working [a] farm for [Henry M.] Porter, one of the bankers and general store merchants at Cimarron. He was one [of the pro-Granters] that we didn't run off in the Colfax County War, although [Asa F.] Middaugh, the other partner, left the country for good. Porter had us put in a little patch of alfalfa, which was not called alfalfa then, except very rarely. Usually it was called "Cuban clover." Out of the whole patch, we had two plants to grow. He didn't know how to plant it or take care of it, and we didn't care much. When I went through there on the train, years later, I saw a number of fine fields of it between Cimarron and Raton, along the Red River.

All of this came in the late 70s. When I first went down there, the Mexicans were the only farmers, and they did very little of it, utilizing only the few fertile spots along the river bottoms, and clinging to their primitive tools. But when the English Company came to New Mexico, and the country commenced to be settled by ranchers and "nesters," in the period previous to the Colfax County War, the walking plow as of today was brought in and used by the settlers. Of course, the Mexicans began using it too, and by the 80s the old wooden plow had practically disappeared.

MEXICANA: THE OLD WOODEN CART

Just as the wooden plow disappeared, so also did the old wooden Mexican cart. This was made entirely of wood, wheels and all. They hewed two slabs to make the wheels. Each slab was three inches thick, hewn from large cottonwood logs, and then crossed so that the grain in one slab ran across the grain in the other. These slabs were then fastened together with wooden pegs, so that they made a circle having a diameter of about four and a half or five feet, and the rude wheel was then cut out, a hole in the center was cut for the axle, which came out through the wheel, and was held in place with a wooden pin. The wheel thus had a six-inch rim, and when that greaseless axle turned inside its wheel, you could hear it coming for half a mile away.

A basket rack was set on a board floor for a wagon bed, a little grass or hay placed inside to serve as springs, two or three sapling poles fastened across the top of the rack, and the cart was done. The family rode inside, with a yoke of oxen to draw the cart. The driver usually rode too, although sometimes if the cart was heavily loaded he would walk beside the oxen. All he needed was a six foot goad with a nail filed sharp on one end of the goad. Then he could poke the oxen through the slats, holler "Gee" or "Haw" in place of using lines, and they were ready to go.

Once when there was a feast-day at Socorro, I caught up with a family in such an equipage. I rode up and joshed them a bit, and they asked me to get in and ride with them and eat watermelon. That was the best watermelon I ever ate. But I will say, the Mexican cart wasn't something to want to ride in.

MEXICANA: FIREWOOD

The Mexican never hurried. He rode a horse at times, but mostly he used a burro. He never used a bridle on a burro, all he needed was a stick whittled sharp at one end. With this he would tap either side of the burro's neck for him to go right or left instead of saying "Gee" or "Haw," and if he wanted to hurry he would punch the burro's shoulders with the sharpened end.

It was interesting to see the Mexicans coming along with their burros loaded with firewood. They would go to the mountains with several burros and cut their stovewood, then they'd make the burro lie down and they would build on each side of him a bundle of wood, and fasten the two bundles together by a rope or a rawhide strip. They would then get the burro up on his feet, generally having to assist him, then they would build the wood up so as to form a half-circle and tie the top down to the sides. The sides would extend out on each side of the burro about a foot, the load generally looking a good deal bigger than the burro which was carrying it. Then the rest of the burros would be loaded similarly, and the Mexican would proceed to town and sell the wood to the townspeople.

MEXICANA: SHOES

Very few Mexicans of the poorer class wore "store bought" shoes. They made their own, using rawhide for soles, and making a leather top from somebody's old shoe which had been thrown away. Whenever possible, they sewed the upper to the sole with sinews taken from the carcasses of small animals. These were very strong and tough. The soles were generally made out of a chunk of hide from a bull's neck, as this is the thickest and toughest portion of the hide, and it was sewed in such a manner that the seam could not touch the ground.

These *teguas* were very comfortable, and easy on the feet except after a rain, or when for some other reason the soles would get wet. When wet, the rawhide soles would become soft and have to be laid aside until they dried thoroughly again. This didn't bother the Mexicans much, for they usually had two pairs. That rawhide when dry was as hard as any factory-made sole, but when wet was so soft that it offered no protection to the feet. This was why it had to be dried before using.

Mexicana: Soap Weed

The Mexican women used the soap-weed for shampooing hair. They would dig up some fresh roots, pound them up into a sort of fibrous mass, and use it for soap. It was very fine for washing hair, and they never used anything else. The name "soap-weed" came from this use of the roots. The plant is also called "century plant" and "yucca." The Mexicans called it *amole.*

Many a time have I had my hair washed with soap-weed root. It was a courtesy, similar to the washing of feet and anointing of the hair in the Biblical days. Very often when I would stop in at some Mexican home, a woman would be having her hair washed, and she would invite me to come and have mine washed too. I usually did, for that sort of shampoo would leave the hair soft and clean and lustrous, and my hair was the one thing about my appearance of which I was inclined to feel vain.

Yucca (soap-weed or *amole*, [as] it was called then) grew tall in New Mexico. I've seen fellows in the southern part of the State make a little hut by digging out a shallow cave in the side of a low hill, throwing up a few logs, and putting *carajo* poles over it. These poles were the stems of the yucca flower. We used them, when dried, for fuel sometimes, although they were too pithy to last long. The word *carajo* was a swear word, something like "damn," but what its exact meaning was, I could never find out. That was one word my Mexican friends wouldn't translate literally for me.

MEXICANA: THE OLD MEXICAN DANCES

If you could find a room big enough to dance in, you could get a dance up any time by paying a fiddler. I used to have a lot of fun attending these dances. It did not matter whether I knew anyone or not, no introductions were made nor were any necessary. The floor was in every case of hard-packed clay. The women and girls would sit together at one side or end of the room, and the men generally stayed near the door or around the approach to the door.

If a fellow was acquainted, of course he had more fun, but a perfect stranger could glance over the row of *señoritas*, select in his mind the one he wanted to dance with, and simply walk over to her and hold out his hand. If he could speak any Mexican he would politely ask her to dance with him. If not, he would hold out his hand, she would take it, and walk out on the floor with him. Once out on the floor, it was no use trying to talk with her, for conversation was taboo, and she would not reply, and you would be sure to get into trouble if you persisted. This, of course, was the country folks' code. It would not apply to the larger towns where they had manners and customs of their own. The Mexican unmarried girls were uniformly very circumspect in their behavior, although they for the most part lost much of this circumspection after marriage.

Most of the dances were what we call "square dances," and you had better know your way through them as there was no caller. Folks just danced to the music, making their changes as it did. If you did not know what to do, you would get a gentle push from your partner in the right direction, and it did not take very long until you could go through the dance pretty well on your own. You always improved as the dance continued, until [by] the time it ended, you knew it pretty well.

One of the favorite dances was the "valse dispacio" (slow waltz). In dancing this, there was always an idle pair of dancers at one end of the room, and sometimes at both ends. Next to these, four hands round would prance half around their spaces, then sashay back to where they were originally standing. Then as the music changed to waltz time, they would waltz around their space, edging toward the other end of the room, and join hands with a pair coming from it. The idle pair would join with the recent partners of the first pair, and leave them to idle. The new pair would work their way thus to the other end of the room and then return the same way. So the dance would go on until every pair had taken a turn at idle and at dancing. The music was usually furnished by a fiddler, sitting up on a table and playing the tunes. Generally, there would be some old man up there with the fiddler, and this old man would sing verses of songs while the dancers were going through the part of the dance which was not a waltz. These tunes were old tunes which had been handed down, and frequently the singer would make up new words as he went along. One of the favorite songs was "Los Benadoa[s]" ("The Deer"). Sometimes it was called "El Benado" ("The Male Deer"), and again "La Benada" ("The Doe"). The song started like this:

El Benado

Benadita, benadita, bien y a usted como ti ya?
El benado estar en la sierra en una penalida.
("Little doe, little doe, well, and how are you?
The buck is on the mountain, doing penance.")

Nowadays we would say "in the doghouse" instead of "doing penance." There were several verses to this song, one of which I remember as follows:

El benado y benada si hueron por Santa Fé,
A vender los benaditos por azucar y cafe.
("The buck and the doe have gone to Santa Fé
To sell the little fawns for sugar and coffee.")

The old man would sing a verse and repeat it, and as he ended it the second time, the music would change and the dancers would waltz around again, ending with one pair near the door as the idle pair. After a while each pair would get to the end, and work its way back to the original position, and by that time a different dance would be called for. The last verse of the song was the signal for this, and although the body of the song might be composed of verses which the singer made up out of his head, the last verse always ended the same way:

Sl preguntan quien compuso, quien compuso "la benada,"
Los diran que don luis di la casa colorada. (repeat)
("If they ask you who composed, who composed 'La benada,'
You may tell them that it was Don Luis of the red house.")
(repeat)
Sl prequnta ne que horas cerca di la madrugada.
Sl prequnta ne que horas cerca di la madrugada.
("If they ask you at what hour, 'getting close to daybreak.'")

The next dance after La Benada would probably be a *valse redondo* (round dance) in which there was no change, you just waltzed your partner around and around as long as you could both stand it. They did not sing while dancing these round waltzes, but they had a song which went to one of their favorites:

El valse di amor
Sobre los llanos del norte si ha vista una placa de grande valor,
De adonde si saca la piesa florista, del diche valse de amor.
("Over the plains of the north has been seen a city of great
   wealth,
From where was brought the flowery dance tune, the
   aforesaid 'Waltz of Love.'")

This verse was followed by a refrain which was simply the same tune played over by the instrument, without any singing. The tune of this old song very closely resembled the chorus of the popular tune recently in vogue, called "The [Daring Young Man on the] Flying Trapeze." I hadn't thought of "El Valse di Amor" for years, until one afternoon when my granddaughters and their friends were dancing around the room to the tune of "The Flying Trapeze," which was coming over the radio. They were paying no attention to me, being intent on their dancing and chattering, until suddenly I burst into the old song, "*Sobre los llance del morte se ha vista . . .* "

"Why, Grandpa!" they cried, "where did you learn that song?" For a lonesome cowboy who could speak Mexican as well as English, there was lots of enjoyment in the old Mexican dances, and I missed as few of them as I possibly could.

64

MEXICANA: PENITENTES

I don't like to discuss the practices of any religious sect, for while I am not a religious man myself, I respect the views of others. The secret organization among the Mexicans which is called the *Penitentes* is after all no more unusual in its ways than any other such belief. Yet so much interest has been taken in the sect in late years that it would not be amiss to complete my dissertation on the Mexicans of the old days, with a few paragraphs telling what little I knew about them.

One afternoon another young fellow and I were riding along the trail near Ponil Creek, when we heard voices and looked to see a small procession of five or six men coming along from the opposite direction.

We pulled out of the trail to let them go by. We were standing right beside the trail, holding our horses, watching as the *Penitentes* went past. They made a weird procession, chanting their hymns and led by their black-robed priest, each one flogging himself with a whip made of yucca leaves, braided together in such a way that the sharp points protruded. One of them dragged a heavy cross hewed out of heavy timber. One end of the cross was laid across his shoulder with a leaf of prickly pear beneath it to make the punishment more severe. He followed the priest, two others followed him, and one or two more behind them. They were bound for the little church which stood outside the village. The church was a little distance from the town, on a knoll on the prairie. It was used by the *Penitentes* for their inner church. No one got into that church but the *Penitentes* themselves.

While we were watching the procession, the cowboy who was with me suddenly raised his quirt and brought it down on the shoulders of one of the followers. And I exclaimed, "Here! Cut it out! What did you do that for?"

"Well," he said, "they was a-floggin' theirselves, and I just thought

I'd help 'em along!"

"Well, let me tell you," I told him quietly, "you'd better get out of the country."

He was astonished. "What fer?" he demanded.

"Because if you don't," I answered, "you'll stay here permanently, pushing up daisies. Them fellas won't stand for any monkey-doodle business concerning their religion, and will certainly resent any assistance from outside." Well, the seriousness of my tone must have convinced him, for he went on, and I never saw or heard of him again. Whether he left of his own accord, riding his horse (which might have been the case, as he was just drifting through anyhow), or whether the *Penitentes* avenged the sacrilege they considered he had committed, I never knew. He hadn't really meant to do any serious wrong; he had simply seen the opportunity to play a typical cowboy prank, but he hadn't realized what a sacred rite this was to those people. I knew it, for I had talked to the Mexicans about it, and I knew what it meant to them.

About a year before, I had been invited to attend their holy week services, a thing very few *Americanos* got the chance to do in those days, in fact, so far as I know, I was the only one thereabouts who did. That was in the little Mexican town of Ponil, on the creek of the same name, near where we two fellows had stood to watch the procession go by.

In fact, it was to that same little "inner church" that the Ponil *Penitentes* would go for their secret rites.

Ponil was not really a town, just an aggregation of houses. There was not a store in it, and the "church" to which I was taken was not a church proper, but a large room in one of the Mexican homes. The *Penitentes* would go from their services in that room to the little church outside the village, but of course, I was not allowed to go with them.

The room set aside for the church in the village house was divided into two sections by a curtain which hung to the floor, being suspended from a wire stretched several feet below the ceiling. The *Penitentes* were on one side of this curtain, and the rest of us on the other.

The inside of the room had been whitewashed before the ceremonies began, and when we went in, the walls and ceilings were snow-white. But, by the time they finished their services, at midnight of Good Friday, the whole surface of the ceiling and wall on their side was sprinkled with blood until it seemed to have been painted crimson. Even a part of the ceiling in the room where I sat was generously splattered.

Promptly at midnight of Good Friday they stopped all religious action and we went over to another house in the village. There a dance was started immediately after the *Penitentes* had ended their services. The only part of the services that struck me as ludicrous occurred shortly before that midnight hour. They put out all the lights in the church room, leaving it in total darkness, and on their side of the curtain commenced making a noise that sounded to me exactly as though they were flipping heavy log-chains on dried cowhides hung on a fence. As soon as the din subsided to where I could be heard, I asked a Mexican sitting next to me, "What in the world are they doin' that for?"

"Hush," he whispered, "they're scaring the Devil away!" That was the only thing I saw that was the least bit funny to me.

The *Penitentes* whipped themselves in public only during Holy Week. They wore a hood over their heads, covering their chins. The hood was white, or at least it was originally white! They were bare to the waist, with only a pair of white muslin drawers below the waist, and bare feet. There was no way of telling who was a *Pentitente* [*sic*] and who wasn't, on account of the hood. I had a young Mexican friend, whom I knew very well, and at the dance after midnight he came in. He was about twenty-five years old, a strapping young fellow, and I thought I'd try out a scheme to find if my suspicions were true. Slapping him heartily on the back, I asked him where he'd been all week? I said I hadn't seen him. He winced, and shuddered away from me.

"For God's sake, friend," he implored, "don't do that again!" That was all the answer he made, but it was sufficient. In it he told me all I wanted to know.

Mexicana: Padre and Port

There was an old padre, I forgot his name, who lived at the old mission at Valeta [Valencia?], down the river a little ways from Albuquerque. I used to make a practice of calling on him whenever I happened to be in the neighborhood. The old monks had planted a fine vineyard at Valeta and they made the best port wine I ever tasted. The old padre would always go down into the cellar and bring up a man-sized jug of that wine whenever I called on him, and we would sit and talk until we had about used up the jug, before I would be going.

He was a fine old man, well-educated and intelligent and sociable. He was well-posted on all subjects, politics, economics, current news, everything. We talked about anything and everything under the sun, or rather he talked, I mostly listened. He liked to talk, and when he had got a couple of glasses of that grape wine into his system, he could really talk! We always used the Spanish language, talking away in it as readily as I do in English this minute. I never remember talking to him in English. I learned a great deal from the old padre during my acquaintance with him, and only wish I could have another session with him and his jug!

MEXICANA: AMIGO MIO

I had many good friends among the Mexican people. I understood them and liked them, and appreciated their many fine qualities. I thought nothing of it at the time, of course, but my knowledge of them and their ways, and my sympathy with them, was to come in handy for me many years later, during my life in Emporia, Kansas. So for the time being, as I have so often bidden good-bye to them, "Hasta la vista"—till we meet again!

CHAPTER FIVE

The Bell Ranch

EDITOR'S NOTE

It is difficult today to imagine a cattle ranch three quarters of
a million acres in extent, but once upon a time in the West
there was such a ranch. It came into being largely through
the efforts of John Sebrie Watts—a former member of the
Indiana House of Representatives and a close friend of Abra-
ham Lincoln—who emigrated to New Mexico shortly after
it became a territory of the United States.

Kentucky-born Watts served as an associate justice of
the U.S. court in New Mexico Territory from 1851 to 1854.
He then resumed the practice of law in Santa Fe and became
a specialist in establishing title to Spanish and Mexican
grants, a fertile field in those days for speculation and the
amassing of wealth. Notably, Watts successfully handled
the confirmation, survey, and patenting of the Baca Location
No. 2 and the enormous Montoya Grant of 1824 for the
Montoya and Cabez de Baca families, taking a goodly portion of their grants as his fee, and later purchasing still more
of the property from the heirs. (It might be also noted here
as a fact of history that very few of the grants remained in the
possession of the original grantees.)

In 1870, Watts—who was also involved in the Maxwell

Land Grant & Railway Company's purchase of the Lucien B. Maxwell properties—sold most of his enormous land holdings to the flamboyant Wilson Waddingham, another major player in the Maxwell sale that same year. On March 15, 1875, after adding other land purchases to his holdings, Waddingham registered the Bell brand for livestock, appropriating the abandoned buildings of old Fort Bascom on the Canadian River as his headquarters. For more than a century and a half, the Bell Ranch would remain a genuine working cattle ranch.

In 1947, however, the ranch underwent significant reorganization, its headquarters, name, and brand being retained with approximately 130,000 acres near the center of the old Montoya grant and five other portions sectioned off. Later purchases of the original grant land enlarged the ranch further, so that today the Bell Ranch covers less than half of the original 719,000 acres. The latest sale of the ranch was closed on August 17, 2010. Comprised of 290,100 acres, it is believed the largest single block of deeded land to sell in the Western United States during the past sixty years. Priced at $115 million in 2007 and then $103 million in 2009, the ranch was most recently offered at $83 million. The final selling price has not been revealed.

"*It was on the Bell ranch,*" *said the raconteur, "that I gained the reputation of being a dead shot. It was not so, of course, and I never was called on to prove it, but I didn't make any attempt to disprove it. That was when I was eighteen years old, and working*

as a top hand on that ranch. I felt pretty perky anyhow, being a
top hand so young, although I was really a man, six feet two in
height and big-framed, yet carryin' not an ounce of fat. Many a
laugh I've had over the way my reputation with a six-shooter was
enhanced."

Bell Ranch was owned by Wilson Waddingham,[1] and run for him
by Mike Slattery.[2] This ranch, we never called them "spreads" in
those days, was the nearest to being an ideal ranch that I ever saw,
in location. It was in a valley eight to ten miles from home ranch to
top, and bounded on two sides and one end by mountains.[3] These
mountains were not as high as the Rockies, but they were high enough
to make a natural barrier which cattle seldom passed. The valley, as
nearly as I can remember, was between two and three miles across,
and the La Cinta Creek ran through it, emptying into the Red River
not far from where it entered the canyon. This canyon was several
miles long. The Red River lost its name when it entered the upper
end of this canyon, and emerged at old Fort Bascom as the Canadian.

Now the entire valley occupied by the Bell Ranch was treeless.
There was a big hill, or low mountain, it might be called, rising between the creek and the easterly side of the valley. This hill was about
a third of a mile long, and had a trail to the top. This trail was rough
and very steep, but a horse could make it all right. From the top of the
hill a man using good field glasses could see what was going on in all
parts of the valley. Old Mike Slattery used to go up on the mountain
every so often to check up on the rider covering that end, which was
my end while I was there.

I would start at daylight, right after I had got my breakfast, and ride the outside edge of the valley, generally on top of the "breaks," as we called the foothills. I would go about a third of the way around, coming back to the home ranch every night. Next day I would commence where I had left off the day before, and make another third of the way around that day. The third day I would ride the remaining part. On the rides I would drive any "Bell" cattle I found near the edge of the range back toward the creek. In that way very few "Bell" cattle strayed off their own range. On the lower end of the range they had two men in a line-camp house who attended to the Red River side of the range in the same manner.

My third day's ride brought me within a couple of miles of the Mexican town of La Cinta, and I would generally hurry that day, and go into town for a drink or so, which kept my financial standing close to zero most of the time. Mike used to cuss me out frequently for that. He didn't make any complaint as to my neglecting my work, for I didn't do that. He only hated to see me be such a fool. However, Mike and I could never see eye to eye on that subject. La Cinta[4] boasted a newspaper, [the *Red River Chronicle*] and the editor [Louis Hommel] had a grown daughter [Mary][5] who was a good looker and good company, so what was the use of Mike's preaching to me? White girls were scarce as hens' teeth in that country those days. And anyway, Mike liked to go to Las Vegas for a week's visit every so often, himself.

This girl was a mighty fine girl, and I liked her very much. I used to write to her occasionally after I left the Bell Ranch, but finally I left the country and lost all track of her. I felt that I had nothing to offer such a girl.

Strangely enough, her brother came as near to killing me as ever anyone did in my life. He cooked for the outfit at the home ranch, and one evening when I came in late, he didn't want to fix supper for me. He got sassy and personal, and I just walked over to the stove and slapped his face. I stood there a minute or two to see if he'd do anything about it, but he didn't, so I turned around and started to walk away. Suddenly the boss yelled, "Look out, Frank!" [and] I whirled around and caught his arm as he was bringing down a flat-iron on my head. Even so, the point of the iron grazed my head leaving a lump the size of a pea. Those irons were solid and heavy, and it would have been "Good-bye, Frank," if the boss hadn't yelled in time.[6]

One day when I was riding into La Cinta, shortly after I first commenced to work at the Bell Ranch, a steer came running up the road to meet me. Some Mexicans who lived in a little 'dobe hut beside the road on the outskirts of town came out shouting and waving at me to head the steer back, which I did.

"What you going to do with him?" I shouted at the Mexes.

"Butcher him!" they screeched back.

"Where you want him put?" I yelled. They jabbed their fingers towards a spot on the ground in the area between their house and the road. "Aqui!" they screeched. ("Here!")

The distance between the 'dobe shack and the road was only about thirty or forty feet, and when the steer and I got to the spot the Mexicans had pointed out, I made a snap shot, which struck the critter just back of the horns and he fell almost at their feet. I couldn't have done it again in a hundred years, but it came to me instantly that here was a good chance for me to get a reputation as a dead shot, so I nonchalantly waved my hand at them and jogged on down the road to town as if what I had done was only a matter of course. They stood and watched me with their mouths open, and before I got out of hearing, they started chattering to each other a mile a minute. As long as I stayed on the Bell Ranch, my reputation as a dead shot was never questioned.

Not long afterward, however, another lucky break enhanced this reputed prowess of mine. One day when I was riding the range alone, I saw a bunch of about fifteen antelope that were nearly a quarter of a mile away. I just raised my six-shooter at an angle that I thought might carry the bullet to them, and shot once. At the sound of the shot, the antelope started to run, of course, but one lagged behind. I could tell that he was wounded, so I took out after them, loosening my rope from the horn of the saddle. When I caught up with the laggard I roped him. I found that he had been struck just back of the heart. I cut his throat with my pocket-knife, let him bleed, "wrestled" him onto the saddle, climbed up behind him, and took him to the home ranch for meat.

Everybody knows that it is hard to get an antelope. It is practically impossible to creep up on them and get close enough to shoot one, even with a long-range rifle. The only way we were successful was for a man to get behind a clump of soap-weed and tie a red hand-kerchief on the flower stalk. They are very curious about anything strange you know, and they would circle around, and circle around, coming closer all the time, until finally they would get close enough for a rifle shot to get one. Now the boys knew I had no rifle with me, nothing in fact but a .45 Colt six-gun. I never told them exactly how I did get the antelope, and they couldn't get over it. They naturally thought anyone who could kill an antelope with a six-shooter must be a lallapaloosa, so I let it go at that. If I had told them I had roped him, they wouldn't have believed me. So, I figured, let it ride, and there you have the true story of my reputation as a dead shot.

While I was riding for the Bell outfit, I noticed a five- or six-year-old mare running with the horse bunch on the range. She was steel-gray, and a beauty. After I'd been working there a couple of months, Mike asked me if I could break a horse to ride. I told him I could. He said he had a three-year-old white colt that he wanted broke carefully as he wanted to make a present of it to a neighbor rancher, a Jew. (I think the rancher's name was Frankenthall, as he was the only Jew I ever ran into that had a cattle ranch.) So the bunch was brought in from the range, and [we all] remarked on what a nice-looking saddle animal that steel-gray mare was. Nothing further was said then concerning that particular pony.

I went ahead and broke the white pony, and found it an easy job. When I got on him the first time, he never even pitched, and inside of a month I could cut cattle out of the bunch with him at a roundup. He was the most tractable horse I ever saw, perfectly gentle right from the start. In talking with Mike about this white pony, Mike remarked, "He's a half-brother to that steel-gray mare you was lookin' at.["] It didn't take me long to make up my mind.

"What'll you take for the mare, Mike?"

He wouldn't put a price on her, but I finally gave him my own forty dollar riding horse in an even swap for her. I brought her in, and proceeded to break her, or rather, to try to break her. She was one of the worst pitching horses I ever straddled. She had a habit of going along with her head down, like an old plow horse, for maybe a mile or two, apparently just thinking of something to do because in a split second she'd be off sunfishing at right angles to the road. It got to be plenty monotonous, but I believed I could tame her in time.

One day [fellow ranch hand] Charley Dorland and I were riding to town together, when she took one of her spells of pitching. Charley had never been with me before and seen her in action. When she quit, and I brought her back into the road, we started on and Charley said, "Some o' these days that mare is agoin' to spill you all ovah the prairie!"

"Hell, Charlie," I declared, "Ain't no horse 'at wears hair can spill me!"

I'd hardly got the words out of my mouth till she was at it again. Usually, after a spell of pitching, she would go quietly for another mile or such a matter, but this time she decided to be different. The worst of it was, that catching me unawares, she put me over the horn of the saddle at the first jump. Then putting her head between her knees, she started pitching right, but she never tried to strike me with her hooves. She'd just stand more or less in one spot and pitch. She wasn't the kind of horse that would fight a man, so I held onto the bridle reins, and when she got through, I straddled her again and we went on.

That's the only time I ever got thrown from a pitching horse, and Charlie laughed at me all the way into town. I rode that mare every other day for six weeks, and at the end of that time, when I got in one evening after riding her all day as usual, I stripped her of my saddle and bridle, kicked her in the ribs as hard as I could, and that was the last I saw of her.

When the ranch boys found out what I had done, they "hoorawed" me plenty, and told me I was about the fourth man who had tried to break that mare. She was, they told me, a confirmed outlaw, and they knew all the time I would never get her broke, but they sure enjoyed watching me try it, so they kept me in ignorance of it. I managed to trade her to one of the boys for his saddle pony, a very poor specimen of a saddle horse, by the way, so I had a horse of my own to ride away on when I quit the Bell Ranch, anyway.

I quit the job in November, a bad time to quit. It happened as follows: Mike Slattery was raising a two-year-old colt for his own use. The colt was quite a pet around the place, and consequently a big nuisance. It would come up and try to steal the other horses' feed, and wouldn't respond to any amount of shouting. So one morning I picked up a little sliver of a cedar stick and threw at him to scare him away. Of course, I didn't mean to hit him at all, but unfortunately the jagged end where it had splintered off struck him in the eyeball, and of course, it ruined the eye. Mike was Irish and quick-tempered, and soon as I told him about it, he cussed me out and said, "You're fired!"

He said it plenty emphatically, so right away I packed up my war-bags and got ready to leave. By that time Mike had cooled off. He knew that I didn't do it intentionally and he told me to stay. But I was already packed up, and I didn't want him to fire me twice, so I left.

This was nearly the middle of November, and a hard time of the year for a cowhand to get a job, as all the extra men were dropped as soon as Fall round-up was over. The big ranches kept only a few old hands through the winter, and did no hiring whatever at that time of the year.

EDITOR'S NOTE

Here, a portion of the manuscript is missing.

It would appear that Wallace recounted some further "adventures" that took place between his quitting the Bell Ranch and his making the decision to look for work in the new town of Tascosa in the Texas Panhandle. For the moment, at least, we can only wonder what they might have been, and skip to the next chapter, in which he relates his side of the story of the pursuit and capture of Billy the Kid.

CHAPTER SIX

An Expedition and a Capture

🌿 *"I've had folks say to me," observed Mr. Wallace, "that they never saw anyone who could have so many things happen to 'em as I could, and still come out all right. Take the time; for instance, when I was out of a job in mid-December, after I quit the Bell Ranch. It does seem odd how a job caught up with me, as you might say."*

A feller by the name of Cape Willingham[1] was then driving the mail route from Las Vegas south. I don't recall exactly where to, but probably to Fort Sill, Oklahoma. He knew I had been working on the Bell Ranch, and since we were well acquainted, he wanted to know what I was doing down there.

I explained, and told him I was striking down, trying to locate myself a job. He shook his head. "It's an awful poor time of year for that, Frank," he said. "Unless a man's a good hand and purty well acquainted."

"Well, I can hold my own at a job of work," I answered, "but I ain't acquainted at all."

We jogged along awhile without saying anything. Finally he spoke up.

"Say," he said, "I think I know where you can get yourself a job.

In fact; I'm almost sure of it, you knowin' the Mexican language like you do. When you get to Tascosa, don't ask anybody about a job. Ask for Tee Silman,[2] [sic] and if he ain't in town, go down to his ranch, the E-Cross-E, about fifty mile below Tascosa. You see, the Canadian Cattle Association[3] is organizin' an expedition to send over into New Mexico to help break up the Kid's gang, and Tee hadn't got anybody to go from his ranch the last account I had. I'll get to Tascosa before you do. I'll send word to Tee to meet you there."

He went on ahead of me. He was driving a team to a buckboard, and naturally he travelled faster than I could. It was a treeless prairie country, called the *Llano Estacado,* or "Staked Plains," so named because the Spaniards, when they crossed it some three and a half centuries before, had driven stakes to mark their way. Since there were no trees, this was the only way they could "blaze" their trail. The plains looked perfectly flat at first but after being on them for a while a person could realize that the land was really composed of slight rolling swells covered with short grass. I pushed on steadily, hoping I'd get the job, or some job, in Tascosa. When I got there, I inquired around for Tee Silman. He was in town, and he took me right on. Forty-eight hours later, the expedition was on its way. I was turning right around to go back to New Mexico.

There were four wagons in the expedition, each with four-up teams, as we called them. That means four horses, or four mules, to a wagon. The wagon I put my war-bags in had mules. It was an LX wagon, with Charley Siringo[4] in charge. There was a combination driver-cook to each wagon and the wagons carried our equipment. This consisted of bedding, war-bags, grub, and anything else we might be likely to need. With the wagons went fourteen riders, representing different cattlemen who ran their stock along the Canadian River, either north or south of Tascosa.

The LX had one wagon and five men. Besides Charley Siringo, their men were Lon Chambers,[5] Lee Hall,[6] a feller known to me only as "Uncle Jimmy," and Cal Polk.[7] The LX brand was written with a lazy L, this way; (—X). (if a letter lay on its side, we called it a "lazy" letter).

The LIT [ranch] had one wagon, with Bob Boberson[8] in charge. Their other men were Tom Emory[9] and Jim East.[10] The Box T ([T]) wagon had one man, whom we called "The Animal."[11] I can't remember his name, nor why we called him by that name, but I do remember the man. He was as quiet, well-behaved a man as you could ask for, a fine fellow all the way through.

The E-Cross-E (EXE) had no wagon, and I was the only man, so I was assigned to the LX wagon. Charley Siringo and I doubled our blankets and slept together all the time. We became the best of friends, and would have backed each other up in any play. Yet I never revealed to Charley my real name.

I have explained how I used different aliases, as I roamed over the country. While I was on the Bell Ranch, I was known as Frank Clifford, and of course, Cape Willingham knew me that way, too. So, when he spoke to Tee Silman about me in Tascosa, it was as "Frank Clifford." I kept that name all the time during the trip to New Mexico and back, until I finally quit the Canadian River country.

The first night out on the expedition, after we had made camp, the boys were sitting around the fire, and some of them started joshing about my big feet.

"Why," said one of them, "you might be old 'Big Foot' Wallace himself, or leastways his son." "Big Foot" Wallace, as everyone who knows about the history of Texas is aware, was a noted character in the early days of that state. Well, the boys called me "Big Foot Wallace," or "Foot," or "Feet," from then on. None of them, not even Charley Siringo, ever knew how apt the nickname was, for I never said anything to any of them about it. I've had many a laugh over it to myself, however.[12]

Well, the expedition kept on going, up the Canadian River until we got to La Cinta, where we branched off to go to Anton Chico, a town west of La Cinta, located on the Pecos River. We were headed for White Oaks, New Mexico, near which town the Kid had a hide-out on the ranch run by Jim Greathouse.

By the time we got to Anton Chico, we were running pretty short of grub, and Charley went up to Las Vegas to get more money from the Canadian Cattle Association. Charley was the financial agent of the expedition.

He didn't get back as quickly as we thought he ought to. In fact, he was gone for over a week. By the time he did get back, us fellows had stripped the wagons of what little grub there was left, and swapped it for what we could get. Charley explained that he had got into a "monte" game in Las Vegas, and lost the first draft the Association sent him, and had to wait for another. We didn't care anyway, for we were having a lot of fun swapping the stuff for whiskey and so on. While waiting for Siringo to return, Lee Hall decided the he would get up a dance which would be different! Lee was a man who constantly looked ahead. He claimed he had been to college in the east somewhere, and he felt somewhat superior to the rest of us ordinary cow-hands. He wouldn't fritter his time away and throw his money about, but held to the thought that he was going to make something of himself some day. I heard later that he became Sheriff of a county in Texas, it was either Oldham County, or one nearby it.[13] Also, I heard that he was a captain of the Rangers. I never verified this, but he was of some official capacity in the Rangers, I am sure. So Lee held himself a little aloof from us and our mode of living, and our easy comradeship with anybody, high or low, and when he decided to get up a dance at Anton Chico, he declared that only the best people were coming to his dance. He would rent a real hall, and ask the best white and Spanish elements, but he would not have any dirty, ragged *pelados* at his dance. "Pelado" (*p'la-tho*, soft th) was Mexican equivalent for "poor white trash," and its literal translation is "naked," figuratively, "skinned" or "broke."

Now when Lee made his proclamation, Bob Roberson and I began to do a little figuring. The hall which Lee rented for the dance was in a hotel run by an old Irishman and his Mexican wife. The main door opened on the street, and at the back end of the hall there was a small room with only one door which opened into the main room. This small room had a window opening onto the alley, so Bob and I skirmished around town and found some of the vilest whiskey we could locate. We went to all the saloons and none of them had any bad whiskey, but we finally located a Jew who ran a store, who had some particularly vile stuff, he said, but he didn't want to sell it to us. So we tipped him off as to what we wanted it for, and he agreed to let us have two gallons of it. He said it was not fit for sale, but we paid him a couple of dollars anyhow, and he threw in a couple of tin cups.

Well, we carried the booze to the alley window, and I went in and opened the window and Bob passed the booze and cups in to me. From then on it was my job. I got a couple of poor Mexes in from the street and throwed a couple of drinks into them and told them it was free, and for them to bring in any of their friends, but to be sure and be on good behaviour coming through the hall. Of course, they spread the news among their friends with enthusiasm.

Pretty soon some of them began to "feel their oats," and became careless. Then they would be escorted to the street door and invited to stay out. Of course, they didn't care at first about the dance itself. What they wanted was to get to that little room, where free drinks were being passed out. By ten o'clock our back room gang was in the majority, and feeling just as rich and important as anybody, and when taken to the street and told to stay out, they would protest and even fight to get back to our little room. How they did strut through that dance hall! Some even wanted to get on the floor and dance, dirt, rags, stink, and all, so the dance wound up in a general row, early.

There was an old Irishman who was about sixty-five years old and hung around the hotel for his room and board. We had him well polluted also, and he refused to quiet down unless the proprietor's wife would give him a kiss. Her reaction to this is unfit for publication. The old fellow was carried out and put to bed, and everybody went home.

Lee did not know for several days how we pulled things off, but he knew Bob and I did it all and he was very offish for some time. But that did him no good, as we neither loved nor feared him. There was no real friendship between him and us, although he had a good head, and was really a cultured fellow. He was always looking out for Lee, and he held to the line of getting ahead in the world. Naturally, we could never have the careless, happy-go-lucky comradeship toward him that we had toward each other and toward Charley Siringo.

Bob Boberson, or Bobinson, or Robertson, I never knew how he spelled his name: it was always "Bobison" to me. Perhaps it was "Robison!" He was a character himself. Smallish, slow-moving, and quiet, he spoke in a gentle southern Texas drawl, and was simply full of devilment. His fun wasn't always harmless, either. He had a ruthless streak in him, and nobody dared to step on his toes. Bob hated "niggers" worse than rattlesnakes, after the fashion of most southern Texas men at that time. I don't know why but they really couldn't tolerate a colored person about them.

One day when we were in White Oaks something happened to show how he felt toward them. We had a Negro cook, our Mexican cook having run out on us, and this fellow got into a quarrel with another Negro, the only other Negro in town, over the latter's Mexican woman. One day our cook came in about to collapse from fright, saying that the other fellow was going to come down and kill him the next morning. Well, Bob bucked him up, and the next morning he bucked him up again, telling him he was as good as anybody, and not to let this feller scare him. Bob took off his own loaded six-gun and said, "Here, take this, and if he tries any funny business, shoot him!"

Well, the cook's foe came when he said he would, and the cook took the gun and went outside. They were doing a lot of talk and blustering, and Bob got a big kick out of it. He whispered to me, "Feet, get your rifle. If they do start shootin' we'll kill both the blankety blanks!"

I believe he would have done it, but luckily they hollered themselves out and nothing happened. I was relieved, for I knew that although I had followed Bob in the rest of the schemes he had cooked up, I wouldn't have gone all the way this time. There is one thing about which I have a clear conscience; I have never killed a man.

When Charley got back with the cash, we stocked up again and started for White Oaks. Grub was bacon, flour, coffee, sugar, canned tomatoes, and canned corn, and we felt as if we had enough to last us this time.

On the morning we left Anton Chico, it was snowing. There

was already about five inches of snow on the ground. By the time we stopped at noon, snow was from eight to ten inches deep. We made a dry camp, and melted snow to water our horses. Before we could get started again, Pat Garrett,[14] Sheriff of Lincoln County, New Mexico, and Frank Stewart,[15] cattle detective for the Canadian Cattle Association, and another man (one of Pat's deputies) rode into camp. Pat told us that the Kid was down by Fort Sumner, and had a large bunch of Canadian River cattle that he was aiming to start for Old Mexico with in the morning. This couldn't be true, as nobody could go any distance through a snowstorm like that with a big bunch of cattle. There would be nothing for them to eat. Bob Boberson and Charley Siringo immediately told Pat so. They demeaned him, and didn't mince words either.

Pat insisted he was telling it straight, and after a long argument, Bob and Charley agreed to leave it to their men personally to decide who would go with Pat. We split up exactly even, seven went, and seven wouldn't go. I was one who didn't.

We took the wagons and went on to White Oaks, reaching there on the day before Christmas. I remember the date, because just at midnight Christmas Eve, a lot of us slipped out of the saloon and turned loose our artillery, firing two or three salvos in to the air by way of saluting the new Christmas morning. When we went back into the saloon the first thing we saw there was Pinto Tom [Longworth], the lanky, red-headed Marshal of White Oaks, crawling out from under a billiard table, which cost Pinto Tom several rounds of drinks before morning. He thought the Kid and his gang had come in and were shooting up the town, as he dived under the table for safety. I never heard of the Kid shooting up a town just for fun, but folks always seemed to be afraid he was going to![16]

We stayed there several days before the boys came in from Fort Sumner, telling us that the Kid had been captured, and from there I must tell the story as they told it to us. The only hearsay about this story is from the lips of the men who were actually present at the occurrences, and told to me and the other boys by these men immediately after the event took place.

Sheriff Pat Garrett and his deputy, Kip McKinney,[17] and five men, together with Frank Stewart and six of our men, formed a posse and went to Fort Summer. Pat hired a Mexican for one hundred dollars to go to the Kid's hideout on the edge of the Staked Plains and tell the Kid that "the Texans," that was us, had turned back home, and that it was now safe for him to come on in to Fort Sumner, which the Kid told the Mexican he would do that evening. When Pat Garrett got that word, he placed his posse out of sight, where they could cover the road which the Kid's gang would ride in on. There were in the gang, the Kid (whose name was "William Bonney"), Dave Rudabaugh,[18] Charley Bowdre,[19] Tom O'Phalliard (they have spelled his name O'Folliard on the tombstone which has been put up for these three, as I notice in a photograph which I ran across, but we always called him O'Phalliard),[20] and one other whose name I cannot be sure of. I think it was "Wilson."[21]

When they got opposite to where Pat's men were hiding, Pat opened fire on them *without calling to them to surrender,* according to the definite words of these men who told us about it, men who were in the posse, Lon Chambers, Tom Emory, Jim East, "The Animal," Cal Polk, and Lee Hall, all men who were from our expedition. Well, O'Phalliard was killed, and the rest of the Kid's gang turned back and headed away from there, but with eight or ten inches of snow on the ground they were easily tracked. They went out to their hideout, which was a crude rock shanty at the edge of the Staked Plains. Pat's men placed themselves just under the edge of a draw where they had full view of the shanty, but were out of sight themselves, and waited for daylight.

Dave Rudabaugh had tied his horse at the door of the shanty. Shortly after daybreak, Charley Bowdre, who was the same size and build as the "Kid," came out with the Kid's hat on, and started to break up some wood to build a fire. Pat, according to the boys' story, shot Bowdre down without warning, the same as he did Tom O'Phalliard the evening before, and the siege was on. Bowdre, the boys said, staggered toward the posse saying, "I wish—I wish," but he couldn't finish. With the words on his lips, he died.

After a couple of hours, the Kid managed to untie Rudabaugh's horse and was getting it into the shanty, intending to make a break-out, but the horse was shot and killed by Pat's men, and it fell with its body blocking the door.

About noon or a little after, Pat's men were cooking themselves some bacon and coffee, as no one had eaten since dinner the day before. The Kid's gang were holed up so they could not even have a fire, and it was pretty cold, and that bacon and coffee must have smelled good. Pat and the Kid had been talking back and forth most of the time, Pat trying to get the Kid to come out and surrender.

In the end, the Kid agreed to surrender if they would guarantee him a fair trial in court, and protection from lynching, which Pat eventually agreed to. On that the Kid and what was left of his gang came out with their hands up. The first thing the Kid said when he saw the posse was, "Pat, you so-and-so, they told me there was a hundred Texans here from the Canadian River! If I'd a-known there wasn't no more than this, you'd never have got me."

But Pat and the rest just laughed, and they all went back to Fort Sumner, where they split up, our men coming to White Oaks to join us, and the Kid's gang being taken to Lincoln, and from there to Los Cruses [sic] or Mesilla, I cannot now recall which.[22] He was tried and sentenced to be hung, and brought back to be confined in the Lincoln County jail until the date set for his execution. I never heard what became of Rudabaugh and Wilson (if that was his name).

Talk about a vicious-looking countenance, Rudabaugh really had one! He was tough all the way through, and he showed it. One look at his eyes gave him away for what he was, mean all the way. I saw him once, when I was working at the Bell Ranch. A man by the name of Wilson was with him, and I think he was the other member of the Kid's gang but I am not sure. Wilson may not have been his name, but it was what he called himself there.

Two men rode up to the home ranch that night, at the Bell Ranch, and asked to stay all night. They ate with us, slept in the bunk house with all their clothes on, and never took off their guns that we saw. They probably slept with them on all night. Next morning they ate breakfast and rode on. We could tell the big fellow was a killer. He looked it. His eyes showed it. We were remarking about it, when along came Cape Willingham with the mail, practically on the heels of the two strangers, who had hardly got out of sight. Cape brought the Las Vegas newspaper, carrying the story of what these two had been up to. That was the first we knew of the men we had been entertaining.

The day before they arrived at the ranch, this fine pair had ridden in to Las Vegas, where Dave Rudabaugh and "Wilson" had tried to rescue a friend of Rudabaugh's from jail. Dave and "Wilson" rode up and told the jailer to let the fellow out. The jailer refused, and Rudabaugh killed him instantly, took his keys, and opened the jail. Strange to say, his pal refused to come out, so Dave and "Wilson" gave up arguing with him, and rode away. There was a lot of feeling in Las Vegas about that, and I guess plenty of people would have liked to see Dave Rudabaugh swing for the killing of the jailer.[23]

Many folks felt sorry about Bowdre's death. He was a right decent fellow, and well-liked despite the fact that he had joined up with the Kid's gang.

CHAPTER SEVEN

The Winter at White Oaks

🖉 *"Durin' the time that the Kid was in jail," said the story-teller, "Charley Siringo, Tom Emery [sic, Emory], Lon Chambers and I stayed in White Oaks. There were several amusing incidents that occurred there, including the story of the old prospector who ate a water tumbler. Before we get to him, however, we'd better start with the day us boys scared Pinto Tom so badly, and continue with the story of Old Man Allen and his family."*

The day following Pinto Tom's fright, I was standing in the saloon, liquorin' up. A feller spoke at my elbow, calling me by name. I looked down and saw Old Man Allen, whom I had known two or three years before down on the Rio Grande, where he and his wife had run a little boarding house. I set 'em up to him a couple of times, and of course, had to go over and renew acquaintance with his family.

I was much surprised to find that his oldest girl had grown up into a young lady, and as pretty a one as ever I saw. It was midnight before I could get away from the house, because we had so much visiting to do. When I got back to camp,[1] Charley Siringo immediately demanded to know where I'd been all this time. Charley would follow a piece of calico five miles to get acquainted, so just for devilment I wouldn't tell him.

"Oh," I said, "I've just been around town, and you didn't happen to run onto me!" Next evening after supper, I slipped away from him again, and spent the evening with the Allens. There were only two single girls in White Oaks at that time. Leonie Allen was one, and Ella [sic, Ellen] Bolton was the other. Ella Bolton wouldn't have anything to do with us, and I thought it would be fun to keep Charley in ignorance for a while concerning Leonie.

White Oaks was just a little mining camp, composed of one main street between two gulches, with a string of shanties on either side of the short street. The business buildings consisted of a post-office, a store, two or three saloons, and that was about all. One of the "residences" was Allen's shanty, and I had a good time there that evening, swapping yarns and eating a bite with them.

The following evening I didn't have any luck slipping away from Charley. So, trying to divert him, I said I believed I would clean up and oil my six-shooter. He said he believed he would do the same with his. After fiddling around with our guns for a while, Charley said, "See here, Feet, if you're goin' anywhere tonight let's start, 'cause I'm goin' with you!"

So I gave up and said, "Come on," for I knew what Charley was. He'd never quit till he found out what was going on, and we went up the street to the Allen shanty. There was no one at home but the old man and the old lady and two little girls. We sat around and talked for quite a while. Charley wasn't interested, but every time he said anything about leaving, Allen would tell him, "Why, hell, man, hit's early! No use leavin' yit!"

I had found out from Mrs. Allen that Leonie was out at a social that evening, but would be back after a while. Before long we heard somebody come running. Now, [the] Allens were very poor, and the house they lived in had no door. They used a blanket for a door. Leonie and her friend came running in, Leonie in the lead. Her companion, Mrs. Henley, a young woman I hadn't met before, stumbled as she was coming in and came in head first. I happened to be sitting where I could throw out my arm and catch her and save her from falling, which I did, and introductions followed. All the sleep seemed to go out of Charley's eyes. Then it was my turn. After giving Old Man Allen the wink, I proposed leaving. Each time I did so, Charley, who seemed to have had a change of heart, protested vigorously. "Why, man!" he'd say, "it's early yet!"

We became very friendly with the Allens and one or two other families in town. Charley made it a practice to go to a store and buy stuff for a party, charge it up to the Canadian Cattle Association, and take it to Allen's. Other people would come in, and we'd make an evening of it. We always had a good time at these parties, which were a welcome change from the monotony of camp life.

We would also go out in the country and hunt up a fat steer occasionally, butcher it, and distribute it among our friends as well as use it for ourselves. This was a common custom among the cowboys, expected by the cattlemen, and as long as it was not abused, it was not considered rustling, although we were supposed to keep it rather quiet!

After the boys came in from Fort Sumner with the news of the Kid's capture and told us that four of us were to stay behind in White Oaks, we made a little change in our way of living. We had been camped in a barn, but Charley rented a small house for the four of us, just across the street from the Boltons. This family consisted of Mr. and Mrs. [John and Ellen] Bolton, their daughter Ella, and a boarder.[2] Old Jack Winters, the fellow who discovered the Homestake gold mine, had been staying with them for some time. The Homestake mine was a very rich mine. It was the mine which "made" White Oaks, and it made a wealthy man of old Jack Winters. What good his riches did him I wouldn't know, for there he was, living on in White Oaks, boarding with the Boltons, and drinking himself to death.[3]

Ella was the [only] other grown single white girl in White Oaks, but she would have nothing to do with "those wild Texans," as she called us. She wouldn't come to our parties, nor have anything to do with us at any time. Naturally we felt a little resentful, and so when she called my name one morning, I didn't answer right away.

I'd been up late the night before, and as a result had slept late that morning, so that I was all alone at camp. Even the cook had left, so I was chopping a little wood. She yelled again, "Oh, Mr. Clifford! Frank! Come here, please, quick! Mr. Winters is trying to get out and go down after a drink of whiskey, and he is not dressed! And Mama is trying to keep him in the house!"

I ran over and found old Jack Winters just inside the door, without his clothes on, and Mrs. Bolton wrestling with him trying to get him back to bed. I picked him up and Mrs. Bolton showed me where his bed was, so I put him in it. I tried to hold him in, but it was a tough job, so I asked Mrs. Bolton if she had any whiskey in the house. She brought a big drink in a glass, and I held it to Jack's mouth, and let him drink it. When he had swallowed it all, he bit a large piece out of the side of the glass and chewed it up and swallowed that! I choked him a little, trying to keep him from swallowing the glass, but I had no luck, so I told Mrs. Bolton to bring another big drink in a tin cup. I fed that to him, and when it took hold he went to sleep.

I may as well say here that that was the end of old Jack Winters, for he died the next day. Whether the glass he swallowed had anything to do with it or not, I cannot say, but I doubt it very much, for he was pretty far gone from whiskey long before that. I never knew what became of his money, since he had no relatives thereabouts.

After he got to sleep that day, I was sitting beside his bed, when I heard more feminine voices in the outer room. As the door was open, I could hear pretty well. I was particularly interested as they were talking in Spanish and Ella (that was Miss Bolton) was telling them about the "Texans" coming up and breaking up the Kid's gang. They were much interested, and I heard Ella say, "There's one of them in Mr. Winters' room now taking care of him. He got rather out of hand this morning." As old Jack was by that time sound asleep, I decided to find out what I could about the visitors. So I got up to leave, and as I went through the front room where the girls were (which was necessary to get out of the bedroom) I paused and told Ella that old Jack was asleep and I was going back to camp.

"I'll be there all day," I told her, "in case you need any help."

Of course, she stopped me from going on and introduced me to her friends, who turned out to be the two Misses Valdes of Lincoln. At first I did not let them know that I could talk Mexican as well as they, so Ella interpreted for us. I had a lot of fun that way for a while, but it got stale, so I took advantage of a little mistake which Ella made and corrected her, speaking Mexican as I did so.

Of course, the girls were astonished, and taken aback, but they were good sports and they also saw the funny side of it. We all had a good laugh over it, and the upshot of it was that I visited with them until long after dark that evening. When the Valdes girls started back home I left, too, and went back to camp, as we still called it

When I got there, Charley demanded to know where I'd been. I told him very [self-] importantly that I'd been visiting practically all day with Miss Bolton and her two friends, the Valdes girls from Lincoln, and that I'd had a *good* time.

"But you just go to sleep, Charley," I told him soothingly, "because the Valdes girls have already gone on home!" Those *señoritas* were very high-class Spanish girls, educated and well-bred. Their parents were quite well-off, and were by no means to be considered Mexicans. The term "Mexican" was used to denote the poorer classes, whose blood was a mixture of Spanish and Indian, whereas the "Spaniards" belonged to the leisure class, and kept their blood pure.

From that day on, Ella Bolton attended our socials regularly, and had as good a time as any of us. She found out that the "Texans" weren't so "wild" after all.

During the winter I got acquainted with the school-teacher in White Oaks, a man whose name was Shelton. One day at noon I met him on the street and stopped for a chat. I noticed he seemed out of sorts about something, so I mentioned it to him, and he told me he was having trouble on account of a feud between two families of children who attended his school. It seemed that one family had a grown girl about seventeen or eighteen years old, and two little girls about eight and twelve years old. In the other family there was a girl of fifteen. When the fifteen-year-old girl would catch one of the smaller girls alone, she would whip thunder out of her, then when the two little girls were together, and could catch up with the fifteen-year-old, they would maul her, and plenty!

The story tickled me immensely, and as I knew the little girl's family well (in fact, it was the Allen family), I said I was going to put them up to maul thunder out of the big girl the first time they could find her. Shelton begged me not to do it, as he said he was already having trouble enough, but I just laughed and went on.

Of course, I didn't intend to do anything of the kind. I had a ride planned for that afternoon, and I did not think any more about Shelton's troubles, but when I got back that evening I heard some more about them.

It was past supper-time, and I sat eating mine alone because all of the rest of the boys were out somewhere, when Old Man Allen came in all out of breath, and told me that Shelton was out looking for me, vowing he would kill me on sight. Allen was too badly scared to explain further, and he hurried away.

I kept on eating for a few minutes, but finally thought if Shelton was looking for me, it was a shame not to let him find me. I couldn't imagine what was the matter, but Old Man Allen was white and trembling, and if he wasn't sincerely scared almost to death, he was a better actor than I considered him to be. So I decided to take proper precautions, and let Mr. Shelton have the chance of finding me.

As we had promised the "law" in White Oaks not to wear our six-shooters down-town, I just stuck mine in my boot, and leaving the rest of my supper for later, struck out down-town. I met Shelton near the post office, a little shack made of pine boards set upright and nailed together. There was just enough moon-light for me to see who Shelton was, and I walked up to him, slapped him on the shoulder in a friendly manner and greeted him.

"Howdy, Cap!" I said. Before I finished speaking, I felt the muzzle of his gun poke me in the stomach. He had whirled and drawn and cocked his gun in that instant. I certainly never came closer to breathing my last, for he pulled the trigger, and the gun should have gone off, and would have except for one thing, my coat was not buttoned up, and it got between the hammer of Shelton's gun and the cartridge. I jumped backwards as far as I could, tearing a hole in my coat where the hammer of the gun had caught as I jumped. Reaching for my gun, I found my pants leg had slipped down over the handle, and I heard Shelton's first shot. It was a bad miss, fortunately for me, and bent over facing him as I was, I heard him shoot twice more, each time throwing the dirt up in my face. By the time he had shot the third time, I was straightening up with my gun in my hand.

When I came upon Shelton, he was standing talking to Johnny Akers [sic, Eakers], a mining engineer. Akers had nothing to do with the fracas except as a bystander. Seeing me stooped over, he thought I had been hit, and he tried to get Shelton to quit shooting, without avail until I straightened up with my gun in my hand. Seeing that, Shelton did quit, and started running. I shot after him once, but missed him, the bullet going through his coat tail. When I shot the second time, he was going around the corner of the building, hoping to be lucky. He was not hit, so he kept on going, right out into the timber, where he stayed all night, he afterwards said.

Akers managed to get into a place where he would be safe from stray bullets, but to his astonishment he found that he had dashed in on a confinement case. He was afraid to come out, as he did not know what he might be running into, and so he stayed, although, being a bachelor, it must have been hard on him, since there was only one room in the shanty and he stayed there until things quieted down.

By the time Shelton disappeared, I was backed up against the side of the post office building, surrounded on all sides by a crowd of men. They were a rough, tough-looking lot, miners and so on. They pressed in as close as possible, and probably were only curious, but I couldn't be sure of this, so I would not let them crowd me. I kept a half-circle of space in front of me clear, by waving my .44 steadily back and forth.

Pretty soon Charley Siringo came galloping down on my horse.

He was bareback, and he dashed right through the crowd. I swung up behind him and we left, telling the men if they wanted anything out of us to come up to our camp and we would be there.

The next morning I was sleeping late, lying on my back on my bed, which was flat on the floor. When I felt some one shaking me rather gently, I opened my eyes and saw Shelton bending over me. I reached for my gun, but Charley Siringo threw himself across me, pinning me down. He said that Shelton had come to explain and apologize, so we had a pow-wow and got things somewhat straightened out.

It seems the girls had done just what I told Shelton I was going to put them up to doing, and the fight occurred on the school ground during recess. Shelton started to whip them for it, but their older sister took his strap away from him and lashed him proper with it. That broke up school for that day, and Shelton, thinking I was the cause of it, took a few drinks and concluded he would stop any further activities along those lines on my part by simply killing me off.

All this Shelton told me as he had told it to Akers and Siringo that evening. He had seen them first, and then he came to me to explain everything. Of course, we had to go to the court of the Justice of the Peace [Frank H. Lea], so as to satisfy the law, but when Pinto Tom, the town marshal, came after me, I refused to go with him.

"But, plague on it, feller," he protested, "Justice Lea said for me to bring ye!"

"I'll be there, Tom," I told him, "but I'll come when I get good and ready, and I'll come by myself!" He finally went back, reluctantly, alone.

Of course, the trial was a farce, as neither Akers nor I would testify to anything serious against Shelton. We were turned free without even a reprimand from the court. Shelton, however, went on a several days' drunk, and when he sobered up he left town. He was done for there, and he knew it.[4]

He went down on the railroad somewhere close to Bernalille [sic, Bernalillo], and got a job on the section. After he had worked only a few days, he got into an altercation with the boss and played the same trick on him that he had tried on me, whirling about and pointing his gun the same way. The only difference was that this time the gun went off, killing the boss. They took Shelton out of the jail that night and lynched him. I guess I had been just lucky.[5]

Both schools and churches were very scarce in that country in those days, but they had both at White Oaks, such as they were. About the only experience I had with church during my residence in New Mexico was the time we "Texans" went to Sunday-school. The rest of us boys went because of Charley Siringo. Charley went because Justice of the Peace Lea, who was also store-keeper and, as so, got to see a good deal of Charley, and coaxed him to go. Then Charley persuaded the gang to go with him to provide a little backing. I have often wondered what the Justice thought about the result of his missionary endeavors.

This experience occurred before the rest of the boys went back to Texas, while "Uncle Jimmy" was still with us. "Uncle Jimmy" was a confirmed kleptomaniac, not over-bright. He would take any little thing any of the boys had that took his fancy, and put it in his war-bag. In consequence, we had to take the old boy down and sit on him every few days, and go through his war-bags and retrieve our property. It made no difference to him, though. He'd swipe it right back again from us the very first chance he got.

About all "Uncle Jimmy" knew about religion was that there was a book about it, and this book was called the "Bible." So that Sunday morning when the Sunday-school teacher would get around to him with a question, all he could do was just to look "dumb," and that was very little trouble to him. Tom Emory, Charley Siringo, Jim East, and I were the others of our bunch who had attended, and in a spirit of deviltry, one of us would whisper an answer to him and he would bawl out what we told him, to the teacher. I remember that one question she asked was, "Who was the strongest man in the Bible?" We whispered to "Uncle Jimmy" an answer, and he bawled it out, *"John the Baptist!"*

In answer to the question, "What woman anointed Christ's feet with oil?" we told him—*"Jezebel!"* That nearly broke up the meeting. That was the only time we went to Sunday-school during my life on the range.

Among the cowboys there was very little religion as taught by churches and preachers, for they were rare in the Old West. Our religion, and we really believed in it, we carried on our *hips.*

Our life in White Oaks was monotonous in spite of all we could do to prevent it. The first break in that monotony came just before Spring round-up started on the Pecos. Pat Coughlin [*sic,* Coghlan] had a cattle ranch in Tularosa and we had information that some Canadian cattle were on it. One day about noon we got word that they had rounded up some cattle and were to start for Fort Stanton with a bunch of beeves. Coughlin had the contract to supply Fort Stanton with beef. He and the Kid had been pretty friendly.[6]

It was too far from White Oaks to the Tularosa ranch, going around by way of the road, for our wagon to make it that night. So Siringo and I took a short cut through the mountains leaving the wagon and the other two boys to follow by the road. Coughlin was not at the ranch himself, but his ranch foreman welcomed us and put us up for the night.

At the crack of dawn, we were out in the corral looking over the cattle and we found a few steers from the Canadian country, also one fine fat steer, about four years old, with a brand we had never seen. We figured it was from the Big Bend country. We knew it was not Coughlin's, so we talked it over, then went to the house and got a sheet of paper from the foreman [George Peppin], and Siringo forged power of attorney covering the brand on the steer. He had a large bundle of these mostly written on common paper in his pocket, so he dirtied up the forged one and put it in with them.

We had to put up a pretty stiff bluff to keep Coughlin's men from taking the cattle, but we stood at the corral gate and held it. About ten a.m. our wagon came in sight, and Coughlin's men agreed to let us cut out our cattle, which we did. We also cut out the four-year-old steer with the strange brand. They protested against our taking him, but we seemed to have our bluff working and we took it anyway.

To cap it all off, we camped in full sight of the ranch house, and when two or three shoats weighing around sixty pounds each came poking around our camp that afternoon, Siringo shot one. We skinned it, and took a forequarter to the ranch house and asked them if they liked "mutton." They took it, and never hinted that it was their pig, although they must have known it.

We got a great kick out of that trick. It may seem a bit crude nowadays, but it was a typical cowboy prank. Shucks, we had to have a little fun, didn't we? The cowboy's life wasn't much fun any way you took it. In fact, the old time cowboy's way of living wasn't exciting at all. He would often be tired, and dirty, and bored. Sometimes he would work hard, and sometimes his job would be easy, but whichever it was, it still was just a job, and the cowboy was just a hired hand. His pay ran from thirty to sixty dollars a month, depending on his "cow-savvy." A man in charge of an outfit, one who knew the country, with its water holes and places where cattle might be found, would draw around sixty dollars. Ropers, too, and men good in the branding-pen, commanded more than green-horns.

Whatever the job, the life was far from romantic. We had to create our own fun, and mostly we did it by such pranks as Charley's, and by going to town and getting drunk. What else could we do? White families were few and far between, and an occasional dance was our only social venture. There were no picture shows or any of the modern diversions. We played cards, mostly "monte" or poker, when in the saloons, for money. We spun yarns and sang songs, and sometimes we rode around just looking at curiosities of nature which we would come across every so often.

There was one wonderful thing to see near White Oaks. I thought perhaps there was a volcano at one time which may have erupted a great quantity of dazzling white dust as fine as flour. It lies in a broad strip perhaps two or three miles long, and as I remember from a quarter to a half mile wide where I crossed it. These dimensions may not be correct, but I am sure that the stretch of sand was just about that size, certainly no less. We discovered it one day when we were riding around, probably looking for a steer. When we came to this white stuff we just rode on across it. Riding across it was rather a punishing job, even though a cowboy was used to common dust. This white dust was not like ordinary dust. It settled all over us, in our eyes, ears, noses, mouths, and it got on the inside of our clothes. We didn't feel comfortable again until we had found a waterhole big enough to wash off in. You take a fellow wearing wool all the time, and get that consarned fine white dust down inside his clothes, and it's just awful!

The place where the dust lay was a sort of shallow valley, looking as if it had been the bed for a stream, which dried up and filled with the white dust. I have often wondered about this peculiar formation, and wish that I had explored it further at the time. The people at White Oaks called it the "White Sands."

The next morning after Charley Siringo and I had made a present to the Tularosa people of their own pork, we started back to White Oaks. When we got there, we butchered the strange steer and gave the meat to our friends.

A short time afterwards we got word that the Chisum round-up was starting, so we packed our war-bags and loaded up our wagon and pulled out for Roswell, New Mexico, where we intended to camp until the round-up was over.

During the months that we were at White Oaks, "Billy the Kid" had been confined in jail at Lincoln, New Mexico. It was while we were at Roswell, and just at the finish of the round-up, that we received word of his escape from jail. Shackled hand and foot, constantly and closely guarded, he had patiently waited and watched for his chance during the long six months of his imprisonment, from December to June.[7]

Frank Clifford's birthplace, The Wern, or Wern House, as it is today.
With the arrival of the railway, the estate became part of an area known as
Sebastopol, south of Pontypool. *Photograph by author.*

Cimarron, New Mexico, ca. 1882. *Courtesy University of New Mexico, Center
for Southwest Research.*

Lucien Bonaparte Maxwell. *Author's Collection.*

The Maxwell House, Cimarron, New Mexico. Built in 1858, it was destroyed by two fires, the first in 1888 and the second in 1924. *Courtesy Audrey Alpers Collection.*

Ruins of the Mutz Hotel in Elizabethtown, New Mexico, now a ghost town. *Photograph by author.*

The plaza in Cimarron, showing the well and former Ute and Jicarilla Apache Indian agency buildings. *Courtesy Audrey Alpers Collection.*

Isaiah "Ike" Rinehart and his wife, Sarah. *Courtesy Chuck Hornung, Western History Collection.*

Colfax County jail, Cimarron, New Mexico. The surrounding wall, once ten feet high and four feet thick, was destroyed in an early 1900s jailbreak. *Photograph by author.*

Clay Allison, ca. 1871. *Courtesy West of the Pecos Museum Archives.*

St. James Hotel, ca. 1900. *Courtesy Audrey Alpers Collection.*

Henry Lambert, proprietor of the St. James Hotel. *Author's Collection.*

Site of the *Cimarron News and Press* office, formerly Carey Hardware & Livery. *Photograph by author.*

White Oaks, New Mexico, ca. 1890. *Courtesy University of New Mexico, Center for Southwest Research.*

Charlie Siringo. *Courtesy Robert G. McCubbin Collection.*

Sheriff Pat Garrett.

Pat Garrett, 1881. *Courtesy Craig Fouts Collection.*

Patrick Coghlan. *Author's Collection.*

Bob Olinger (right) with Tony Neis, March 1881. *Courtesy Harold B. Lee Library, Brigham Young University.*

Billy the Kid. *Author's Collection.*

Frank Clifford, ca. 1882, wearing Billy the Kid's hat. *Courtesy Michael Winter.*

Lake Valley, New Mexico, ca. 1900. *Courtesy University of New Mexico, Center for Southwest Research.*

Frank Wallace about the time he moved to Emporia. *Courtesy Michael Winter.*

CITY OF EMPORIA
ORGANIZATION OF THE CITY COUNCIL
April 23, 1908.

Mayor . . . . . . J. H. GLOTFELTER
President of the Council . . . . J. F. WALLACE

COUNCILMEN:
- *First Ward*—D. D. Williams, Jonas E. Eckdall
- *Second Ward*—M. J. Grosz, Fred Baird
- *Third Ward*—N. J. Jorgensen, J. F. Wallace
- *Fourth Ward*—J. O. Graham, Adam Mishler

Regular meetings of the Council first and third Mondays of each month.

Time of Meeting—April 1 to November 1 . . 8:00 o'clock p. m.
November 1 to April 1 . . 7:30 o'clock p. m.

Committees:

City Property—Grosz, Mishler, Jorgensen
Claims—Mishler, Eckdall, Wallace
Fire Department—Wallace, Graham, Grosz
Light—Mishler, Graham, Grosz
Ordinance—Wallace, Eckdall, Baird
Police and License—Baird, Jorgensen, Eckdall
Printing—Williams, Grosz, Graham
Sewers—Jorgensen, Baird, Graham
Streets—Graham, Jorgensen, Eckdall
Unfinished Business—Grosz, Williams, Jorgensen
Water—Eckdall, Mishler, Wallace
Ways and Means—Eckdall, Wallace, Baird
Special Paving—Williams, Baird, Graham

Emporia City Council cards showing Frank Wallace as president. *Courtesy Michael Winter.*

William Allen White. *Courtesy Kansas State Historical Society.*

Walt Mason. *Courtesy Kansas State Historical Society.*

Sarah Frances and Frank Wallace, ca. 1935. *Courtesy Michael Winter.*

Frank Wallace with his daughters, Little Rock, Arkansas, ca. 1940. *Courtesy Michael Winter.*

Grave of Frank Wallace in Bradford, Arkansas. *Courtesy Michael Winter.*

CHAPTER EIGHT

Billy the Kid Escapes from Jail

"I'd never have lighted that match," said Mr. Wallace, "if I had known who it was I was talking to." He meditated, started smoking, and then went on. "I suppose I had better start at Roswell," he decided, "and carry the story straight through."

Roswell wasn't the town then that it is now, for it consisted of Cap Lee's [sic, Lea]¹ store and his residence and no more. We had a lot of fun there, raggin' Cap Lee about his trees. He had just set out a nice young peach orchard, which was absolutely unheard of in that country then. We told him that he was just wasting his time, because that land wasn't fit for anything but to run cattle on. It seems we were slightly mistaken, for while I haven't been to Roswell since that time, I have been told that the peaches raised there now are as good as any peach produced in Georgia. It makes me wish I could get down there some day, and sink my teeth in one!

Roswell had a big Artesian spring, which flowed into the Pecos River. The spring was a river itself by the time it entered the Pecos, and so it was called "Spring River." That spring was really a big one, and I notice that it is now called, on the maps of New Mexico, "the largest Artesian well" in the United States.

Another curiosity which I saw in the Pecos valley was as follows:

right on the river bottom there is a small hill, probably seventy-five feet high, with a spring of water *at the top of it.* The hill is cone-shaped, like an ant-hill, and the spring flows right out of the top.

While we were in Roswell, we got up a dance that was a little out of the ordinary run of dances which we attended in New Mexico, in that it was not a Mexican affair. There was a little creek a short distance down and a few miles west from Roswell.[2] Scattered along the creek, the name of which I do not recall, were the farms of several "nester" families. We fellows decided that it would be fun to get up a dance where we could dance with white girls instead of Mexicans. As usual, the parents were kind of reluctant to let their girls have anything to do with us "wild Texans," since that type of person was ignorant of cowboy customs and suspicious of people who lived as we did. Accordingly, we were told that we probably could not get up a dance, but that our one chance was to get the two Corn girls[3] to come. If we could do that, our dance was sanctioned, for this family naturally led the rest, and if they would come, we'd have no trouble in getting the rest of the women-folks out.

First, we got hold of one of the nesters who had in his house a fairly large room with a board floor in it. Most houses, even among the white population, consisted of one room with a dirt floor. We got this fellow to agree to let us have the dance in his room, if we could get the dance up. Then we went to the head of the little creek, and told the first family that the Corns had promised to come. When they heard that, they also agreed to come, so we put their names on our "list," then went on to the next family, and got their names, and so on until we got them all on the list in the end. We went to the Corns last, and of course, had no trouble at all getting them to agree to come, with the names of all the settlers to back us.

We had our Mexican cook bake us some dried apple pies in the dutch oven. We killed us a nice fat calf, and got some canned goods from Cap Lee. These were the "refreshments" at our dance.

We had a really good time. It was a refreshing change for a bunch of cowboys to dance with the pert, independent, white girls instead of the silent Mexican *señoritas*. I remember one little happening which will show how we carried on. I was dancing on the floor in an old-fashioned square dance, which had in it a movement called "cheat or swing." In this movement the man joined arms with the girls and swung them on to the next one, unless one of them decided to "cheat" the other. When I got around to the point where I met Molly Corn, who was the "belle of the community," she "cheated" me. When I got around to her the second time, she held out her arm for a swing and I deliberately "cheated" *her!* We were an ornery, independent outfit!

The dance turned out very successful and ended rather unusual. It commenced raining about midnight, and we all stayed until the rain quit, which it did the next morning! Then we rolled back into Roswell and went right on working.

We did not have as much time for sociables and dances as we had at White Oaks, for the round-up kept us pretty busy. We worked at it steadily until it was over, and we were then ready to start back to our home range. We had in all nine head of cattle to take home with us, all steers about four years old.

I well remember how we heard the news of the Kid's escape. It is as fresh and clear in my mind as if it had happened yesterday. It was the day before we were to start back to our home range, and we were eating our supper in our camp, which was located just at Roswell, some distance from the Pecos River.

It was June, and a nice still evening, between sunset and dusk.

The day was Wednesday, and the Kid was to be hanged the following Friday.[4] While we were sitting around, eating, we heard a rider approaching, and wondered what was up. It turned out to be a feller who had come in from Lincoln, and who told us that Billy the Kid was on the loose again. He had escaped that day, after killing a couple of deputies.

I was not present in person either at the time of the Kid's capture, or his breaking jail, or his death, but I recall vividly the stories of these events as told to us at the time *immediately following their occurrence,* by men who were present, and whose word I knew to be good. I have not read any published reports of the Kid's adventures, nor have I seen a photograph of him at the present time.[5] Sixty years ago is long to remember, but these events were dramatic, and concerned people I knew, and my memory is very clear. All the things related in this book are accurately described, either as experienced by me or as related to me at the time. I have always designated as to whether I was actually present at an occurrence, or not. In the matter of Billy the Kid's escape from jail, I must tell the story as it was told to us on that night long ago.

The Kid had been kept in the Lincoln County jail, awaiting execution, which was to take place during the early part of June. Pat Garrett's chief deputy, Bob Gillinger [*sic,* Olinger],[6] and another deputy, John [*sic,* James W.] Bell,[7] were guarding the Kid on the Wednesday preceding the Friday that he was to be hanged.

Bob and the Kid were enemies of old, and really hated one another. Bob took delight in tormenting the Kid every chance he got, and one of the ways he used was to show the Kid his shot-gun, and say, "Kid, this here gun's loaded 'specially fer you! Both barrels is loaded with buckshot, and I'm sure anxious to try it out!"

He would beg the Kid to make a break to get away so he could use the gun. Such stuff as that, he would keep up all the time, but the Kid's chance to make a break didn't come until this Wednesday noon, when Bob went across the street to get the Kid's dinner and bring it over to him at the jail. Bell, the other deputy, was left alone with the "Kid." Bell was sitting in a chair in the main office, reading a newspaper, while the "Kid," shackled hand and foot, was doing as good a job as he could of walking around in the office. He had been allowed to leave his cell to get some exercise that way. Bell was interested in his paper, and paid little attention to the Kid, walking back and forth, back and forth in front of him. Then, seeing his chance, the Kid changed his directions so as to walk behind Bell's chair, instead of in front of it.

When he got directly behind Bell, he smashed down with both hand-cuffed hands on Bell's head, stunning the deputy. The Kid then took Bell's six-shooter and killed Bell. Then he hobbled over to the armory room and took out the shot-gun which Bob Gillinger had boasted was loaded for the Kid himself and went to the window facing the street.

Bob heard the revolver shot and was coming back across the street to investigate. The Kid hollered at him. "Hey, Bob!"

Bob looked up at the window where the Kid was, and the Kid let him have one barrel. Then he gave him the second barrel, and yelled, "That's for Dolores, Bob!"

Dolores was a Mexican girl. It was over [her] that Bob and the Kid had had much of their trouble.

After that, the Kid hobbled downstairs and over to a nearby blacksmith shop, where he had the blacksmith cut his shackles off. When he was free, the Kid walked over to the court-house. The county clerk's horse was tied to the hitching-rail. The Kid appropriated the horse, and jogged slowly down the main street and out of town. Jogging along like that, when he got to the end of the street, at the outskirts of town, he waved his hand and hollered, "So long, everybody!" and he rode away.[8]

The time of day when Billy killed his jailers and escaped is fixed in my mind by the fact that Charley Siringo and I were eating dinner with Bob Gillinger's mother[9] at noon of that day, and we often remarked about it later. We had left the few cattle we had gathered at that time for Lon and Tom to take care of while we took a ride down the Pecos from Roswell. We went, partly hoping to pick up another head or two of steers, but mostly for the ride and to see that part of the country. We happened to reach the Gillinger house near the mouth of Seven Rivers just at noon, and of course we gladly accepted Mrs. Gillinger's invitation to eat dinner with her. She seemed to be a grand old lady of the frontier type, but we felt some surprise at her attitude toward her own son.

She spoke of Bob in a very disparaging manner, saying that he was a blow-hard and a blusterer, and didn't always have the nerve to back up his plays. Billy must have been shooting Bob at that very moment, for we got the news of the Kid's escape while we were eating supper in camp at Roswell that day and we particularly noted at the time, the fact of our having supper with Mrs. Gillinger, and the way she spoke of Bob.

This was the biggest surprise, to hear a mother speak so harshly of her own son [*several lines illegible*].

As soon as we heard of the Kid's escape, Lon Chambers made me a present of the Kid's hat, which I had been trying to trade him out of. Lon thought that because he had been with Garrett when the

Kid was captured, it might not be healthy for him if he should happen to meet the Kid while wearing that hat. So I got it in the end. The hat had cost the Kid about twenty five dollars originally. It was a wide-brimmed, light-colored felt hat with a really artistically braided band around the crown. The crown was of just ordinary height, as the so-called ten-gallon hats were unheard-of in those days.

I kept the Kid's hat for several years, and finally traded it in on a new one at a store in Las Vegas. I kept the band and after I was married my wife wore it as a belt until it wore out.[10]

On Thursday morning, the next day after the Wednesday on which the Kid broke out of jail, we four fellows started up the Pecos with our nine head of Canadian River steers. It was a two days' drive to Fort Sumner, where we would leave the Pecos and strike across the Staked Plains for the LX ranch twenty-five miles below Tascosa, Texas.

About half-way between Roswell and Fort Sumner, we stopped at an old deserted house to make camp. There was a brake of cottonwoods at this place, running down to the river, and this in itself was memorable, because in those days there was very little timber on the Pecos. It may have been because of the cattle keeping it down, or it may not; anyway, you would ride right up to the river and drop off into the water. Therefore, a clump of cottonwoods such as surrounded that old house was something to stay in the mind. The dirt was hard-packed and gravelly around the house, which was the usual one-room hut, with the old-time dirt roof on it. This roof was decorated half-way across the front edge with human skulls. There they sat, grinning cheerfully, and *each skull with a bullet hole in it!*

The place was called the "Bosque Redondo," which means "round timber." It was formerly one of the camps used by the Chisum boys on their round-ups, but no one had been there for years except the occasional passer-by such as ourselves. Consequently, we didn't ever learn for sure where the skulls came from. We were told afterward, without authority, that they were the skulls of "bad men" who were killed there, and their heads stuck up on the hut as an example. This, however, was just a rumor, so far as I could find out, and it is possible that the skulls were collected by somebody who had a notion to see how many he could find, and with a gruesome sense of humor, thought it would be funny to decorate the house with them.[11]

On the second day of our drive, we were nearing Fort Sumner about the middle of the afternoon, when a horseman came in sight behind us. He was travelling the same direction we were, but of course he could go faster, as we had the cattle. When he got within a hundred yards or so of us, he left the road and eased around us, keeping some fifty yards away from us all the while. He circled completely around us and went back onto the road again, and rode on ahead. Now I knew the fellow instantly, and I told Charley Siringo who it was.

"Charley," I said, "that feller ridin' around us is the Kid!"

I knew him by sight, even at such a distance, being [as recounted below] fairly well acquainted with him, and we were much interested to see him avoid us as he did, making a complete semi-circle around one side of us, instead of passing us in the usual manner. Readin' sign, we knew he was going to Fort Sumner, which was his favorite hideout place.

As we went on, Charley started planning for us to make a dry camp a couple of miles the other side of Sumner, and leave Emory and Chambers to take care of the steers until midnight, when it would be my turn to relieve Chambers on night herd. While the other boys were on duty, Charley planned, he and I would get Pete Maxwell's hall and have a dance. So we did just that.

Pete Maxwell's "hall" was really just a room in his house.[12] The dance had been going full swing for some time, and it was warm inside, so I stepped out on the porch to cool off. When I became accustomed to the dark, I noticed that somebody else was out there. He was a slight feller, as I could tell, but it was too dark to see more. I took him to be one of the Mexicans, and spoke to him.

"Buenos tardes, amigo." [sic]

"Y a usted, amigo," he answered easily, as if he were perfectly at home in the language. We chatted on for a few minutes, and most people would have taken him for a Mexican, from the way he handled the language. But I had been among the Mexicans so much that I really talked it like a native and my ear detected a slight difference in the stranger's accent. I couldn't lay my finger on it exactly, but something about his Mexican speech wasn't quite right.

"This ain't no greaser," I thought. "I'll take a look at him."

I still couldn't tell who it was, although my eyes were now used to the dark for the fellow loitered in the shadows, and there was no moon. He'd been standing at the window, watching the dance, but he swiftly moved back as I came out. I wouldn't have been so curious if I had even vaguely suspected who he was, but under the circumstances I had no thought of such a thing, and so I rolled me a cigarette, still chatting away, and struck a match to light it.

In the brief flare from the light, I directed a glance at the fellow. I knew him at once, and I knew that he must not realize it! Still seeming casual, I lit my cigarette, tossed the match away, and stood smoking and talking to him for about ten minutes, still in Mexican of course. Presently, to make it seem more certain that I did not recognize him,

I asked him why he didn't come in and dance a while. "We're havin' a good time in there," I told him.

"No-o," he said, "I don't feel like dancin' tonight. Guess I won't."

So I told him I guessed I'd go on in and dance some more myself.

"Bueno, amigo," he answered. "Adios."

I turned around and went back in the house, wondering what would happen next. Nothing did happen, but I figured then, and I still believe, that it was a very close call for me that night, for I was playing with dynamite, and I knew it. The glimpse I caught of him in the light of that match revealed his identity to me at once. It was *Billy the Kid.*

He must have known me, too, for we had met several times, and we'd talked and had drinks together in saloons. He was a likeable kid until he was crossed, and then he was as swift and deadly as a rattlesnake. He didn't "take nothing from nobody," as we expressed it, and mostly nobody tried to cross him.

I still wonder, sometimes, how I ever escaped with my life that night, for he was being hunted by a posse which must have had orders to shoot him on sight, and he must have been nervous. Also, he had been standing on the porch of the Maxwell house, watching through the window. He could hardly have failed to see me as I went by inside, wearing his hat, and dancing with his girl. She was Pete Maxwell's sister [Paulita], and the Kid was very much in love with her, and she with him.[13] He was trying to persuade her to run off with him, to Mexico, which was the reason for his hanging around instead of getting off to safety as he could easily have done after he broke jail.

I have decided that he let me go because he didn't want to start anything, and he surmised I wouldn't. I had nothing against him personally, nor he against me, so he probably knew that I would not reveal his presence there that night. But just the same, I'd not have been so careless, if I'd dreamed of who he was, standing on that porch in the dark.

As it turned out, though, I'm glad I did, for that was the last time I ever saw Billy the Kid. The following morning we four "Texans" started on toward the Canadian River country, and the next time I heard of the Kid, he was dead, shot by Pat Garrett in Pete Maxwell's house.[14]

CHAPTER NINE

Various Stories Concerning Billy the Kid and Contradictory Stories of His Death

"He was a likeable kid," asserted Mr. Wallace, with emphasis. "He was popular with everybody except the men whose cattle he was stealing, and those who wanted to collect the reward that the cattlemen set on his head. Even a great many of the cattlemen liked him. He was well thought of by the cowboys, and as for the Mexicans, well, he was their friend, and they were his. He talked their language fluently, and he was not niggardly with his money, and he was always square with them.

"I liked him, too, and I would have liked to see him make his getaway with Paulita Maxwell and make a man of himself. He would have done it. He was a square-shooter and a good companion, and never went out of his way to make trouble. Contrary to the reports, he never killed a man unless he had to, and in the first place he was only doing what all hired hands were expected to do if necessary in those days, kill to protect the cattle or lives of the men they worked for."

In appearance he was smallish, very deeply tanned but not swarthy, with, to the best of my recollection, bluish-gray eyes, and brown hair. He was slightly buck-toothed, that is, his teeth protruded a little. In manner, he was pleasant, soft-spoken, never ugly, and he never tried to pick a fight. He was full of fun, and quick-witted, and very loyal to his friends.

The Kid was really outlawed when he was working for [Alexander] McSween, an Englishman [sic] who had established in Lincoln County. McSween was a lawyer in Lincoln, with a ranch out of town a ways. According to the story as it was told to me, McSween was resented by old John Chisum, who was king of cattlemen in New Mexico at that time. He had two brothers, Pitts [sic, Pitzer] and Jim, but John was the dominant one of them.

The quarrel between the two factions grew into a minor war, and the militia was called out to help quiet things down. Since I first put down these reminiscences, I have been told that it was a man named Murphy who was McSween's foe; but I am telling it here just as I heard it in the 70s in that country.

One day the Sheriff of Lincoln County, assisted by colored soldiers, surrounded the Englishman's house and called on them to surrender the Kid. This being refused, the result was a pitched battle between McSween's household and the Sheriff's party. Seeing he was making no headway, the leader of the besiegers decided to set fire to the house, and smoke them out.

Now to show how rich McSween was, I have only to say that his wife had a piano! So far as I know, it was the only piano in New Mexico. And to show her contempt for the besiegers, Mrs. McSween played the piano during the time their house was burning, but, as the fire gained, it got too hot for them to stay inside, so the Kid said, "I'm getting out of here and give you folks a chance to save your lives!"

Throwing open the door, he dashed out through the soldiers. Sometimes he seemed to jump ten feet at a leap, and when he lit he'd throw his gun down and kill off a soldier. Even though the entire posse, soldiers and all, was shooting at him he got through without a wound, and again made his getaway. McSween, however, was killed, and so were several others. This occurrence created a good deal of excitement at the time, and formed the climax of what was called the "Lincoln County War."[1]

A story which was told at the time with considerable enjoyment, was as follows: the Sheriff's office heard that the Kid was out at a certain Mexican house, which was built on a piece of open prairie. It was a two-room adobe, or as we called it, 'dobe, shack, occupied by two families, each family living in one room. Each room had an outside door, and there was a 'dobe partition between the rooms. In this partition was a window-like opening, rather small and high up, but no door.

The posse surrounded the house and entered one of the rooms by its door, and proceeded to search that room thoroughly. The Kid was in the other room at the time, so the posse failed to find him. So, like chuckle-heads, they all went around to the door of the other room, not leaving any of their number in the room already searched. While they were going around the house, the Mexican women (there were no men at home) pushed the Kid through the opening in the partition, into the room already searched. The women in that room promptly covered him with old bed-quilts and the posse rode away deciding they had been given a wrong tip.

This story was told for the truth at the time it was supposed to have occurred, and I believe it is true. It certainly is typical of the Kid's coolness in danger and his ingenuity.[2] The following story of the Kid I can really vouch for, because I was present when the incident occurred. A cattle buyer from Las Vegas was down at Fort Sumner buying some butcher stock for the Las Vegas market. He was ready that morning to start back home with cattle he had been able to buy, and he came into the saloon where "Billy the Kid" himself, and several others were irrigatin' our systems. He came up to the bar and set up the drinks for the house, and told what his business was down there. He said that he had been very disappointed that he hadn't been lucky enough to see "The Kid," as he had heard so much about him. He had hoped to see him, for he had heard that this was one of his favorite sections of the country. He was rather indiscreet in his talk, saying he had heard so much about the Kid's quick draw and straight shooting that he would have liked to watch him in action.

"I'd have probably been disappointed," he added, "for I don't believe *any* man can handle a gun as they say the 'Kid' can!" The Kid was leaning up against the bar, but he stepped away from it. The cattle buyer was also at the moment three for four feet away from the bar. The Kid spoke up.

"So you don't believe anyone can handle a gun like that?" he answered softly.

"I'd have to see it to believe it!" stated the cattle buyer. With one swift motion the Kid drew his six-shooter and shot the buyer's hat off his head. The fellow didn't faint, but he must have come close to doing it.

"Well," smiled the "Kid," "guess you'll have to believe it now. And I'm the feller you wanted to meet. Folks call me 'Billy the Kid.'" After the atmosphere had cleared up and we had all taken another drink, at the Kid's expense this time, he asked the cattle buyer if he'd bought all the beef cattle he wanted. The buyer said he'd like to get a few more, but couldn't find them there.

"Why, I've got a couple of steers," said the "Kid," "that are fat enough for beef. I'll sell 'em to you. What are you payin'?" The cattle buyer said forty dollars was about the average for the kind of stuff he wanted, but he was starting and wouldn't have time to go after them that day.

The Kid said, "Why, they're right on your road. I'll ride along and we can make our dicker, and you can take 'em right along!"

So he and the buyer rode on and joined the buyer's men. When they were about a couple or three miles up the road, the Kid pointed over to some cattle grazing on a little *vega* (meadow), and said, "There they are now. Let's go over and look at them."

They rode over, and as the steers were in fairly good flesh, the cattle buyer immediately closed the deal at forty dollars a head. The Kid helped him drive them to the rest of his bunch, and bid him good-bye.

The cattle buyer proceeded on his way, and the Kid rode over to a Mexican house on the other side of the vega. When he got to the house, he called the man out and told him, "I have just sold that fellow goin' up the road them steers of yours. You'd better go get them."

Then he rode back to the saloon and told the rest of us about it, and had a good laugh over it. We learned later that the Mexican got his cattle back, but the buyer didn't come back after his money. The Kid was like Charley Siringo that way. He was a prankster, full of "devilment," as we called it, and if his pranks turned out profitably for him so much the better. Billy looked a great deal like Charley, too. They were the same build, and complexion, and even both slightly buck-toothed.[3]

About the first news that we heard after getting back on the home range in Texas, with our Canadian River cattle, was that Pat Garrett had killed the Kid. Pat's account of the killing was as follows: he had got word that the Kid was hanging around Fort Sumner, which was true, so with his new chief deputy, Kip McKinney, and the cattle detective for the Canadian River Cattle Association, John Poe, Pat went to Fort Sumner and dropped into Pete Maxwell's house after night. Pat slipped quietly into the house and into Pete's bedroom, Kip and John staying on the outside. Pat was holding a whispered conversation with Pete, who had told him the Kid was sleeping in the house that night. While they were whispering, the Kid opened the door of Pete's bedroom. The Kid was dressed only in his underwear, and held a butcher knife in his hand. He saw someone was there, and said, "Quien es?" (Who is it?). Pete whispered to Pat, "That's him!" Pat immediately shot, killing the Kid instantly. And that was his story of shooting "Billy the Kid."

There was, however, another version of the shooting of the Kid. Of course, there were no witnesses to the shooting except Pete and Pat, but it was generally believed that the Kid must have been killed as he lay asleep in his bed, for no one believed that the Kid would have come out clad in only his underwear, and bearing a butcher knife. In fact, he probably would not have taken his clothes off when he slept. Certainly he would not have moved from his bed without his gun.

I was back in Fort Sumner a few months later, and stayed a week or so, and I found that this was the version which was believed by all the people whom I talked to, as Pat was pretty well known as a man who took no chances on his own hide, and never gave the other fellow a chance if he could help it. Also, the Kid never carried a knife for a weapon, and certainly not a butcher knife.[4]

Pat's reputation was not enhanced by his handling of the Kid's gang, for he shot three of them down without giving them a chance to surrender, and that was plain murder then, and is today. It was a common custom in those days, when a reward was posted on a man's head, to shoot him first and then claim it was done while he was trying to get away, or in self-defense.

This pretty well ends my recollections of the Kid. I may as well say here that Frank Stewart, who was then cattle detective for the Canadian River Cattle Association, got his share of the reward money for the capture of the "Kid," but he did not share a penny of it with the men of the expedition, as he was supposed to do. Frank did, however, buy himself a spread of his own shortly after the Kid's capture.

To complete the chapter; some time after that, during my perambulations about the country, I landed in Albuquerque after several weeks on the plains. I was dirty, and tired and dressed just like all cow-hands dressed then when they were doing a job of work, in pants and boots, shirt, neckerchief, and old corduroy coat, ragged, at that! I saw a photography shop on the outskirts of town, and some whim decided me to have my picture made. Just as I was, I went in and had a tintype made of myself, wearing the Kid's old hat.

I don't know how I happened to hang onto that picture all this time. For years I wanted to forget that old life, and the picture just lay around, but finally, I resurrected it, and now I wouldn't part with it. You can see the ragged edge of a hole in my jacket sleeve, and I bet I hadn't washed for a week!

The crown of the hat and hatband do not show as well as I'd like for them to, but otherwise, the picture is very plain, and is certainly typical of the old western cowboy, just as he was.

CHAPTER TEN

Back to the Canadian

"Did I ever tell you," asked Mr. Wallace, "how four men took three thousand cattle three hundred miles across the Staked Plains? It seems almost unbelievable, but I know it was done; for I was one of the men."

The morning after the dance at which I saw "Billy the Kid" for the last time, we started to head back towards the Canadian River country. The Staked Plains, the *Llano Estacado,* was then a large area of trackless wilderness. The only road across it was the old Government road from Fort Sill, Oklahoma, to Fort Sumner, New Mexico. The four of us, Emory, Chambers, Siringo, and I, had to make a trip of three hundred miles "by the sun." There was no road, and nobody ever thought of carrying a compass. We went by the stars and by the sun. We had to know the plains, and the direction to the next water, and how to find it. Water was from twenty-five to forty miles apart, one water here, and another there. I came to know all the plains, eventually, but at the time we four took our herd of Canadian cattle home, I had only been over a part of them, and there was a gap I did not know anything about. Our orders were to bring back all Canadian River cattle that we found, and this, combined with our ignorance of the route, came to be a large order indeed.

By the time we reached the headwaters of the Brazos River, a small spring at the head of Double Mountain Fork, we had about four hundred head, and the next water was the big spring at the head of "Running Water," located on the Staked Plains about sixty miles south of the Canadian River. Running Water was an important watering place, as there was no other water closer than forty miles.

None of us knew the exact direction to Running Water, but a couple of buffalo hunters came in for water while we were camped on the Brazos. They told us Running Water was a little east of south, forty miles from where we were. While that did not seem to fit in right, we had to take it as it was told to us, so we started out. We made a dry camp that night, and the next day we kept on in the same direction all day without finding any water. We made dry camp again the next night. We had covered a lot of ground that day, as it was now in June and hot. The cattle were thirsty, and did not stop to graze any. We knew we were lost by then, but we kept on going in the same direction.

The following morning, when the cattle got so we could not hold them on the bed ground any longer, we had to let them string out. It was before day-break, and Charley Siringo and I had doubled up to try and hold them, but we were not able to do so. Before the sun came up they smelled water, and we let them go. We went ahead of them, fighting them out of one end of a grassy lake of rain water, so we could have some fairly clean water for our own use. After about two hours, the cook wagon and the other two boys caught up with us and we enjoyed a hearty breakfast.

Now a real problem confronted us. We had only one horse each. We could use two of the wagon mules to help out a little, but it was still a problem to handle the cattle with so few horses. Our herd had now increased to about twenty-five hundred head, as there was a lot of cattle around the "lake." We knew we were off our course, and the other two boys did not want to try to take the cattle any farther, since our grub was also running very low. We had very little coffee, no flour, and |still had more than a hundred miles to go.

Charley and I talked it over, and we decided to go ahead on a new course. We started on again about mid-afternoon. The other two fellows had no choice, they had to stay put, as neither of them knew a thing about the plains. We now headed about north-east. We made a dry camp that night and next day continued on the same course. Close to two hours before sundown of that day, we struck the draw of Running Water, below the water itself. We pushed on up it till we got to the water. The spring kept water in holes for about two-and-a-half or three miles below it. The cattle filled up with water at these holes, then Charley and I rode on up to the spring and found signs of an outfit that had pulled out that morning for the Canadian. We at once rode back and helped Lon and Tom to shove the cattle along, and we followed the plain trail of the fellows that had left that morning. We had to go about forty more miles to the next water, and we caught up with them there, after a two days' drive. There we parted company with Tom Emory, as he was a rider for the LIT, and that outfit was going to the LIT ranch, while we were headed for the LX. It was at the head of the Palo Duro canyon that we caught them, for I remember that we could see their outfit away down in the canyon when we were still on top.

We were out of everything to eat but fresh meat. I would have given a dollar for enough tobacco to roll one cigarette. We got grub from the LIT outfit, and a fresh horse apiece, and the next day we took the herd across the Canadian to the LX home ranch, and met the round-up there.

That trip really was a tough one. Heat, dust, the knowledge that we were lost, the lack of water, and for the last days the lack of all supplies except fresh beef, united in making a journey that was far from pleasant. Charley and I used to ride on ahead of the herd and leave the other two boys in the rear. And when we'd come to a place where the outfit ahead had camped for a meal, we'd race to see who got there first to pick up any biscuits they had thrown away. Sometimes we'd find one, and were we tickled! The first one to get there got the biscuit, and he ate it! The other two boys didn't have a chance to find any. It was always either Charley or me.

It was not easy to handle so many cattle at any time, with so few men, but when they are thirsty, the job was really hard. It was especially difficult to keep them bedded down at night. I was pretty good at soothing them down. Lon Chambers was on duty just before me, and he would get them all riled up, milling around, and generally restless. He had a rasp in his voice, and he was a nervous type of person anyway. He'd try to bunch them up too tight, and they didn't like that, either. Then I'd go on duty and loosen them up, so they didn't feel crowded; talk softly to them, and sing to them, and they'd bed down with very little trouble. My voice was just the opposite to Lon's as mine was deep and sort of soothing, and the cattle seemed to quiet down to my singing.

These cattle were not the white-face or Hereford cattle, which had not yet been introduced on the range. Ours then were the old Texas longhorns—scrubby stock, half-wild, and quick as race-horses. We had a hard time holding them on that trip, and we were worn out long before the end. Well do I remember one night when we had them pretty well quieted down, with Lon Chambers on guard. I was to follow him, and I was getting some needed sleep, along with the other two boys, when in came Lon all excited and woke us all up. From a bright moonlight night everything was getting dark, and Lon he was mighty excited. That fool boy had never seen an eclipse of the moon or knew there was such a thing! Well, we were sore! But we explained, and did we cuss him out!

When we got back to the LX home ranch, they said we had three thousand head of cattle, and they swore that we could not have brought them in with no more men than we had. But there we were, and we had the cattle to show, so that settled it.[1]

CHAPTER ELEVEN

Life on the Staked Plains

🌿 *"Cattlemen got their start in various ways in those days," observed Mr. Wallace. "Most of 'em came by their herds legitimately. And their word was good to the last penny. Some of 'em made out like a feller who came down from Colorado to winter his stuff on the Staked Plains, the same winter that Siringo and I and the other two boys spent in White Oaks. I was told how he had done in the Fall and winter, and in the Spring I had personal experience with him." He paused and mused as he rolled the inevitable cigarette. Presently he continued.*

LIFE ON THE STAKED PLAINS: AN INCREASED HERD

The two Canadian River round-ups, one working up the river from Adobe Walls ('dobe Walls, we always called it), and the other working down the river from Fort Bascom, New Mexico, set close to Tascosa, Texas. The next day after we four boys got in from the plains with our three thousand head of cattle from Tascosa, all the outfits started back to their home ranges, taking their cattle with them.

The fellow from Colorado did not belong on the Texas ranges at all. He had a ranch somewhere not far from Pueblo, Colorado. The summer before, it had been very dry in that section of the country, and there was not enough grass on his range to winter his cattle, so he rounded them up and struck down into the Canadian River country. He brought down about eight hundred head, and when they were near the LX home ranch, he saw there was plenty of grass thereabouts, so that night he let his cattle all get away from him.

Next day he rode to the LX ranch and asked John Hollicott for help to round up the cattle so he could take his farther on. Hollicott was in charge there, and he told the Coloradoan that it was too late in the season, that he couldn't afford to have a round-up at that time of year, as it would take too much flesh off the cattle right at the time they would need it most, going into the winter. Hollicott told him to leave his cattle right where they were and bring an outfit down for the Spring round-up, and gather up his stuff then.

As this was exactly what the gentleman from Colorado wanted, he agreed to do it, and went back home. Next Spring he came back to Texas with his men, and a tough, hard-looking lot they all were. Both he and his men proved to be of an accumulative disposition, and any cattle they found with brands that did not belong to the Canadian Cattle Association members were branded at once with the Coloradoan's brand, if he could possibly get by with it.

The Canadian River men caught on to his little scheme, and when he started back up river, Hollicott, who was captain of the round-up, detailed me to go with him and see that he had no cattle branded with a Canadian River Cattle Association brand, when he passed Fort Bascom. So I took my bed over to his wagon, and worked with his men up the river.

I remember this man's name well, but I don't want to use it out of consideration to any family he might have still living in his part of the country. We'll just call him "Buck," and his brand we'll call the "BOK." for it was similar to that. It was stamped in large letters on the left side. I have occasion to remember his name, for I nearly made a serious mistake concerning it.

We were sitting around the camp fire, eating our suppers one evening, when he said something about his name being "Dutch."

"Why, Buck," I says, "are you *Dutch?*"

"Sure, I'm Dutch!" he answered. "Whatsa matter with that?"

"Why, hell, Buck," I drawled, "I thought you's a white man!"

Now that was just my fool kid idea of a joke, not meaning a thing by it, and not realizing how sensitive he was about being "Dutch," as we called it. Really he was German, but all Germans were "Dutch" to us then. I certainly realized in a second how he felt, for those hard-faced hombres stiffened and their hands fell to their six-shooters, while their eyes moved to "Buck" and they waited wooden-faced to see what he'd do next. Well, he stiffened, too, for an instant, then he relaxed and laughed, and his men did the same, and of course I did too. Yep, we had a *good* laugh over my little joke. Nobody laughed harder than I did, but I never tried making any more jokes with "Buck" about his nationality. Such an incident could lead to very serious consequences, and I should have known it. Many a gun-fight has started as innocently as that, and often has led to a killing.

I rode with "Buck's" outfit all the way to Fort Bascom, according to my instructions, and it was really interesting to see his technique as we went along. He and his men made a practice of taking in any stray cattle along the way, providing they were other than Association cattle, and at the first stop, they would put the BOK brand on the "strays."

Maybe the same day, maybe the next day, a fellow, usually a Mexican, would catch up and accuse "Buck" of driving off his cattle. Sometimes it was a milk cow, sometimes a steer, but whatever it was, "Buck" would immediately order his men to stop the cattle, and he would ask the Mexican to show him what his brand was, and then they would ride into the bunch and the Mexican would show "Buck" his animal. "Buck" was a very smooth talker, and on finding the Mexican had pointed out his brand correctly, would say that he was very sorry he had made the mistake. He would say that he had bought some cattle, back along the road, and thought that they were what he was branding, but that he never sold any BOK branded cattle to anyone except when he shipped them to a distant market. He would then ask the Mexican what his price was for his cattle that had been branded BOK, and he would pay whatever the Mexican asked, at once.

This was a profitable procedure, for where he paid a big price for one animal, he got away with about ten free. When I parted from him at Fort Bascom, he laughed and said, "Well, I brought down eight hundred head last fall, and got 'em wintered free, and I'm takin' twelve hundred of them back. I didn't do so bad this trip! And I'll come back and get the rest of 'em on the fall round-up!"

Of course, it was none of my business what he did about taking cattle other than Canadian Association cattle, and a man with common sense didn't butt in where it was none of his business, those days. So I turned back at Fort Bascom and he went on, but I never forgot that experience. It was just a sample of how some of the cattlemen would increase their herds.

Life on the Staked Plains: Tascosa

After I got back to the E-Cross-E from the trip with "Buck," the Spring round-up was finished and there was very little to do, nor would there be much until Fall round-up time. Of course, the boys had celebrated in Tascosa when the round-ups met, and a wild, rip-roarin' time they had, too, after being out on the range so long. But now all was fairly quiet. Tee [Sillman] and I made a couple of trips to Tascosa. That was a wild little cow town! Tough as Dodge any day! I have often wondered what became of it. I finally found it on a Texas map, so it evidently didn't disappear, but apparently its most important era was its brief moment as a "cow-town."

Cape Willingham was sheriff at Tascosa after he quit driving the mail route. It was told to me that one day a fellow came riding into town, roarin' drunk, and he'd ride up and down the main street, flipping his six-shooter back and forth, back and forth, shooting it not up in the air (as was customary when a cowboy was having a little fun), but right down at the feet of such folks as those who hadn't got out of the way.

He wouldn't pay any attention to Cape, who ordered him to stop; and so he shot once too often, killing some ducks right near a woman who fainted of fright, and then Cape let him have it with his "Betsey." He shot the drunk right in the head. The fellow was really dangerous, you know, and Cape had to get him before something worse happened. If he'd fired a few salvos into the air it wouldn't have been so bad.[1]

Cowboys were frequently doing that, and the townspeople expected it. But they couldn't be allowed to go along firing at people's feet from a running horse that way. I have often seen them fire at a fellow's feet to make him "dance" in saloons, but that is a different proposition.

The rest of that summer I knocked around on the E-Cross-E ranch, passing time as best I could, riding around, taking a rifle and hunting deer or turkey, whichever I happened to see. Sometimes antelope, too, when sighted, but I never had another such experience with antelope as when I was on the Bell Ranch.

LIFE ON THE STAKED PLAINS: BUFFALO

One time that summer I had an experience I've always been ashamed of. I was sent back out on the plains with some of the boys. One day we were camped at the head of Running Water for dinner, and shortly after we had eaten, a herd of about five hundred buffalo came in for water. Some of the boys proposed a buffalo hunt, which we all enthusiastically agreed to, and we ran those buffaloes for ten or twelve miles, killing possibly fifteen to twenty of them. We had no use for the meat or the hides. We just did it for sport, and left the carcasses where they lay. This was the last sizable bunch of buffalo that was left on the Staked Plains.

It was just this sort of foolishness that caused the buffalo to disappear from the open range, and almost become extinct. It was an exciting sport, but I was ashamed of it even then, and I haven't felt any better about it since.

Coming back along the trail, Tom Coffee and another fellow, whose name I can't remember, and I found a wounded young buffalo bull that immediately showed fight when we rode up on him. There was only one cartridge left among the three of us, and that was in my six-shooter. Tom had a good rawhide rope on his saddle, and in a spirit of devilment he roped the bull. On being checked by the rope, the bull immediately turned and charged Tom on his horse. Tom tried to spur his horse into a run, but our ponies were so badly played out chasing the buffalo, that there was no speed left in them. Tom yelled, "Shoot the son-of-a-gun!" I was afraid to take a chance with my one bullet by shooting at the head, so I took a snap shot at the small of his back. Luckily, it dropped him, so Tom took his rope off the bull and left him lying there and we rode on.

LIFE ON THE STAKED PLAINS: COW SAVVY

I drew sixty dollars a month that summer, as I was in charge of the outfit. That was the top pay for a hand, and I thought I was doing pretty well. My job then was to handle the men, direct them to the next water, and look out for and pick up Canadian River cattle, by which was meant all cattle having brands of the ranchers who belonged to the Canadian River Cattle Association. I used to get a good deal of satisfaction out of being able to roll in at night and let somebody else stand guard, with me drawing sixty dollars a month and them thirty! Of course, there was much more to the job than that. The man in charge of such an outfit had to know the plains. He had to know where the best grass was, and where the water holes could be found. He had to know where low places were located, that were likely to collect rain water when the season was wet, and that were likely to collect cows at certain times! Scattered over the plains were many little flat alkali spots, where water would gather in the rains, especially in the spring season.

During the winter the cattle had got weak, and sometimes they would get in these ponds and get stuck there. Sometimes it was a "cow-brute," as we called the cows, but mostly it was steers who would get caught. They would be too weak to move, and the sticky 'dobe mud would be deep and hard to get out of, and they would just stand there, waiting to be got out, or to die. This was especially tedious when the hot sun began to dry up the mud-holes, and the weak "critters" would sometimes stand there until the mud had baked hard. I've found them in such a state that I knew they had been there at least a couple of days.

If the mud was hard and caked about their feet; we would have to break it away, or sometimes they would be lying on their sides, having grown too weak to stand up. Then we'd have to drag the critter away from there, and "tail him up." That was done by twisting the tail and giving a little pull, and then a lift, and if they were able to start at all that would start 'em. Then you'd better have your horse handy, and get on him as quickly as possible, for invariably that critter would come after you and try to hook you! They wouldn't bother you if you were on your horse, but afoot they would go for you.

It was this process of "tailing up" that gave rise to the expression "on the lift," used amongst us to denote a siege of illness. I have been asked why we got the cattle up by lifting their tails. That was because a cow always got up hind legs first. You could tell a cow from a horse as far as you could see them on the plains by this way. The horse got up by raising the front legs first, always. This knowledge came in handy for the cowboy many a time.[2]

The cowboy's pay started at a low of thirty dollars a month, but as he became more proficient, he would draw more. Ropers commanded more than greenhorns, as did men that were good in the branding pens.

There was quite an art in branding. You had to be careful to burn through the hair-roots and yet not all the way through the hide. A young calf's hide was thin, and if the brander was not careful, the branding iron would go through and burn the flesh, which in healing would cause the brand to be blurred. A brand properly put on would be as clean as if it had been written with a pen.

Life on the Staked Plains: A Close Call

Tom's narrow escape from the buffalo bull reminds me of one of my own. It was when I was riding to Fort Bascom with the BOK outfit, and it was really a close call.

I was riding a rangy, claybank horse, a four-year-old. He was one of the best horses I ever rode on the range, but as yet he wasn't thoroughly broke. I could do the usual work with him, however, except for cutting out. This he had not yet been taught.

One day a steer broke away on my side of the herd as we were driving it along, and of course, I started out to head him off and bring him back. The steer was running his best which was plenty fast, but I finally got a little ahead of him and he checked to turn back. Just at that moment my saddle turned. I guess I'd been careless that morning and neglected to tighten the cinches, as was usually done after riding awhile.

Those old range horses soon learned to swell up when we were tightening the cinches while the saddle was being put on, and unless we re-tightened them after about a half-hour or so of riding, they would be so loose that there was danger of the saddle's turning when a sharp turn had to be made with the horse.

Well, my saddle turned, and when I struck the ground I found my left foot hung fast in the stirrup. The horse, of course, had kept his feet and was dragging me across the prairie. I reached for my six-shooter, but it had fallen out of the holster when I fell off the horse. I thought that was my last trip, but I braced myself on my elbows, letting my arms and back take the brunt of the dragging. The horse had taken me this way for nearly a hundred yards, when one of the other boys caught up with us with his rope swinging, and put it over the claybank's head. That got me out of as tight a place as I was ever in, I believe.

Life on the Staked Plains: The Claybank

This claybank was a splendid swimmer. Several times when I had to swim the Canadian when it was running full on account of rains up above somewhere; he would carry me across without wetting my clothes more than a few inches above my belt.

I remember one time when I was going to cross the river, and found the ford swimming deep. A covered wagon was camped on the other side, waiting for the water to go down, so it could be got across in safety. Looking across, I could see two or three womenfolks in the party on the other side, so I thought I would show off a bit. I rode to the edge of the water on my side, and when they saw I was going to cross, they stood in a bunch and watched me. The claybank swam over as easily as usual, and came out about twenty steps below their camp. He climbed up on the bank, and without pausing I rode straight on away from the river. Were those folks astonished! I believe I could have thrown an apple into any of their mouths without touching their teeth. "We fellers" sure enjoyed pulling off a stunt like that in those days.

This claybank was fast on his feet, also, and he would cross on quicksand without getting bogged down. The quicksand was always packed slightly for a depth of about four inches on top, and if an animal was fast enough he could cross with safety, but a slow-moving animal would sink half-way to his knees, and find himself unable to go farther, whereas the quick-stepping one could get across. I could always rely on my claybank to carry me over quicksand, and also through water.

A claybank is a drab yellow horse, really a clay color, or a dun color, you might say. If he had markings like a burro (black mane and tail, with a dark streak from the top of his shoulders down a short way onto his leg) he was considered the toughest and most reliable of all cow-ponies, for he'd take you there and bring you back every time. A solid black horse was considered a good color, too, but the claybank with burro markings was picked first every time.

Life on the Staked Plains: The Rodeo

While we are on the subject of horses, let me say my word about rodeos. In the Old West there was, of course, no such thing as the modern rodeo. "Rodeo" (and it should be pronounced "ro-thay-o," with the "th" soft as in "then") means "round-up," and we had no time for any "monkey-doodle work" on a round-up. Course, we generally had several pitching horses in the remuda, but we rode the kinks out of them for necessity, not for fun. The *remuda* pronounced "r'moo-tha," again with the "th" soft) was the "horse-bunch" which contained the extra horses needed by the cowboys in their work. Each man at a round-up would have six to eight horses assigned to him as his "string." As fast as he needed a change, he would draw out one of his "string," and ride it until it became necessary for him to have a new mount. Of course, there would be several horses that would pitch every time they were saddled up, but we merely rode those like other horses; as the pitching would not last over four or five minutes. In the larger outfits it was a common practice to have a genuine outlaw horse in the remuda. If we got a chance, we'd get a green hand to saddle up one of these, and then we'd watch him get thrown. The outlaw also came in handy for a rider who was out of sorts and hating the world in general. Such a one frequently would put his rope on the outlaw and take out his grouch on the horse. The job of conquering such a horse would get a bad temper out of most anybody's system!

In those days, when you rode a pitching horse, you rode him until he quit pitching, or threw you. There was nobody to take you off at the end of a few seconds like they do now at the "rodeos." I've seen many times a man bleeding at the nose before his horse quit pitching, in fact, that has happened to me several times.

I went to see one modern rodeo in my life, and I wouldn't cross the road to look at another. Looked to me too much like circus play, with trained animals. Those horses knew all about it, you could tell that! They quit pitching when the whistle blew, and waited for the men to come up and take the rider off!

There is something else that I have seen in rodeos, and occasionally in illustrations of Western stories in magazines that I take exception to. That is, girls wearing pants! In my whole experience on the range, I never saw a cow-girl. Girls in those days rode side-saddles, and wore long skirts to ride in. Under no circumstances would they be seen wearing trousers and riding a horse a-straddle. There were plenty of good riders among the girls, though, and we often would have some of them looking while we were cutting out our cattle from the bunch after the day's gather.

Life on the Staked Plains: White Women

There were very few white women at all in the country then, but if we happened to round up our day's gathering near a ranch where there were women-folks, it was a common thing for them to come over and watch us work and eat their dinner with us at the chuck-wagon. There were no snobs in the cattle-country in those days. If they had any stuck-up ideas in the first place we soon got those ideas "hoo-rawed" out of their systems.

The code of the Old West was very strict in regard to white women of good character. Sometimes even mentioning the name of a white girl in a saloon with a lot of half-drunk fellows in it would lead to a fight right away. No cowboy ever offered disrespect to a respectable girl.

LIFE ON THE STAKED PLAINS: THE VISIT AND "PERFUMERY"

This made it all the funnier when something untoward did happen without intention. At the time, I won't say exactly where or mention any names, but it was while I was in the Panhandle; a bunch of four or five of us made up a plan to ride over and eat supper and spend the evening with a family which had two grown girls. It was around forty miles from our home ranch. We picked out the following Sunday as the day to make the visit. One of the boys [Lon Chambers] rather fancied himself as to looks and ability to charm the girls, so he got all fixed up for the occasion. He rode up to town and bought himself a clean shirt and two clean handkerchiefs, one for the neck, and one for the pocket. When Sunday came; he even washed clean the back of his neck and behind his ears. He had also bought in town a small vial of perfume, and after dinner Sunday, before we started for the other ranch, he put plenty of perfume on the pocket handkerchief!

In that day people liked perfume. The women-folks would get sweet-smelling herbs, such as rosemary and thyme, and especially lavender, and they would keep these herbs in the bureau drawers where they kept their Sunday-go-to-meeting clothes. Perfume in bottles wasn't easily come by, but the girls kept their things smelling sweet with these herbs.

Well, we fellers got there and finished our supper, and afterwards we were all cuttin' up with the girls in the "settin' room," the old folks sitting by and having a good time watching us. Suddenly Lon remembered his perfumed handkerchief, and prancing across the room, he flipped it under one girl's nose!

"Say!" said he, "Smell o' that!"

"Bah!" she retorted, "that's nothin'! You oughta smell my drawers!"

160

Poor Lon was speechless for an instant, then he stammered out, "S-smell your wha-at?"

With a little swish of skirts and a slamming of a door, the girls vanished into their room. Of course, we just howled with glee, and the old folks right along with us. When he could get breath enough to speak, the old man gasped out, "Well, boys, you might as well ride on back home now. You'll not see them gals no more tonight!" So we did, and alternately cussed and hoorawed Lon all the way home. I guess we used up our entire vocabulary of cuss-words on him.

LIFE ON THE STAKED PLAINS: THE RANCH HOUSE

Home life in those days was very simple and often crude. The home ranch house was always a very plain affair, usually built of adobe bricks. In the mountains or foothills it would be of log or stone, but not on the rockless plains. The Bell Ranch house, in New Mexico, was typical of the way the house was designed, having a large main room with the beds and chairs on one end, and the cooking stove and table on the other end. The house on the LX home ranch was more pretentious. It had four or five rooms, in the "main room" of which was a large fire-place. The top of the mantel was a full-length solid petrified log. This house was also a 'dobe house.

Erskine Clements was the financial secretary of the LX at that time. He was an Easterner, a very well-educated man, and a fine fellow. I had many a long talk with him. He was very gentlemanly, and knew how to mix with his men. As we expressed it, he was not "stuck-up."

Of course, there were no flowers and shrubbery around those frontier homes, as there are now, in so many places. What flowers the frontier people enjoyed they had to get from the prairie itself. I don't remember many flowers on the Staked Plains. They certainly didn't grow in any profusion, or I would have noticed them. I do remember a bright red one called, I believe, the "Indian paintbrush." There was of course, much cactus, which would bloom in the spring and then bear fruit. We called this fruit the "prickly pear." We would wipe the little thorns off of them and then eat them. I've ate many a batch of them. They have a somewhat sickly taste, not particularly palatable.

Life on the Staked Plains: Cuttin' Sign

One thing that interested people, and which few non-Westerners understand, is the manner in which we would trail and find animals or men in the trackless wilderness. "Cuttin' sign" was what we called it, or "readin' sign," as the case might be. "Cuttin' sign" was looking for a sign of the person or persons, or of the animals, being hunted.

"Readin' sign" was figuring out what the sign meant. After cutting for sign and finding it, you would follow it and make deductions from the sign itself, for instance as to how many were in the party you were trailing, and how long they had been at each stopping place, and what they did while they were there. You could trail these things by observing their campfire and tracks, and any other little signs or clues that had been dropped by them. That of course applies to trailing men. In trailing stock, you [would] follow the tracks of the animals after you had cut the trail. It was easy if a man was fairly proficient, but it was also quite an art in itself.

Life on the Staked Plains: A Man's Word

An interesting example of trailing a man occurred while I was in the Las Animas placer district near Hillsboro, New Mexico, at the edge of the Black range, between Socorro and Silver City. A man rode in on a claybank horse, both horse and rider showing evidence of having come a long distance. From what I gathered from him, he had been a Texas cowboy. He had been there about a week or two, when his horse disappeared one night. He seemed to set great store on the horse, and looked for it afoot for a couple of days, but could not find it. Then he talked a fellow into loaning him a horse to ride while looking for his own. After he had been gone for about a month, the owner of the borrowed horse gave up all hopes of ever seeing man or horse again. But, sixty-two days after his departure from Las Animas, the Texas man rode back on his claybank horse, leading the borrowed one behind him. The led horse was carrying a man with his feet tied together under the horse's belly.

The Texas man said he had trailed the claybank and the thief over a lot of country, sometimes losing all trace of them for days at a time, then he would pick up the trail again from some one who had happened to see them and would follow it until he finally caught up with them near Fort Windgate [*sic*, Wingate], Arizona. From my talk with the fellow who owned the claybank, I figured he had done a little horse-stealing on his own hook in his time, and thought he'd better let the law deal with this horse thief. So he turned the thief over to the deputy at Las Animas, who promptly locked him up in jail. But stealing horses was a capital crime in those days and that same night the thief was taken out and hung by an improvised vigilante committee.

The job of trailing this man down was done by word of mouth, and not by actually tracking him. The Texas man just followed the thief from ranch to ranch, getting closer and closer until he finally overtook him. This incident also illustrates well the value a man put on his word in those days. "Tex" might have stolen a few horses on occasion himself, but when he said he would bring back the borrowed horse to Hillsboro, he meant just that, and he did it.

This insistence on a promise being binding held true all over the western country. It was as true on the Staked Plains as it was in New Mexico. And in like manner, the method of trailing man or beast was the same all over the west. Some very pretty work was done in this respect, especially in the treeless, trackless country of the *Llano Estacado.*

CHAPTER TWELVE

Cowboy Equipment in the '70s

Mr. Wallace studied with interest the illustrations of a Western novel in a magazine.

"Well, that's not bad," he said, laying down his eyeglasses. "So often they don't have the details correct in these pictures. I noticed they have used a swell-fork saddle here, which means that the story took place somewhere from the late 70s onward."

COWBOY EQUIPMENT: SADDLES AND ROPES

Up until the late 1870's, the narrow-forked saddle was in use. About that time the swell-fork saddle appeared. On a narrow-forked saddle a pitching horse could easily hurt the rider by throwing him forward onto the horn. The swell-forked was a great boon to the rider, as the swell (bulge) below the horn would come just above a man's thighs while riding, and with this class of saddle it was almost impossible for a rider to get injured in that manner. The horn of the old narrow-forked saddle was all wood, and had a bolt running from side to side to prevent its splitting. The new style (swell-fork) had a metal horn, the metal (steel) continuing below the neck of the horn to reinforce it. The top of the horn on both styles of saddle was covered with leather. Both styles had rawhide thongs, one on each side of the horn, and one on each side of and behind the saddle. A rider could tie his blanket and war-bags on behind the cantle, and frequently he would tie a blanket across the saddle behind the horn, when he was going to ride a pitching horse, which helped to prevent injury.

Generally we carried on the horn a sort of endless loop, made of a thong of buckskin or rawhide, about fifteen inches long. The ends of this thong were fastened together by a little knot, forming a smaller loop at the end of the larger one. This little loop was just large enough to slip over the horn of the saddle. Our riatas were carried in the large part of the small loop. By passing the loop under the riata, then around, making one complete turn, then slipping the other end of the loop over the horn of the saddle, we could get our rope in quickly, and there were no knots to untie. Sometimes this quick action of the rope was very necessary. If we knew we weren't going to be roping, we put a double turn of the loop over the riata. In the Panhandle country of Texas, the end of the riata was never tied fast to the horn of the saddle. When a critter was roped, we used the "dally," which was merely wrapping the rope around the horn. "Dally" comes from the Mexican "*da la huelta*," meaning literally, "give it a wrap." In other sections of the cattle country, the custom was to fasten the end of the riata to the saddle horn by tying but we did not like that, because, for example, if an accident occurred in which the steer threw the horse instead of the horse throwing the steer, the tied riata left the horse and steer tied together, while by using the "dally" there was no danger of such a thing occurring. These accidents rarely happened, but they did occasionally, and we thought it was the sensible thing to prevent them when something of that sort did take place. It could put the rider in a very embarrassing position, if not actually in a dangerous one.

Another thing which made for safety in our opinion was the double cinch. All our saddles at that time had a double cinch (two girths around the horse's belly, one in back and one in front, to fasten the saddle on). In California I have heard that the single cinch or "center fire" was mostly used, but a double-cinch saddle always remained on the horse's back (if properly fastened), while the center fire would frequently get slipped out of place and sometimes would be stripped off the horse.

When a man had a saddle which fitted him perfectly, it was a toss-up as to whether he would part with his six-shooter or his saddle, in order to get food. If he was forced to make the choice, he would generally part with the gun and keep his saddle.

COWBOY EQUIPMENT: BRIDLES

Nearly everybody used the ordinary leather bridle, which had "conchos" (metal disks) on each side of the head where the browband covered the cheek-strap. "Concho" means shell, and shell was originally used by the Mexicans for these ornaments. Later they were made of metal. They were also used down the sides of chaps.

Occasionally you would see a really fancy bridle made of horsehair. An Indian who rode for the LX had one of these, which was really a beauty. I had offered him as high as fifteen dollars for it. He wouldn't sell to me at all. But when we parted for the last time, knowing it would be just chance if we ever met again, he got up in the middle of breakfast, and walked over to where our horses were standing nearby, both of them saddled and bridled and ready for the day's work. There he took the bridle off my horse, and put his fine horsehair one in place of mine, then he went back, and put my leather bridle on his horse. Then he came back and finished his breakfast.

It would have been wasting words to thank him for the bridle, so I reached over and shook hands with him, and that was enough. I never saw him again. I kept the horsehair bridle a long time, but it was finally stolen from me in Las Vegas at the livery stable where I'd put up my horse. I remember its being Las Vegas, because it was at that same time that I traded the "Kid's" hat in on a new one.

I had been wearing the old hat for some time, and I figured it had seen its best days, so I traded it in at a Las Vegas store, retaining the hatband. I happened to remark to the Jewish proprietor as I was about to throw the old hat in the street that it was Billy the Kid's old hat. The store-keeper was almost in tears as he begged me to give it to him. I did so, but have wished many times since that I had kept it myself.

To return to the bridles in use at that time: the bridle-reins were usually two-and-a-half feet longer than was necessary, the straps being narrowed down to the end much like the lash on a whip. At a convenient length from the bit was a braided leather knot, which could be slipped back and forth on the reins and was generally kept at the right length so the reins could be slipped over the horn of the saddle. The extra length of the reins on past the knot was used as a quirt if the rider was not carrying one. When the reins were "grounded" (that is, left hanging on the ground) the horse would stand quietly for hours. The reason for this was, that if they started up they'd step on the long reins, which would jerk their mouths and hurt them. They didn't like that, so they would soon learn to stand still as long as the reins were "grounded."

Cowboy Equipment: Bridle Bits

The usual bit on the range was the plain "snaffle" bit, which has a toggle joint in the center, and is an easy bit on the horse's mouth. Another is the "curb" bit with sides extending up past the horse's mouth on the outside, and a strong strap or chain running across from each side of the bit under the horse's chin. The lower ends extended down three or as much as four inches from the bit bar. A pull on the reins would tighten the curb back of the horse's chin and it was plenty severe when a chain curb was used. Usually, however, the curb used was a leather strap.

Once in a while you'd run onto a rider who used the old-style Spanish "spade" bit, which was built much like the curb bit except that it had a solid piece running from the center of the bit into the horse's mouth. This piece was flattened at the end so that it lay flat and spade-like on the horse's tongue. A quick jerk on the lines would cause the "spade" to rise off the tongue, in some cases even striking the roof of the horse's mouth and lacerating it. The use of this style of bit was generally discouraged, as only a man who was cruel to his horse would punish him by the use of such a torturous device. A man who used this bit couldn't hide the fact from his fellow-riders, because his horse would usually be bleeding at the mouth. You had to have a gentle hand to handle the spade bit properly, and you must be constantly on the watch to keep from hurting the horse's mouth. I have used one occasionally when no other was available, but I did not like to do it.

A rider who abused his horse in any manner was looked down on, and the habitual use of the spade bit was indulged in only by a man who was a brute at heart. It was a good index to a man's character. And did we read character in those days! You often had to size a man up quickly and correctly, for if you made a mistake it might be too bad for you.

Cowboy Equipment: Quirts

The quirt was a short iron bar about three quarters of an inch in diameter, and about a foot long, with a loop at one end by which the quirt was carried, dangling from the wrist, and a double leather popper (lash) at the business end of it. The bar, which formed the handle, was covered with tightly stretched or braided rawhide, which in turn was covered with either braided horsehair or with slip knots of leather. In an emergency this quirt was a very effective black-jack, although seldom was it so used. Still, it was there if needed. I have known a man to stun an outlaw horse with a blow from one of these improvised billies. If a bunch of cowboys happened to be in a saloon, and a heated argument started which apparently was not going to end in gunfire, you'd notice that the boys wearing quirts on their wrists would slip the loops over their hands, and hold the quirts by wrapping the poppers around their right hands. These made very effective weapons in a free-for-all "fist-and-skull" fight.

Cowboy Equipment: Chapaderos

Chapaderos or "chaps," as we called them, as worn by the cowboys told us in most cases what part of the country the wearer came from. On the southern and southwestern Texas ranges, leather chaps were worn on account of the thorny mesquite thickets. Some of the mesquites had straight thorns, and these were plenty thorny but others had curved thorns, shaped like a cat's claw and as sharp. They were called by that name *"una de gato"* (claw of the cat), and they would tear off a man's clothes if unprotected. Therefore, smooth leather chaps were worn for such protection by the southerners.

On the other hand, a plainsman (or northern Texas man) most frequently wore chaps made of goatskin with the hair on the outside. Some of these were white, others were black. I remember that mine were white, and Charley Siringo's black at the time we were in the Panhandle together. The Fall after our return from New Mexico, we both got into a watermelon patch down on the E-Cross-E ranch. By the time we got out of the patch, the goat hair on our chaps was completely matted with sandburrs from the knees down. It took us two hours to clean them out by wetting them and using a curry-comb followed by a regular hair comb. We didn't go into that patch any more! But we had the melons. We carried them over to our camp from the patch. Of course, the boss didn't care if we got into the patch and took a few melons, but nobody told us the burrs were there, either. And did they rag us as we were cleaning them out, nor did they offer to help us, either.

COWBOY EQUIPMENT: SPURS

By the time I was working in the Panhandle, the old-fashioned spur with the big rowel that dragged was fast going out of use. The spur that took its place was a band of steel, nickel-plated, which fitted around the shoe just above the heel with a small chain running down under the instep, fastened at both ends to hold it down in front, and a strap going over the instep to hold it up. These spurs made no noise when you were walking, but the old Spanish type with rowels dragging was a noisy thing, and death on wood floors.

I wore a pair of the old noisy kind for a long time, however, and I remember with amusement an incident connected with them when I was in Las Vegas one time. George Boward and I were together on that trip, and we had stowed a few jiggers of whiskey under our belts. Off the main square in Old Town (there was no New Town then)* we somehow strayed into an office of a Mexican Justice of the Peace, where a trial was being conducted. We both had on the old-fashioned

---

*New Town, Las Vegas, sprang up following the arrival of the railroad on July 4, 1879, as a result of which the earlier settlement half a mile away became Old Town.

spurs, and we walked up near the justice's seat before we found a place to sit down. The old *alcalde* reprimanded us for making so much noise. Well, we didn't want to stay in there anyhow after we found out where we were, so we tiptoed out, careful as could be until we got fairly near to the door, then we turned our feet sideways and made all the noise we could, and those old spurs could certainly make plenty when you turned them sideways and tried to see what you could do.

"Arrest those men!" shouted the *alcalde* to the policeman, but we ducked into a saloon which was next door to the *alcalde's* office, and were at the bar soaking up another drink by the time the policeman got there. We convinced the policeman that he was on the wrong track, and got him to go back without us, then we immediately left for other parts. That old *alcalde* would have stuck us at least ten dollars apiece if he could have got us back in there, and we knew it.

You would hardly ever see the mark of a spur on a horse unless he was very lazy, as most of the cow-ponies were quick to respond to the lightest touch. A rider who brought his horse in with bleeding flanks was looked upon much as the one who rode a horse with a bleeding mouth.

Cowboy Equipment: War-bags and Knives

Whenever we were taking a trip, we used to put our things in what we called "war-bags." A "war-bag" was made of what was then termed the "seamless sack," which were the grain sacks that ranch wives used to make towels. Those towels never got soft! They almost never wore out, either, and that was one reason why they were handy for carrying belongings from place to place. They were easy to make, for all you had to do was sew up the open end, cut a slit in one side about the center of the sack, and throw it over the horse's back behind the saddle. Stuff your extra shirt (if you had one) and some grub and whatever else you had to carry into either end of the bag, and you were ready to travel.

In Western stories every cowboy carries, besides his six-shooter, a Winchester rifle and a Bowie knife in his belt. The truth is that the ordinary cow-hand of my time carried only his six-shooter most of the time. Knives were used among us only in butchering an animal. We never thought of using one for a weapon. The Mexicans generally did carry a Bowie knife for a weapon, but not the white cowboy. I still have a Bowie knife that I took away from a Mexican in Lyons [*sic,* Lyon] County, Kansas, years after I had left the range. I was a deputy Sheriff then in Emporia, and handled the Mexicans because of my knowledge of them, and their language. We still use that knife in our kitchen.

Cowboy Equipment: Guns

In my day a cowboy never carried a rifle unless there were Indians on the war-path in that section of the country. The old six-gun was good enough for him for all ordinary uses. In the 70s the .45 Colt's revolver was the usual one carried, and the Winchester .44 carbine would be the saddle gun if one was carried at all.

The change from the .45 to the .44 revolver (both Colts) came in the late '70's. We all changed as soon as possible because the same cartridge fitted both the Winchester .44 rifle and the Colt .44 revolver. Then we had to carry only one belt full of cartridges for the two guns. One thing I noticed as being misrepresented in the pictures and stories which I have run across, is the way in which a revolver was used to club a person. He brought the butt of his revolver down on the other man's head, they'll say. Well, he didn't do any such thing, not if he was living in my day in the Old West. He brought the barrel of his revolver down on the other fellow's head, so that he would still be in a shooting position, and what is more important, he wouldn't shoot himself. Nobody ever turned the barrel of a gun to any direction where he didn't want a bullet to hit! Once in a while a man would shoot his gun at the same instant it struck the other fellow's head, that was a very effective way to put the fear of God into them.

Besides the Winchester rifle there was the old buffalo gun, long and heavy, with an octagonal barrel. Good for close shooting at long distances, it was used by buffalo hunters. I never was a buffalo hunter, but have talked with them, and they have told me of their practices. If they could sneak up on the buffalo without being seen, so as to make a sure shot, they could keep on shooting as long as they could kill an animal with each shot, and the herd would keep on grazing and would not run, but if a misplaced shot wounded one, that one immediately started on a run and got the whole herd in motion. Shooting the buffalo in this way was called "getting a stand on them." Of course, the heavy buffalo gun was practically useless when the herd was running. The Sharp's .50 caliber rifle was also used by buffalo hunters.

I remember when the old-style rim-fire "Henry" was superseded by the later center-fire Winchester. I used to own an old Henry rifle myself, and it was the best-shooting rifle I ever had in my hands. The firing-pin of a "rim-fire" struck on both sides of the rim of a cartridge, whereas the "center-fire" had a cap in the center of the cartridge that the needle struck. I finally got rid of my old Henry rifle in a peculiar way.

It was while I was still living in Colfax County. I was riding around one day, doing a little hunting, and I shot at an antelope. The bullet hung up in the barrel, and I concluded I'd drive it out with another bullet, so I pumped another cartridge in, and fired it off. That bullet also stayed in the barrel. When I had three of them in there,

I commenced to get scared that the barrel might burst, so the fourth cartridge I exploded by laying the rifle flat on the ground and tying a string to the trigger, but it also stayed in the barrel. I finally gave up and rode on.

Before I got into town, I met a Mexican on the trail. He had a .45 Colt s revolver, and in talking he said he'd like to have a rifle like the one I was carrying. I offered to swap him my rifle for his six-shooter, and he agreed at once, not knowing the condition the rifle was in. I rode off, thinking I'd like to hear his language when he found out the barrel was practically choked with bullets! But I never saw him again, so I never knew what happened. Of course, I could have laid the rifle over a fire and melted the bullets out, which is probably just what he did, but I never thought of it at that time. I was just a kid then, about sixteen, and didn't have too much sense.

Practically every Sheriff had a sawed-off shot-gun, a "Betsy," as we called it. It was really a deadly weapon, and whenever it was pointed at a man he put up his hands right away, if he had time at all to do so. The "Betsy" was made by sawing off the end of a double-barrelled shot-gun to within a foot or fourteen inches, and loading it with buckshot, and when it was fired those buckshot would spray all over everywhere! It didn't do to fool with a man who had one of those weapons in his hands.

COWBOY EQUIPMENT: CLOTHES

The "cowboy outfits" folks wear at dude ranches and in the movies, or in rodeos, are highly entertainin' to behold! Maybe the later cowboys dressed a little more fancy than we did in the 70s, but I doubt it. Of course, when we went to a dance we'd put on a clean shirt, maybe, and grease up our boots, and wash a little better than usual, but there were not any silk shirts or fancy pants those days. Flannel shirts were the rule, winter and summer. In winter we wore them for warmth, and in the summer to keep the sun from scorching us.

Sometimes people ask if those woolen shirts didn't itch and irritate our skin. One time they did, plenty. It was the time we took a bath in the salt-water pool. Down by Matt Devine's home ranch-house there was a pool of water as black as your piano, filled with salt. It was like Great Salt Lake, only smaller. It was just a round pool of water, not far from the Canadian River, and the water was so heavy with salt that it was impossible to sink in it. Your body would roll around on top of the water, like a log.

One day one of the boys came in telling us about it, and we wouldn't believe it, so he said, "Well, come on! I'll show it to yuh! You can see for yourselves!" We went and we saw, all right. We all stripped off and took a bath, and when we came out and dressed, and dried off, was when the wool shirts got in their work. Every hair on our bodies was stiff with salt, and sticking to the fibers of those flannel shirts! We simply could not stand it. We hit out for the Canadian at a lope, no jog-trotting about it, and we weren't comfortable till we'd plunged into the Canadian and washed that salt off good and proper!

Sometimes we'd get a fine silk handkerchief from a Mexican who had just come from Old Mexico. These were beautifully embroidered in rich colors, large in size, and of excellent material. I was lucky enough to buy two of them once, for three dollars apiece. I really felt dolled up proper with one of those on. It came way down to the belt in front. I don't know what ever became of mine, I gave one of them to my little La Cinta girl. Except for these Mexican handkerchiefs, the ordinary red bandanna was used by the cowboy, both for his neck and for his pocket.

Cowboy boots didn't interest me much because I had too big a foot to be fitted in one. The ordinary cowboy boot had a high heel, so that the heel would strike the wooden stirrup and keep the foot from going in too far and getting fastened in the stirrup. The tops were usually of soft leather with a fancy shape and stitching or other decoration. We always wore our pants tucked down into the boot-top. My foot was too big for me ever to find a pair that would fit me in a store, so I had to take the coarser boot such as was generally worn by farmers. This had the effect of making my feet seem much larger in comparison with the other boys, and finally resulted in my being nicknamed "Feet," or "Big Foot."

Laced boots were unheard-of in those days, and shoes were never worn by cowboys. Neither did they wear blue denim pants, although I understand that those later became very popular among the boys and were called "Levi's." In my time we wore just flat-woven wool or cotton pants. This was during the late 70s, while I was working on the Staked Plains, and roving here and there. Before that in the early 70s, the buckskin-faced pants were much used by riders. These were ordinary pants with Indian-tanned buckskin sewed over them at points of contact with the saddle. The Indian-tanned buckskin would take any kind of wetting, and would dry soft and pliable. They had a way of tanning to produce this effect. It was referred to as "smoked" buckskin. The "faced" pants would outwear an ordinary pair three to one. I don't know why they quit wearing them.

We didn't spend much on our wardrobe as a rule. Take a good pair of chaps and a pair of buckskin-faced pants, and you wouldn't need to buy more till they just naturally fell off of you.

Underwear was a very simple matter. Plain muslin drawers were worn, but most of the boys never wore an undershirt.

Silk socks were something else we never saw in those days, we wore ordinary cotton socks for all purposes.

Another thing that we never saw in those days was the "ten-gallon hat." Hat brims were rather wide, but not extraordinarily so, and crowns were just of average height. I have already mentioned this in referring to the "Kid's" hat, but I wanted to emphasize it. The tall-crowned, excessively wide-brimmed hat was the type used by Mexicans, and called them "sombreros." It was usually woven of straw.

The cowboy may have had his little vanities, such as perfumery on a pocket hand-kerchief, but for the most part, he was just a cow-hand, and dressed as such. His company clothes were very little different from his working garb.

Cowboy Equipment: The Buckboard

There was one piece of equipment used on the range which I have not touched on, and that was the buckboard. When it was not practical to ride a horse or have a wagon along, a buckboard would be used. The buckboard was a light vehicle having a seat right in the middle, centered between the front and back axles. The spring in a buckboard was five of the wooden slats which formed the bottom. These slats were about two and a half inches wide, and from a half to three quarters of an inch thick, and they served to take the jolt out of rough places in the road. They made for smoother riding than the old Concord stage coach which was swung on leather straps for springs. The buckboard, having no real bed on it, just the slats, and having the seat just large enough for two, made a very convenient vehicle for Star mail route carriers who had to cover long distances, also for bringing back groceries from town. A buckboard was very light draft. You could take one in one hand and run all around the yard with it. A wagon was a heavy draft, meaning it pulled very hard. The light draft vehicle, such as the buckboard, was very easy on the team.

There was no shelter in a buckboard. It was a tough old thing to be caught out in a snow or rain storm, especially if you had to go any distance, but it had its place in the range life, and a very valuable one it was, too. The cowboy, however, used it very little. His means of locomotion was the horse, and he was likely to feel ill at ease when travelling by any other method. With his own saddle and a good horse under him, with his blanket strapped behind him, and his clothes on his back, with his quirt and six-gun at hand, he was ready to ride, wherever his trail might lead.

CHAPTER THIRTEEN

The Fall Roundup on the Staked Plains

🌿 *"We never pronounced the 'a' in 'adobe,'"* mused Mr. Wallace. *"It was always 'dobe, without exception. Adobe Walls was 'dobe Walls, and nothing else. Certainly nothing like the pronunciation the feller gave it when he was telling me about the little town in Texas called, 'AY-dob,' with an accent on the 'a' and a long 'o.' He had been down in that country and I was inquiring of him as to whether there was any town marker at 'dobe Walls. I have yet to find any mention of it on a modern map, and I don't understand that, for at one time it was important, both as an historical landmark, and as a starting point for the round-ups down the river from Tascosa."*[1]

FALL ROUNDUP ON THE STAKED PLAINS: ADOBE WALLS

Adobe Walls was located a few miles down the Canadian from the E-Cross-E ranch, which was at the mouth of the Blue Creek, running into the Canadian river some forty-five miles down from the LX. Part of the walls were still standing when I saw them in the late 70s. They were perhaps two or three feet high then, the house having mostly melted down. At the time it received its name, it was the walls of an adobe shanty, behind which a handful of white men, buffalo hunters perhaps, took refuge when surrounded by a swarm of Indians. Those old 'dobe houses were built substantially, and the whites stood off the Indians for two or three days, finally driving them away.

Naturally the spot came to be noted among the people of the Texas Panhandle, and beyond that. I remember riding down the river to see it, and noting how it stood all alone in the flat, wide, treeless bottoms on the north side of the Canadian River, with not a stick or stone or rise of land for shelter except the walls of the little 'dobe hut.

I cannot recall exactly how far it was from the mouth of the Blue, but certainly it wasn't over five miles, and perhaps nearer two or three. I do recall, however, exactly how it looked, and how the country looked thereabouts. What a farm that flat bottom land would have made! And doubtless, has made long ago. Then, however, it was treeless, as was the rest of the country about it. The bottoms stretched out on either side of the Canadian for a good distance, till they met the bluffs which formed the bound[a]ries of the Plains, northern and southern. The bluffs were broken by arroyos, running down off the Plains. These did not extend very far into the Plains, however, soon fading out to leave the flat, slightly rolling country as level as before.

There were absolutely no trees or even shrubbery, except occasionally in a draw where a creek ran down. Even then such a specimen would be very rare.

The Blue Creek was a little stream which flowed through an arroyo of some size, entering the Canadian River from the north. It was here that the E-Cross-E home ranch was located where I worked most of the summer.

Fall Roundup on the Staked Plains: To the LX Ranch

Just before the Fall roundup started, I was talking one day in Tascosa with John Hollicott, who was runnin' the LX ranch then for Bates and Beal[s] of Boston. He told Tee Silman [*sic*, Sillman] he was a little short of hand[s] for the Fall roundup and asked him if he would spare me to the LX. Tee was glad to do it, as he was plenty full-handed himself, and didn't really need me, so I went from the E-Cross-E to the LX, and worked there the rest of the time I was on the Staked Plains.

The stockmen had been trying for years to improve the old Texas stock, which was runty and rangy and wild as deer, almost. The method was to bring young bulls down in the spring of the year, close-herd them all summer, feed them a little grain through the winter, and then turn them loose on the range the next spring. They had tried the polled Angus and the Durham and Galloway breeds, but these bulls had invariably died out on them the following winter.

This year they sent Jay Barnes and me out on the northern plains to close-herd about four hundred head of Hereford bulls, yearlings to two-year-olds. "Close-herd," of course, means to hold that particular bunch of cattle together, and keep them from getting with the rest of the cattle. We held them that way for about a month, and then John Hollicott came out and said he was short-handed for the Fall roundup, and for us to turn the bulls loose and let them rustle for themselves. "They'll die before Spring, anyways," said he, "like the others did."

This particular bunch fooled him, however, as they came through the winter in as good shape as the range cattle or perhaps better, and from then on the Hereford, or whiteface, cattle were found to be the most adaptable to life on the plains, and as they were better beef cattle, and not so wild as longhorns, they quickly displaced the old type of steer. Now they are seen everywhere in the western United States, clear to the coast.

One thing that happened while we were holding those cattle, sticks in my mind. Jay Barnes was a cowhand about forty years old, of stocky build, with a ruddy face, and a real genius for expressing himself originally and entertainingly when aroused. Jay had accumulated a felon [an archaic term for a whitlow, an abscess near the fingernail] on his left front finger, and it bothered him considerable. One evening we were eating supper, and he picked up his biscuit from where he had laid it on a cow chip while he was otherwise occupied. Some dirt from the cow chip clung to it, and Jay went to knock it off with his knife so he could eat the biscuit. Well, he hit his sore finger, right on the felon! Now Jay started in on his systematic way of cussing, and he sure used up all the strong words he knew in the next five minutes. I remember how he started out, but only a very small portion of it is printable.

"May the black coals of damnation be piled up on your head higher than the pyramids of Egypt! May lightning strike you on top of your head and ball up in your damned belly!" was his beginning, and from there on he gave out the whole chapter and verse. By that time I was laughing too hard to remember the rest, but the longer he went on the stronger it got, with an occasional phrase flung in my direction for laughing! I wish I could remember it all. It was really uproariously funny, as well as artistic.

Before I go on to discussing the roundup that fall, let me remark here upon something which always seemed to me in the nature if [sic] a miracle. I used to marvel at it, and I still do. How can the little bit of a calf, just born, know to lie still beside a soapweed while its mother goes maybe for miles to water? It will lie there and absolutely not move a muscle until she returns to it. I have seen it happen over and over, when I was riding the range. How does she communicate her knowledge to the calf, and why does it pay no attention to anything until it hears her coming back? Then, when it hears her bawling and running toward it, it will jump up and run to meet her. They say that the young of deer and other wild animals "freeze" like that, but I have not observed them. The range cow was almost as wild as a deer, at that.

Fall Roundup on the Staked Plains: "Moonshining"

When Jay Barnes and I got back to the LX ranch, after Hollicott had bidden us to leave the Hereford bulls and come on in to the roundup, I was sent to work the east end, starting up the Canadian River from 'dobe Walls. Some days we would have to cover a larger area than usual and then we would resort to what we called "moonshining" on the roundup. Generally the evening before, six or eight men were sent out to the extreme outside points, two men at each point. These would carry out their breakfast and sleep there, then in the morning they would eat a cold breakfast and start riding at peep of day, pushing all cattle that they ran onto toward the roundup grounds a half-mile to a mile away. Then the men, riding on, would repeat this until they came to where two other Moonshiners had started. Then they would turn back and give the cattle they had started another boost in toward the roundup grounds, then reverse again. By that time the main roundup riders would be pushing the cattle in all around. On reaching camp, the "moonshiners" would change horses, eat a fine large meal, and then ride to the big bunch of gathered cattle and help with the separating of the cattle. Each would take his own brand and the rest was turned loose, as this would be on their home range.

There would be maybe fifteen to twenty outfits in the roundup, each with its own cook-wagon and each holding separate what cattle they would find carrying their brand until the final day of the roundup. Then all would head out for their different ranges. Arriving there, their fat cattle would be cut out and shipped up the trail, and the rest turned loose and forgotten about until the next roundup.

One day after Lon Chambers and I had been moonshining the night before, and the roundup work for the day was concluded, we were eating supper with the rest of the boys when some of them asked where we had been between daybreak and sun-up that morning. We had spent the night at the head of a long draw that ran down in the direction we wanted the cattle to go. There was quite a bunch of cattle near the head of the draw, and we wanted to give them a good start so they would keep going a little while, so we stampeded the cattle, yelling at the top of our lungs. Lon Chambers was with me that morning. He had a very good pair of lungs, too, and we whooped and hollered for all we were worth.

The head of this draw was estimated at seven miles distance from the main camp, and several of the boys said they had heard us plainly, and could hardly believe that we were where we said we were, at the time. Sound carries a long way out in that country, especially in the early morning when it is very still, but that was the farthest I ever knew a human voice to carry, by actual measurement, in my experience.

We kept on in this way until the two roundups met at Tascosa as usual, the east end from 'dobe Walls, and the west from Fort Bascom. About three hundred cowboys met there and when the roundup disbanded we celebrated for three or four days. The LX had a bunch of about eight hundred and fifty head of fat three- and four-year-old steers which they had gathered in the Fall roundup, and were ready to take to the rail-head (in this case, Caldwell, Kansas) for shipment, as soon as enough of the boys, that they wanted to keep over the winter with them, got sober enough to make the trip.

FALL ROUNDUP ON THE STAKED PLAINS: RAIN

I never would go on the trail with cattle myself, for I didn't like it, but I would go with them as extra help for the first day or two. While we were waiting for the boys to sober up, the Fall Equinox rains came on.

One day after John Hollicott and I had eaten dinner we rode out to where the boys were holding the bunch. On the way it started to drizzle.

John said, "Looks like it's goin' to rain, Feet, and if it does get to rainin' purty bad—" (I thought he was going to say "You can come to camp," as he was always showing me favors). But what he did say was: "—just let it rain, don't try to stop it, but *hold them steers.*"

Well, it rained. It rained all night and all the next day, and all the next night, and all the next day, and it was still raining the next night after that! Every man in camp was out there ridin' round those cattle—John Hollicott and all. Sometime after midnight John turned his horse, and as he met each man circling the cattle he said, "Go to camp. No man can stay out when I can't stand it any longer!"

So we all turned in to our wet beds, and it seemed to me about fifteen minutes after I hit the blankets I was being waked up, told to "Saddle up and get after them cattle before they scatter!" It had stopped raining, and the sun was coming up clear. We were riding in a very few minutes, and luckily caught them before they got mixed with the range cattle again.

FALL ROUNDUP ON THE STAKED PLAINS: DRIFTING ON

I went with them a couple of days longer, until they had things in hand, but that siege in the rain had cooled me off. I decided to quit and try some other way of living. However, I stayed at the LX without pay until I'd made up my mind where I wanted to go. When I got ready, I decided to go first back to White Oaks, New Mexico, and as the shortest way was across the plains to Fort Sumner (in place of going around by way of La Cinta and Anton Chico), and as I knew my way across the plains, which then had no trail whatsoever across them, I decided to go that way.

It was about three hundred miles between Tascosa and Fort Sumner, New Mexico, and a really hazardous ride it was for a lone horseman to make, but I felt completely confident about trying it. The saddle horse that I had traded for at the Bell Ranch had disappeared by that time, but there was another unclaimed horse ranging on the LX, and according to common custom at that time, I took him in place of my old one. So, again in December, but this time completely alone, I started on the long ride across the Staked Plains to White Oaks, New Mexico.

CHAPTER FOURTEEN

Rambling Around

🖋 "*Three hundred miles alone across the Llano Estacado was no joke, sixty years ago,*" *observed Mr. Wallace. "As you know, Llano Estacado means 'Staked Plains,' and this nearly flat country in the Texas Panhandle had been known by that name for many, many generations. The plains were, as I have mentioned, uncharted by any trails, but I possessed a natural sense of direction, and I knew them by now, so I was not afraid of getting lost. There were, however, several dangers which might interrupt my journey, and I had to consider them carefully, but because for personal reasons I wanted to miss La Cinta, I decided to risk them.*"

One chance I had to take was the danger of a "blue Norther" coming up. With no fuel or shelter of any kind, I would have frozen to death if I had been caught in one. A "blue Norther" is a sudden blizzard coming down from the north. The weather can change from balmy to below zero in an hour, and the storm would last for at least one day, and usually more. Neither man nor horse could survive such a storm without shelter. The wind would blow violently, sending the snow streaming against the body, and piling rapidly in deep drifts.

A second danger concerned navigation. No one carried a compass in those days. We travelled by the position of the sun by day, and the moon and stars by night. If it should cloud over so that I could not see the sun, I would have to stop until the clouds cleared away, and at that time of year it was hazardous to stop on account of the danger from storms.

Third, even as late as 1881 there would be some danger from Indians. If a party of Indians should happen onto a lone rider, they would be tempted to wipe him out, and he would stand no chance against them with no cover to make a fight from. There were still quite a lot of buffalo on the plains, and Indian hunters would come out for a supply of meat even that late in the season.

The boys tried to dissuade me from trying it, but I was determined to go that way. So I tied up my blankets and a little grub behind my saddle and pulled out. However, as it happened I had only one bit of trouble. It did cloud over and start spitting snow one day about noon. It caught me half way between Portales Lake and the head of Running Water [Draw]. I stopped at once and did not stir from that spot until the sky cleared the next day after that, and from there on I was all right, as the old Fort Sill–Fort Sumner military road ran by Portales Lake.

Nobody at all lived between Tascosa and Fort Sumner at that time. I never met a soul, neither a single rider or a mail carrier, nor anyone else. About ten or twelve days after I left Tascosa, I arrived at Fort Sumner, reaching there the evening of the twenty-fourth of December [1881], just a year after I had arrived at White Oaks with Charley Siringo and the other boys in the expedition sent from the Canadian River country.

When I got in I was too tired for a spree, and went right to bed. The next morning I got up feeling pretty grouchy, and headed down towards the saloon for an eye-opener. My way led down through the avenue of cottonwoods, which was a long straight lane running between two rows of tall cottonwoods. This was a noted street in those days, as most of the towns were as devoid of trees as the country thereabouts. The saloon was at the end of this avenue, and I was making tracks for it, when I met a Mexican. The Mexicans had a habit of claiming a Christmas gift from white folks, generally getting the price of a drink, varying from fifteen cents to a quarter of a dollar. So this Mex I met called out "Keesmas gif'!"

I wasn't feeling any too amiable, so I pretended not to understand him, and snapped out, "Get the hell outa here!" Before I got much further, there were as many as a dozen of them, jogging along beside me and begging for their gifts. Just to be ornery I kept up my assumed ignorance of what they meant, but I think one of two of them must have recognized me and known that I talked their language, for they commenced to get nasty and threatening, so I backed up against one of the cottonwoods and drew my six-shooter and made them stand away from me in a half-circle, so none of them could slip up and stick a knife into me.

I was standing there, waving my six-shooter slowly back and forth and holding them at bay, when two or three white cowboys came out of the saloon and came up to us to see what the trouble was. When they found out, they scattered the Mexicans with hilarity and enthusiasm, and I went to the saloon with them and set up the drinks. That afternoon I went with them to their home ranch, where I spent a couple of days before proceeding to White Oaks, where I had determined to land. I can't remember the name of the ranch or its brand, but I can see the cussed thing! One thing about it was that it had the vilest water I ever drank on the range. It was a gypsum spring, and by far the worst one I ever came across. The water smelled rotten and tasted worse, and soap curdled in it till it looked like curdled milk. I was glad to get away from there.

I went on to White Oaks, but I wasn't [as] satisfied with the change as I had thought I'd be, so I drifted on again, down onto the Rio Grande. I met up with a feller by the name of George Howard, and he and I dealt "monte" to the Mexicans from Santa Fe on down to El Paso. While we were at El Paso, we concluded we'd go to the front on the Mexican central railroad, which was then built as far as Ojos Calientes, (Hot Springs), Mexico. When we arrived, we found that there was nothing but desert around there, so we decided we did not want any of Mexico. There was a nice pool of water at the spring, which was covered with a shed roof. The shed had no sides, but nice clean flat rocks completely encircled the pool, which came up level with them, and seemed to be about twenty feet deep, and not too hot to bathe in comfortably. I asked one of the Mexicans living near by if there would be any objections to our taking a swim in the pool, and he laughed and said, "No, friend. That will be all right. Go ahead and help yourselves."

Bathing suits were unknown to us, and we just stripped off and plunged in. We were having a very nice time swimming around when a Mexican woman with a large bundle of dirty clothes came into the edge of the pool and commenced to do her laundry. Inside of ten minutes there must have been over a dozen women encircling that pool, washing their clothes.

The pool, as I remember it, was about thirty feet in diameter, and the women would dip their clothes in the water, soap them well, and beat the dirt out of them, either on the rocks themselves or with a stick, then rinse them in the pool again. We soon got tired of staying in that water, and I commenced trying to get those women to go away till we could get out and dress. They politely informed us that they had to get their washing done. If we wanted to get out, they said, why go ahead and get out, what did they care? And we finally had to do just that. It didn't bother me as much as it did George. I was used to them, and he wasn't. He practically crawled like a snake getting out of that pool, and how those women laughed. No wonder the Mexican fellow laughed when he told us to go ahead and take a swim. But we didn't swim in that pool again.

It is a curious thing that with all the streams and [a] whole ocean to swim in nearby us in England, I did not learn to swim until I went to live on the dry, almost waterless plains of New Mexico. But after I did learn, I became very proficient and am a good swimmer to this day.

The next day after the swim we took at Ojos Calientes, George and I went back to El Paso. We had then about six hundred dollars in our "monte" bank, and were hoping to increase it. One night I was not feeling very well, and I advised George not to open the game up, and I'd try to sleep off my trouble, but George didn't take my advice. He went ahead and dealt on his own, and the next morning we had an even dollar bill to divide between us. This really disgusted me, for George was not one to get the best of those Mexicans or even to hold his own with them. I considered that he had not done the right thing by going against my advice, and thus losing our money, and so, although we didn't have any harsh words, we parted company the next morning, and I never saw George again.

One day while we still were in partnership, George and I were heading toward Santa Fe, striking across country as I always did. If we had followed a trail, we would have missed one of the most interesting things I came upon while I was in New Mexico. That was the ruins of Gran Quivira.

We had no idea they were there, we just rode up on them and stopped to investigate them, meaning to camp there overnight and go on the next morning. But the ruins interested us so much that we spent all the next day looking them over.

They lie on a rise between the Pecos and the Rio Grande rivers, south of Santa Fe and east of Socorro, and south by east of Albuquerque. They are undoubtedly the ruins of buildings erected by Indians centuries ago, and are built of blue undressed limestone, the only buildings made of that material which I ever saw while I was in the range country.

The stone was put together with a mortar made of clay. The walls were at least three feet thick, I believe a little more than three feet thick. One room was apparently an assembly room of some sort, for it was larger than the rest. It was about sixty by one hundred twenty-five feet, and had over the main entrance a cedar beam fifteen or sixteen inches square.

This beam was really beautiful. It was hand carved in as pretty a pattern and as nice a job of carving as I ever saw. The pattern was perfectly balanced starting in the center with a sort of medallion and spreading out on either side. If the beam were sawed through the center of this medallion and folded together, the pattern on each side would match perfectly. The large room over the entrance of which this beam was placed must have been a city hall or meeting place, as it was by far the most important in the whole village.

Another thing about those ruins which caught our attention was the old, old trail which ran along for a little way just outside of the village proper. Some very old cedar trees grew in the middle of this old road, showing the age of the trail itself. They had grown there since the road was used, obviously, so that the age of the road was clearly indicated.

George and I spent two nights there, and all of one day, just wandering around and trying to figure things out. We examined the cedar beam and the old road, the buildings and the manner and material of which they were built. We were puzzled by it all, but the thing which amazed us the most, and puzzled us as well, was the ditches.

There were several of them, quite long, and evidently used to carry water, yet there was no water near now except the Gallinas River, about twelve miles away and downhill from the ruins. To get water into the ditches from this, the water would have had to be run uphill! We couldn't figure out how this could be done, so we decided that there must have been a spring, or some other source of water nearby, placed above the ditches so that the water would run downhill to them. It really seemed impossible that the source of water was the Gallinas (pronounced "ga-yeen-as," and meaning "chickens").

The ruins lie in broken, rollin' country, and we didn't see anything else like them during our travels. We heard that there were somewhat similar ruins in the Chaco Canyon west of the Rio Grande, but we didn't run onto them. We were told, however, that they were nothing like or as fine as the Gran Quivira.

After I parted company with George Howard, I started sowing my wild oats right, and it was not long until I had a good horse and saddle of my own. I rambled around in different places, now here, now there. Sometimes I'd stop and work a few days or so. Sometimes I'd sell some feller a fat steer or cow-brute, but I never dug in too deeply on that life, and the law was never looking for me. They'd have had a hard time locating me if they had looked for me, for I resorted to my old trick of using a different name in different sections of the country, for the reasons I mentioned before.

Something that sticks in my mind which I saw then was a pool of hot water on the west side of the Rio Grande, above San Marcial. As I was riding along I was attracted by a small outcropping of volcanic rock, not over eight feet high, and perhaps ten feet wide. It was a dark brownish red color, and it jutted up out of the flat Rio Grande bottom in a very conspicuous manner. The Rio Grande bottom had at that time no trees on it between the river and the upland and this served to make more noticeable the outcropping of rock. There was no house of any sort within a mile or more, nothing but the flat bottoms and that jutting rock.

Naturally I rode toward it to investigate it further, and almost without warning, I stumbled onto a pool of water at its feet. It was just a hole in the ground, not very large, perhaps ten or twelve feet in diameter. A cottonwood log was thrown across it, and I wondered why. I felt the water and found it not too hot to bathe in, so I proceeded to take a bath in the pool, but I soon found out what the log was there for. Hanging onto it in an upright position with my legs stretched full length, I found the water too hot for comfort on my feet. There must have been an underground hot spring which fed this pool but no indication of it was to be seen above-ground. Then another thing on which I have often pondered, wondering if it has been made a tourist attraction. It was a very unique formation.

The wisdom of using an alias when a rider was roaming around as I was doing, and almost all young fellows down there took a fancy to ramble at some time or other, was proven by an experience which really caused me to change my ways. It happened at a dance.

This was another Mexican dance, and I was dancing every set

I could with the girl I considered the best looking in the hall. She didn't object to my monopolizing her, but her fiancé did, and tried to make me quit dancing with her. Just for devilment I refused to do it, and redoubled my attentions to the pretty señorita. Finally her boy friend tried to make me get off the floor, after I had her out on it and we were dancing. This resulted in a brawl between us which might have resulted in disaster for me, and did make things bad for him. He came at me with a wicked-looking knife. As I never liked the looks of a knife anyway, and certainly didn't when it was coming towards me, I stopped him with a bullet across his cheek before he reached me. Of course I had to get out of there quick, as I was the only white man at the dance, so I held them back with my gun and faded away from there.

This young Mexican was a strikingly handsome fellow, and the bullet-wound scarred him for life, stretching as it did from the corner of his mouth to his ear. His father and uncle had plenty of sheep, and they resented the scarring of that fool boy so much that they put out a reward of $500 for my scalp. This was not within the law, for I had shot in self-defense, and they knew they would not be able to make it stick, but it was a common custom with many a deputy Sheriff at that time to arrest a man who had a reward on him on any pretext, and kill him before getting to jail with him. Then the deputy would say that the prisoner had tried to break away. The reward would be collected then and no questions asked. For this reason, I knew that I would not live long in that country, so I started drifting away from New Mexico. I went by easy stages, because I did not want to be run out. If I had to go, I chose to *saunter!*

CHAPTER FIFTEEN

Drifting

"*Everyone, at some time,*" *said Mr. Wallace, "must have experienced the fulfillment of the ancient promise that bread cast upon the waters shall be returned a thousandfold. Certainly, I had it fulfilled for me after many days, and got out of a very tight spot thereby.*"

Sometimes I would get tired of rambling from point to point, and so I would stop and work awhile. At that time the Santa Fe road-bed was being graded between Las Vegas and the Rio Grande. I rode into a grading camp run by the firm of Blush and Ellinwood [Ellenwood]. Blush was in charge of that camp. I put up with them, intending to stay overnight, but while eating supper Mr. Blush told me he was having trouble with one of his mule teams. He could not get a driver who seemed able to get the proper work out of them, and he asked me if I could drive a team. I said I could, and he induced me to stay and drive that particular team. There was a little Mexican town by the name of Tecolote about a mile from his camp, and as I knew, I could work for him and get plenty of recreation too while I was there. I took the job. He was working Mexicans mostly, and one morning about nine o'clock they stopped working and got in the shade and went to making cigarettes. The Irish boss kept cussing them and trying to get them to pick up their shovels and go to work, as he wasn't used to anything like that on the section. The Mexicans talked to him in Mexican, which he couldn't understand a word of. I was taking it all in and laughed my head off. The boss came over to where I was and asked me if I could understand what them so-and-so's was saying? I told him I could, and he said, "Phwat the divil are they doin'? Have they sthr-ruck on me?"

"Hell, no," I told him, "they're just smokin' a cigarette. Leave them alone and let 'em smoke. And take it good-naturedly. You'll get more work out of 'em. Mexicans got to take a little rest now and then," I explained to him.

Well, he agreed to do it, but he couldn't stand to sit and see them not working when he figured they ought to be on the job, so he told me to tie up my team and stay with them till they got through smoking, and then call him. After that he made it a practice to do that every time they started to smoke. On account of this arrangement I always knew when there was going to be a dance or any other kind of fun going on at Tecolote ("tec-o-lo-ta" is Spanish for "owl").

One day the Mexicans and I agreed to hold a session of draw poker at Tecolote that night, and I mentioned at supper-time what we had planned, so the camp boys knew where I was. That was a lucky break for me, as it proved later on.

About six o'clock that evening, while our game was going full swing, I was told a man outside wanted to talk to me alone. So I went out to him, exercising due caution as usual. The caution was needless, as it happened, for the man was Jack Cozart, and I knew him well. I became acquainted with Jack in Hillsboro days. While I was at the Las Animas mine, a tramp, more than half sick and stony broke strayed in there, hungry and ragged and too weak to work. That tramp was Jack Cozart. Bill, Tom, and I took him in, letting him eat and sleep in our "dug-out," and he agreed to do the cooking for us in return. Jack was a joker, and liked to tell what a snap he had. He said he did not have to buy any grub, just cook his meals and eat and sleep, and of course (he always added) it was very little trouble for him to throw a little extra into the pot for us! We got along fine with Jack, and I was glad to find him waiting outside the saloon in Tecolote.

When I found it was Jack Cozart waiting outside, I relaxed, but not for long. Jack was really all worked up. He told me that he had overheard a Mexican and two deputy Sheriffs talking in a saloon that evening about supper time, down in Las Vegas. Hearing my name mentioned, he had listened closely, and he heard them plot to come to the grading camp and arrest me next morning. They said, according to Cozart, "Hell, he'll try to get away before we get back, and we'll collect that five hundred dollars!"

Jack wanted to know what that meant. I told him, then I went back to our poker game. The first hand dealt after my return I could see was a "cold-deck," fixed up by the Mexicans while I was outside. I let them win a few dollars on it, then pretended I was sore because they had pulled that stunt, and I quit the game.

I immediately went to our camp, where I saw the light still burning in Mr. Blush's tent. I went in and asked him for what was coming to me. He told me that I would have to wait until pay-day. I argued, but he opened a drawer in his desk and took out a .44 Colt and laid it on the desk as a hint.

I said, "All right, then. If I have to, I can, I guess."

Passing behind him toward the door of the tent, I reached over his shoulder and picked up his gun. Then I said, "Now, Mr. Blush, you will please pay me off in cash and I will leave!" So he did, and I did.

Neither he nor I had raised our voices during this interview, and we parted with a hand clasp and a smile, and a hearty "Good luck to you, Frank!" from him. He was a good sport, and he was learning western ways fast.

By sunrise next morning, I had passed through Las Vegas. I was heading away from Santa Fe, because I figured that they would be certain to look for me over Santa Fe way if they decided to follow me. As I jogged along, I thought of Jack Cozart, and the fix I would have been in except for him. This was certainly one time when bread that I had cast upon the waters returned after many days, and took me out of a mighty tight spot.

Well, I studied the matter over, and decided that I had had enough (at least for the present) of running wild, so I made up my mind to get a steady job somewhere. I soon found myself in El Paso, Texas, and started from there, figuring to get back into the cattle country, again. I "clumb a freight" in the El Paso yards in spite of warning from hobos that no one could bum his way on a Southern Pacific freight train. It was a bright moonlit night, and I found three flat cars together in about the middle of the train. I got onto the middle flat car, and one of the "bos" joined me, but the rest shook their heads. When the train had cleared the yards, a brakeman came along and asked where we thought we were going.

"We-ell," I said, "I do not know yet exactly, but we are going to ride as far as Sierra Blanca with you anyway, and catch a Texas Pacific train from there on." I had spoken very pleasantly to him, but he at once erupted.

"Like hell you are!" he exploded. "You're a-gettin' off this train *right now!* Now jump off before I *kick* you off!"

I quietly slipped my .44 Colt out of the holster and held it with the business end a couple of feet away from his belly, and gently told him he would have a better chance to live to a green old age if he immediately got the hell out of there and stayed in the caboose. He started back, but said as he left, "I'll get the rest of the crew up here and show you, you blankety-blank so-and so!"

He did get them, but my faithful pard, the six-gun, stopped them flat when they got on the first flat car. After a short talk they decided to go back to the caboose, and they did not bother us any more.

We reached Sierra Blanca just after sun-up, and got off the train as it was going to the front on the Southern Pacific, and we wanted to take the Texas Pacific out of there. We waved the train crew good-bye, and got a fairly good cussing-out from them in return, to which we responded with a few big laughs. We then proceeded to look for some breakfast. My pal, the hobo, was rather poorly dressed, to put it mildly. He was unshaven, and really very much in need of a bath. I was none too clean myself by that time, so we did not try to get breakfast at the Southern Pacific eating-house. Instead, we eased down the track to some boarding-cars set on a side track, close to a derrick very much like the oil driller derricks of today. We found the crew at breakfast and I gave the head man fifty cents for our breakfast.

It turned out that he was the owner of the rig. His name was McDougall, and he was a man of forty or fifty years of age, and as Scotch as his name. He seemed rather interested in me. I then weighed about 190 pounds, stood six feet two inches tall, and was pretty full of vital energy. He kept spearing questions at me all the time I was eating and finally he asked me to go to work for him on the well which was to supply water for the two railroads. He wanted a man to fire the engine and to help the driller on ground work. I told him I did not know how to do anything but ride a horse, but he insisted he could teach me enough about the engine in one day so that I could get along all right with the driller to advise me.

Finally, I agreed to stay and work a while anyway. He was to pay me $2.50 a day from the start, and if I stayed over six months, he was to pay me $2.75 a day from the start. Mac explained that he had no regular pay-day, as he could pay his men only as he could get a payment from the railroad. He had four or five rigs along the Southern Pacific drilling for water, and he got a payment only when he had got an additional five hundred feet on any well, or when a well that had water in it would stand up to a test of pumping through a two-inch pipe for a specific number of hours.

I thought it might be a good idea to work steady for a while, and the job would teach me something new. I got along fairly well after I learned how to get water in the boiler. I seemed to have the knack of keeping up a good fire and consequently a good head of steam. I worked for old Mac for nearly a year before drawing any money. I got what clothes I had to have, as well as tobacco and other necessary supplies, from our little commissary. And I really enjoyed myself. For one thing, that was the summer that Hal[l]ey's Comet was so bright that we could see it in daylight. Many people thought it was the end of the world.*

Sierra Blanca was at that time just a spot on the prairie. No one lived there permanently. The employees at the Southern Pacific eating-house lived in it. That summer the first residence, a one-story board dwelling, was built. I did not see a law-enforcement officer while I was there. True, a detachment of Texas Rangers camped there one night. That was one of the few times that I saw anything

---

*This seems dubious; the only year the author could have seen Halley's Comet was 1910. It did not appear again until 1986.

of the famed Texas Rangers, as their work was almost over at that time. Also, a company of soldiers from Fort Bliss, Texas, was at Sierra Blanca once. The C.O. offered me a job as scout at $75 a month, but I turned that down flat. The Texas Rangers were more successful in fighting Indians than the regular soldiers because the Rangers fought the same way that the Indians did, hiding behind rocks and trees and bushes, and using other Indian tactics. But I never hankered to work with either of them.

Mac's rig was set right out on the open prairie. The only water there was hauled from the Rio Grande by a water train, and pumped into the big tank, just like they have now. Engines watered from the tank much as they do at present.

Doris Freeman was driller in charge of the well, and we really enjoyed ourselves. For a bath we would blow out our boiler on Saturday after work, as Mac was too religious to let us work on Sundays, except in an emergency. We would all strip off and get out in the spray of water and have a real shower. One Saturday a "nester" family drove in and camped thirty or forty yards from the rig. There were two grown girls in the family besides the father and mother, and of course we thought we were beat out of our bath, but Freeman said, "Hell, they can't see us in that steam! Let's bath[e] as usual!" So we slipped out behind the steam and were enjoying our bath when suddenly our water spray quit us cold. Freeman had slipped into the derrick and shut it off. He was full of hell anyway. We raced to the shelter of the derrick and there we wallowed Mr. Freeman in the cinders plenty!

It was here that I wrote the only poem I ever composed. I had got to be good friends with the telegraph operator at Sierra Blanca, and when I was leaving there he brought out a little autograph album and wanted me to write something in it, and sign my name. I thought a moment, and then a verse of four lines came to me, and I wrote it down. I can remember only the last two lines, now. They are as follows:

"We meet and we speak and we wander apart,
But the impress of friendship remains on the heart."

The memorable thing about this verse was the reception my friend gave it. He read it and stared at me with his mouth open. "Well, I be dogged, Frank!" said he, "how come a rough-neck like you could think up something like this?"

In the late Fall old Mac got a payment on the Haskell well about thirty miles east of us, and he paid us all up in full, in gold, which was very foolish of him, for we had all been so long away from the joys of civilization that we were yearning for the fleshpots of Egypt, you might say, and we all quit to have a good time and spend our money. That left Mac without a crew, and he had to shut down until he had rounded up another one.

I had close to five hundred dollars, so I went to San Antonio for my spree. When I got there I got myself a couple of suits of clothes, and all the other things I did not have that I needed, and that night I got myself pretty well soaked. I got up the next day in the hotel with the usual head, and decided to find a private place to board and room for a few weeks. That afternoon I was loafing around on the Alamo plaza and got to talking with a hack driver. I told him what I wanted to do, and he said he knew a good place. So he drove me around and around, crossing over about a dozen bridges. He didn't confuse me much, though, as I had a naturally good sense of direction, and I knew that the place where we stopped was not over three blocks from where we started. But I was really glad to pay him his charge of two dollars for the ride, as the house where he left me was run by a grass widow, and both the place and the landlady were very attractive. She was in her late twenties, very intelligent and companionable, and she had a black nanny cook who was a real culinary artist!

The landlady's name was Theresa, and I called her "teaser." We took up with each other and went to theaters and other places of amusement together. We always went to church twice on Sundays, as she was quite religious. I thoroughly enjoyed myself while I was there, but somehow money always had a habit of getting away from me, and at the end of six weeks my five hundred dollars was shrunk to less than fifty. So I had to leave for new pastures, and rather reluctantly took a train out of there.

My first stop was at Temple, Texas. There I ran into a Mr. Richardson, who had a small steam well rig, and he told me he had the contract of putting down a well for the Gulf, Colorado, and Santa Fe [Railway] at the roundhouse. He was not a driller himself, and he talked me into going to work for him, as I had learned how to drill and was qualified to do the job. So I took the rig over.

"Red" Ward was the master mechanic at Temple then, and he liked to come to the rig and talk with me when he had time to spare, so that we got pretty well acquainted. He was a pretty rough guy, who had been a saloon keeper at one time, and he felt himself the equal of anybody.

Before long we had an accident at the well and broke a casting, and we had to shut down and wait until we could get a new one from Fort Scott, Kansas. I was boarding with a Mr. James, who had a planing mill in Temple, and he got me to agree that I would work for him while the rig was shut down. We went over to the mill for the first time one day after dinner, and before I had been there an hour, I laid my hand down on a buzz saw, cutting a gash to the bone across the palm, and nearly splitting the thumb. Well, that was that. The doctor wanted to amputate, but I would not let him, so the hand kept getting worse. However, I could walk around with my arm in a sling, and did so. One day I met "Red" Ward down-town, and he demanded, "Now what the hell have you been doing to yourself?"

I explained everything to him, and he exploded, "To hell with that doctor! Come up to the office with me, I'll fix that hand up!"

When we got to the office, he told his clerk, "Put this fellow on the payroll and give him a pass to Galveston and an order to the hospital." So I took the next train to Galveston, and there my hand got well in a short time. The doctors there never even mentioned amputation to me. I never could quite understand how "Red" could get away with what he did for me, but he made it.

By early spring, I was able to use my left hand considerable again, and as that would not handicap me much on range work, I concluded to go back to punching again, although I was by now losing much of my old hankering for that life. I had been cogitating pretty deeply while I was in the hospital, and I remember wondering just how old I would probably live to be if I stayed on the range. I gave myself about ten more years, if I was lucky. I remember deciding that I might live to be thirty!

I couldn't see what else to do but go back on the range, so I lit out again, and kept going until I got to Las Animas, Colorado. I got promise of work there as soon as Spring roundup started. I had no saddle, so I went to work on the section to get money to buy one, and a bed roll. I worked there for a month or so as Spring roundup was starting late that year.

One evening after supper a covered wagon drove in from the west and stopped about a hundred yards from the section house. A small-sized woman got out and started unhitching the horses, and I could see she did not savvy much about it, so I went over and offered my help, which she gladly accepted, saying her husband was very ill in the wagon. They were from Emporia, Kansas, and were on their way back there. Her husband had taken ill in Emporia, with lung trouble, and she had tried to get him over into New Mexico for his health., but the doctor at Trinidad told her he would die before she could get him over the Raton Pass, on account of the altitude, so she was taking him back home. She decided to stay over for a day at Las Animas and do a little washing.

She was a seamstress by trade, and her husband was a veterinary [*sic*, veterinarian] and an inveterate horse trader. I took quite a liking to them both, and offered to take her place driving the team back to Emporia. She gratefully accepted my offer, and took the train home while the husband and I followed with the team and wagon.

We made a couple of horse trades on the way, he having got on his feet a little. One horse he traded for was loose in a box stall, and the owner said if we traded for him we'd have to get him out ourselves, for he was next thing to an outlaw. I took him out, and put the harness on him and drove him to the wagon the rest of the trip.

We got into Emporia about the first day of July, 1885, and there began a new life for me. We found that Mrs. Williams had a house all ready for us. I stayed with them for three or four days, while I located myself a job. I had called plenty of people "tenderfoot" in my time on the range, but now I was the tenderfoot. I was absolutely ignorant of life in a town like Emporia, and found it hard to adjust myself, and to find a job. But finally I did, and so began the third phase of my life, which proved the longest part of it by some sixty years.

CHAPTER SIXTEEN

A Changed World

EDITOR'S NOTE

In 1883, when John Francis Wallace (or Frank Wallace, as he encouraged people to call him) arrived there, Emporia was already a quarter of a century old, a thriving midwestern town with fine buildings, good schools, and paved, tree-lined streets. Founded in 1857, it was named after the great Carthaginian financial center by Emporia Town Company president George W. Brown, secretary G. W. Deitzler, and founders Lyman Allen and Columbus Hornsby, all of Lawrence, Kansas Territory, and Preston B. Plumb of Xenia, Ohio, who brought with him a printing press on which he published the town's first newspaper, the *Kanzas News*.

Situated on the top of the rise between the Cottonwood and the Neosho rivers on land that had once belonged to Wyandot Indians, Emporia at first consisted of only three buildings; by 1859, its population had increased to 541 souls and boasted four stores and a school operated by Mary Jane Watson with sixty children attending. The town charter forbade the sale of liquor and gambling, leading Emporia to claim itself the first prohibition town in the world.

Free State in its politics, Emporia remained on the

sidelines of the Civil War and never experienced an Indian raid. The town's first bank, Emporia Banking & Savings, was opened in March of 1867, and the first train of the Missouri, Kansas and Texas Railroad ("the Katy") reached town from Junction City on December 22, 1869; the Santa Fe Railroad came in the following September, the same year that marked the incorporation of Emporia as a city of the second class.

Thirteen years later, when Frank Wallace first arrived in Emporia, the city's population had risen to over nine thousand, the first gas for lighting was in use, a franchise for a street railway had been granted, a telephone company was organized, and the first electric lights were being installed at $12.50 a month for users. For him it was a new world, so he remade himself once again and proceeded to find himself a place in it.

"For many years I strove to forget the old life in the West," said Mr. Wallace. "After I went to Emporia I thought for some reason that it was better not to think of my range experiences. I decided to build a new life, and to get married and establish myself in a community like this one. I had begun to feel lonesome, for I had in all the United States, so far as I knew, no one of my own. And by now my ways and mode of living had become so foreign to those of my English relatives that I had no desire to go there. Did I ever tell you how I came to get married, and how my wife's mother received me?" He chuckled and began the story.

I looked about me and soon found a young girl whom I concluded I wanted to marry. She was agreeable, so we went to a preacher and got "hitched up," and rented a one-room apartment to live in. The next morning we went to her mother, and told her we were married. I have never forgotten the first thing the old lady said. "Why, Frankie, have you *married him?*" She sounded so disgusted with the girl for doing such a foolish thing. I suppose I didn't seem to her such a good catch, for in the established Kansas towns, cowboys from Texas and New Mexico were held in very low esteem. However, the old lady came to be very fond of me as she knew me better, and she was my friend for the rest of her life.

My wife's name was Frances, and they called her Frankie. My name is Francis and I was called Frank. Having assumed the responsibility of marriage, it was up to me to provide for Frankie as well as Frank, so I set out to look for a job.[1]

I had worked in all, about ten days in Emporia, in a little café on the main street of the town. I had been perfectly ignorant about finding work in such a place, but Frank Bomaine, the night marshall [*sic*], owned a little café, and he offered me the job of running that, of all things for me to do! As I was flat broke or very nearly so when I got to Emporia, and as I was never afraid to tackle anything, [I] took the job on. At the end of ten days, Mrs. Williams, the friendly wife of the sick man I had brought in from Colorado, came to see me and said that her husband was very bad sick again, and he wanted me to come up and take care of him. Of course, I did. I quit the café and stayed with Williams until he died, about a week or ten days later. It was shortly afterwards that I married.

As luck would have it, the next man I spoke to was a dragman,[2] Silas Holloway. He wanted a married man, and when I said I was married he took me on at once. The wages were seven dollars a week, but we could live all right on that in those days. My wife's people were not well-off, and she knew the ways of economy. It took very little to satisfy me.

At the beginning of the next winter, Hank Lowe came to me and said there was a fellow who had a range up in the Flint Hills. His name was W. P. Herrin, and his ranch was called the "Big Spring Ranch," or as it was locally called, the "Red Ranch." Hank said that Herrin had over a hundred thoroughbred polled Angus and Galloway bulls he was feeding there through the winter, and he asked me if I would consider the job of taking care of the cattle at thirty dollars a month and board for myself and wife. I took the job.

I stayed with Herrin for just about a year. That first winter I fed the bulls for him, and they were moved out in the spring. That summer, starting with 525 head of two-year-old native steers, which was increased by another batch of about 400 before the middle of the summer, I took care of them all. That was the summer that my first child, my daughter Mary, was born.

In late summer Herrin sent another three hundred head of steers out, this time, of Arizona cattle that were just skin, horns, and bones. They were turned loose on me, too. This over-stocked his range badly. There were then three of us at the Red Ranch, but the cattle rambled so badly, especially the Arizonians, that the other two boys did about all the herding. It kept me busy bringing in the strays they let get away.

The last ones I brought in I had to "steal" out of a fellow's pasture down by Eureka. He wanted to be paid two dollars a head before I took them home, but when I went to get them out of the pasture, I took them right through the fence and on home, and so managed to get them out without paying anything.

Big Spring Ranch, called Red Ranch thereabouts because of the good-sized red house on it, was a large ranch in the Flint Hills. There was found the finest grazing in the world, long blue-stem grass about a foot high. It was especially good at the head of Fall Creek. Little India [*sic*, Indian] Creek is the source of the south fork of the Cottonwood River, which branched off at Cottonwood Falls. This side of the Flint Hills was the "Big Flats," a level piece of country stretching off for miles, coming down to within about twenty miles of El Dorado. It was grazing country, entirely uninhabited at that time. It was like a section of the Staked Plains.

Big Spring Ranch itself was in the Flint Hills, however. The Walnut River heads up in the Big Flats, the south fork of the Cottonwood runs off them and flows on down in a northerly direction. Big Spring itself is on the north side of Little India Creek. I couldn't recognize the country when I visited it more than fifty years later, as big trees were then growing along the creeks where no timber had been when I was there, and the old red house had entirely disappeared. If it hadn't been for the old spring, I couldn't have found the spot.

It was a large spring of very cold water, so cold that the cattle would not drink out of it in the hot summer any closer than fifteen or twenty yards from where it flowed out of the ground. Cattle are like that about cold water. From the spring down towards India Creek when I was there the last time (fifty years and more after my first experience there) it was full of growing watercress. Watercress must grow in living water that does freeze. The only place I know of that any watercress grows south of the Cottonwood River is there at Big Spring. It grows on the north side up towards Nebraska. I used to get the engineers on the Santa Fe to bring me some after I went to work for that railroad.

A few days after I got the wild cattle out of the fellow's pasture by running them through the fence, Herrin sent a gang of men out and they took all his cattle off his India Creek range. It was again late Fall, and the grass had dried. I had had enough of it anyway, as the only team that was there was a yoke of oxen, and we had to drive them about ten miles to Matfield Green for our groceries. H. S. Lincoln ran the post office and general store at Matfield Green. When I visited there at the same time I did at Big Spring Ranch, half a century later, it took two old-timers a couple of hours to recall his name.

When we broke up at Red Ranch, I drove the wagon to Strong City and turned it over to Herrin's man there, and from there I returned to Emporia.

As winter was coming on and work was very scarce during the winter months, I took a job hauling cinders with a team of mules, away from the cinder pit at the Santa Fe roundhouse. I got $1.25 a day for that, and often could make an extra fifty cents selling a load of cinders to somebody that needed them to put under their rocks for sidewalks. There were no cement sidewalks in those days. They used quarried rock entirely.

The blacksmith shop was close to the cinder pit, and it didn't take all my time to keep the cinders hauled away, so I would loaf between times in the blacksmith shop. I would always pick up a sledge [hammer] and help them make a weld when they needed it. This resulted in the blacksmith asking the master mechanic to give me a job in there when an opening came. That was $1.75 a day, so I bid my mules goodbye.

They put me to helping a fellow by the name of Wyatt, a high-tempered Virginian. We made a great team physically, both of us six feet two inches tall and weighing 190 pounds each. Alf Taylor was master mechanic at Emporia at that time. He was the last master mechanic Emporia has ever had. He didn't like Wake Wyatt very well, and one day he came in in a bad humor and commenced to "eat on" Wake. It so happened that Wake was not in a good humor either, so he jerked the strings to his blacksmith apron, letting it fall, took Taylor outside by the collar of his coat and proceeded to knock the stuffin' out of him. Then he led Alf through the roundhouse and up to his own office by the ear and made him give him his discharge check, and pulled out of town. Taylor was not a well-liked man, especially by the engineers and firemen, and as he immediately had a warrant sworn out for Wake and they knew there would be a fine to pay, the engineers and firemen said they would chip in and pay his fine if they could find anyone to hold the money until they had enough. I volunteered to do it. I would not accept more than fifty cents from any one man, and soon had to stop taking contributions entirely, as I knew the fine would not be over twenty-five dollars.

Wake had left town and I did not know where he was, but about a week later I was eating supper one evening and Wake walked in on me. He told me he had a job at El Dorado, on what was then the Fort Scott, Wichita and Western Railroad, and is now the Missouri Pacific. He asked me to come down there and be his helper, as he had that also arranged for, if I would come. So I quit the Santa Fe and joined Wake at El Dorado, which was then the division point (moved there from Reece). I worked there about a year and a half, then my wife talked me into moving back to Emporia. We had lost one of our little daughters while living at El Dorado, and she was too lonesome to stay, as she had no kinfolks nearer than Emporia.[3]

While I was at El Dorado the boiler maker had a hard time trying to cure a horse of his, which had [a] fistula. Several people had tried to cure him but had failed. He was a race horse, a trotter, and if he could be cured he would be fine. I bought him for twenty dollars and cured him in about three months. This was the old "horse and buggy days," so I bought a fairly good mate for him, and a light express wagon, loaded in my household goods and family, and went back to Emporia.

When I arrived in Emporia I put my team and express wagon on the street picking up odd jobs until I could land something that suited me better, but in a short time I was offered a house and lot for my team (small houses and lots were very cheap then) so I traded off the team.

Then I went back to the Santa Fe roundhouse and was hired in the wiper gang, following which I took a job as boiler-washer and was working at that when the A.R.U. (American Railway Union) strike was called in '94. Of course, I went out like the rest of the darn fools, thinking the strike would only last a week or so, but we lost, and I had to look for another job. Jobs were so scarce in Emporia that year that a man was very lucky if he could find a day's work at a dollar and a half a day now and then. I saw I could not keep my family on what I could pick up that way, so one day I was down on the street and met a friend who lived in the country. He asked me if I knew any of the boys who could build a house. I told him I could (I had built my own chimney once).

So I went out and rebuilt the chimney on the Bethel Church for him. He liked the job well enough so he got me to go to his house and tear down and rebuild the tops of two of his chimneys. I got $4.50 apiece for those chimneys. That was the regular price which brick-masons charged and I knew it, and felt rather puffed up over it.

When I got back to town after doing that job, and showed up at the strikers' usual loafing-place, the street, some of the fellows wanted to know where I'd been for the last couple of days. I told them very importantly I'd been out in the country rebuilding some chimneys.

One of them spoke up, "Why, say," he said, "Judge Cunnin[g]ham was asking me a while back if any of us boys could do that kind of work! I didn't know you could."

I started at once for the judge's office and told him I wanted the job and got it. He said it was a rental house, and as it was empty just then, he was going to have it papered and painted on the inside, the shingle roof patched, and otherwise fixed up. I was so elated over my success with the chimneys that I told him I could do all of that! So he said to go ahead.

I had worked as helper some with a painter, but knew nothing about paper-hanging, never having done any except a little in my own house, but I waded into the job anyway. I soon found out I could not hang the ceiling paper, so I talked the Judge into letting me calsomine [sic] it, and managed with my wife's help to get the room papered. I charged regular mechanic's prices for the work I did. Judge [E. W.] Cunningham was satisfied and I was more than pleased with my earnings so I took up that line of work, learning as I went along, and I made a comfortable living for my family, even hired helpers part of the time, but mostly I got along with the help my wife could give me.

However, that kind of work was very slack during the winter months, and when I got a letter from one of my old Santa Fe friends from Pittsburg (Kansas) in December, saying he had landed me a job on the P & G [Kansas City, Pittsburg & Gulf, now the Kansas City Southern] railway, as boiler washer at night, I went there, arriving December 25, and went to work the same night.

This was an old Indian-built railroad, originally built for a logging route and called the "Split-log Railroad." When I was there Tom Woodhouse was the master mechanic and Charley North was general foreman. Both were old "split-log" men.

Now, while I worked at night at Emporia, I had learned how to handle engines and was pretty good at it, so when an engine came in with washout reported, and was not brought into the roundhouse soon as it was ready to be, I told one of the night laborers to set the turntable and I would bring it in.

"My God, fella," he told me, "Mac'll fire anybody that moves an engine!"

"Mac" was the night foreman. I thought that would be just as good a time to be fired as any, so I said, "Go ahead, set the table, and I'll bring one engine in, anyhow!"

When I stopped the engine in its stall in the roundhouse, sure enough Mac was there, waiting for me. He was a thickset, bullnecked Irishman. He watched me put everything in order in the cab before I got down, and when I hit the floor and stood beside him he looked up at me and said, "Where the hell did you learn to handle an engine?"

Speaking carelessly, I told him, "Oh, up on the Santa Fe. I always handled 'em up there for the night foreman."

"How long [did] you work there?" he demanded. I told him about five years, at night. He grinned a little, and said, "You're just the feller I've been a-looking fer. I can't trust any o' these yaps to touch a throttle, so I can't get in a wink o' sleep at night on that account. After this, you and me will handle 'em between us. That'll give me a chance to slip off an' get an hour or two's sleep once in a while."

The next night when I came to work Mac was sitting on a workbench talking with the master mechanic. They had both worked on the old split-log road before the P&G bought it, so they were very well acquainted. Mac was pleading to get off that night to celebrate Christmas Eve, but the master mechanic (Tom Woodhouse) told him he had to work as there was no one to take his place, and they were having it hot and heavy. When I walked up Mac got himself an idea. Said he, "Why, here's a man, Tom, can handle it! Put him on in my place!" That was the first time Woodhouse had seen me so he asked who I was and if I could handle it. Mac told him my name and assured him I was as capable of handling the job as he was, so Tom told him all right. Mac gave me a few instructions on the side, and left me on the job. I had not got as far as the coal chute from the roundhouse when they left me in charge of it.

There was an old Santa Fe engineer in Pittsburg who was one of the men Mac told me about. He had lost out in the '94 strike, and they had promised to put him on as soon as they could. Mac said not to use him unless I had to as a last resort. But I knew what it was to be out of a job, and also what seniority meant to a road man, so I found an opportunity to send him out on a trip that night.

I worked at Pittsburg for over a year, and as long as I was there I had to take Mac's job whenever he laid off. I remember one time I held it down for him for six weeks. They put me on days the next Spring, running the stationary engine (which made steam to run all the machinery). One day I thought the general foreman was getting a little bit too uppity and so I told him to take his job, and what he could do with it. It was very hard work and it was breaking me fast. In fact, when I got back to Emporia to establish myself again, I got down sick and was partially paralyzed, so badly that the doctor didn't think I would ever walk again. But I fooled 'em all. One night I was so near gone that the reporter for the *Emporia Gazette* reported me dead, and they had my obituary in the next day's paper.[4] But I got well, and am still going strong at eighty-two years of age. I still get a kick out of that headline, "*Frank Wallace Dead!*" that appeared in the *Gazette* almost fifty years ago.

When I did get on my feet and was able to get around with a cane, smallpox broke out in Emporia, and that was really what restored my health. As I wasn't strong enough to work yet, I wangled myself a job of running the pesthouse which the city established on the forty acres on which the city reservoir was built, about three miles from town.[5]

I had had smallpox in New Mexico, so I was of course immune. At first they had two sisters of charity as volunteer nurses. One of them took a very mild case of it, and they sent the third one out to take her place and help nurse her.

These sisters were very jolly and full of fun after they became acquainted. The first time we were out there we all had tents. One night when the doctor and I got back from a ride, we found our tent all roped up, wound around and around, decorated with weeds stuck in the ropes. Once inside the tent we found that our cots and bedding were all gone. Finally the little Dutch sister told us probably we didn't go far enough to look for them or we might have found them. So we went clear down to the corner of the forty and found them where the sisters had carried 'em. By the time we got back with our beds we were wet with dew to the knees.

The next evening while the sisters were at supper I slipped a piece of three-inch pipe, that I'd found up by the reservoir, under the edge of the sister's tent and after they had got to bed I got a nice piece of dry rag and slipped it into the end of the pipe and touched a match to it. When they smelled the smoke they thought the tent was on fire, and each one tried to outscream the other. So we had to remove the pipe and pacify them or they would have roused everyone who was out there. But they didn't play any more tricks on us!

I remember that the Mother Superior used to bring them wine by the gallon, and they always divided with us. These sisters were very fine people, and the fact that they could unbend and have fun along with us served to raise them in our estimation still more.

As appears evident, the disease never reached a dangerous stage that whole time. It was quite wide-spread, but never very serious. I was out there three times in all. The first time for about four and a half months, the second time for a shorter siege, and the third time another minor epidemic. That time it got into the State Normal School, and we had nothing but State Normal students out there for nearly two months. One girl even had it the second time before she got away. This is a very rare occurrence, but it can happen. However, both were mild cases.

Several colored people were out there with it, too. We used separate quarters for them, of course. By then the city had built frame houses to replace the tents which were first erected, so things were much more comfortable. The doctor and I rigged up a "tick-tock" on the colored folks' house, and when we got to working it that night, they thought ghosts were wailing and all of 'em stampeded out of the house, and would have left the place entirely but we capitulated and explained what we done and got them back into their quarters, before they got away. We never tried that again.

I really had a good time out there. Old Doc Poindexter kept his horse and buggy out there while he was out there, and on moonlight nights he and I would drive all over the surrounding country. It was from one of these drives that we came in to find our tent roped up. The doctor and I would have some good talks, and we really became good friends. He was a smart old man, and a good doctor.[6]

The city treated us very well. Anything on earth we wanted to eat we could order. I'd drive the horse and buggy to the alley back of the store, and they'd throw out the packages of groceries. The city furnished us with good whiskey for medicine for the patients. So whenever we got sick we had our remedy.

By the time the smallpox epidemic was over, I had earned over sixteen hundred dollars from the city, most of which I had saved. So I bought a lot and built a house on it, doing all the work myself.

After that I took up house repairing again. I had tried to get back on the Santa Fe, but was blackballed on that road on account of the strike, and could not get a clearance, as long as general manager J. J. Fry lived. After his death, I got a clearance, through the mail without even asking for it. At that time my old night foreman, Pete Dorach, was day foreman, and one day when I was down town, I heard that they had an engine in the turntable pit. As it was directly on my way home I went through to see it. When I got there, there was not only one, but two engines in the pit. There was a slope to the turntable from the cinder pit, and the pit man had let an engine get away from him, and rolled down and into the pit of the turntable, a drop of four or five feet. Before they had hardly started to get the engine out, another one had rolled in on top of that one through the carelessness of another pit man.

As soon as Pete saw me he asked me if I would go to work for him, if he'd get me a clearance, as I had handled engines a great deal when I worked under him at night. I told him I had had a clearance for six months, and was doing pretty well without working for the railroad. But he rushed me right over to General Foreman Goodhue, and insisted that Goodhue should put me on at once as a hostler, assuring him that I was really capable in handling an engine, and would never have an accident.

It was getting late in the Fall, winter was coming on, and I had my family to think of (I had five children by then) [dating these events post-1892] so I agreed to do it, and went to work that night for them. I worked two nights. The next morning I waited for Mr. Goodhue and told him he either had to give me a day job or my time. I wouldn't work nights any more for nobody. I'd already put in over five years at it, and that was enough.

After arguing a while he told me to come back the next morning and he'd have something for me. He was a cantankerous kind of a cuss, and he and I never got along very well, as he put me on the dirtiest job around there, working at the cinder pit. But I stuck it out, and early in February he came out one day to the pit and told me he wanted me to take the boiler washing job, wet and dirty. I told him I wouldn't even consider it as, if I took it, it'd be no time till the night boiler-washer would claim seniority, and I'd be back on night work again. But he agreed that I should have the day job regardless of seniority, if I would take it. So I did, as it was a better-paying job than the cinder pit one. Late that summer I found the store-house-keeper was quitting and asked Goodhue for his job as by then I thought I had acquired enough education to handle it. And for a wonder he gave it to me. That gave me a good inside job for the winter.

The next summer the Santa Fe put the bonus system in operation, and I was given the job as bonus clerk at a raise in salary. A few months later they promoted the chief clerk to a job in Topeka, and the (at that time) General Foreman, Billy Deveny,[7] put me in as chief clerk. I held that job under four different General Foremen, Deveny, McDonough, Ugden and Collier.

During the time that I was chief clerk for the Santa Fe in Emporia, I served on the city council for two terms, the second year as its president. This period of my life was very enjoyable. It was for me an expanding world. I provided well for my family, I was active in the political life of the city, I had stimulating friendships among "the great and the lowly," from district judges to ordinary laborers. I was constantly striving to improve my education, my speech, and my field of knowledge.

But all things come to an end, and my good job did, too. I had unfortunately incurred the enmity of a higher official by speaking too freely about him, using western range language, and he was out to get me fired. This he succeeded in doing after a couple of years from the time I made him mad at me. I worked as chief clerk for about six years in all, and by the time I was fired I was getting old enough that it was hard for me to get a job, so I had to look about for some other means of making a living for myself and my family.

After some consideration of the matter, I started a little corner grocery store. Then my good friend County Attorney McCarty[8] got me appointed a deputy Sheriff on account of my knowledge of the Mexican language, and the Sheriff turned over to me the handling of all Mexican matters that came under his jurisdiction.

Between the two jobs, I made a very fair living, but again it came to an end. My wife's health was failing, and the doctor ordered a change of climate, so I bought a team and wagon and drove through to Little Rock, Arkansas, with the intention of settling there if she should be benefited by the change. This was in 1916, and I had lived in Emporia for thirty-three years. I had come there a "roughneck" cowboy and had pulled myself up by the bootstraps, as they say, and become chief clerk of the Santa Fe and president of the City Council. I thought I had a right to be somewhat proud of what I had accomplished, against considerable odds.

CHAPTER SEVENTEEN

The Expanding Years

From the first, I had noticed my new friend's extensive vocabulary, and his seemingly unending fund of knowledge and experience upon various topics. Not yet, however, having heard of anything he had done beyond his cowboy life, I asked him about his knowledge of words. "Mr. Wallace," I inquired, "where did you get your vocabulary? You haven't mentioned your schooling, beyond saying that you didn't go to school after you were eleven. Yet you have a wonderful command of words. Where did you get it?"

"From lawyers, partly," he answered. "From reading, for I have always been a voracious reader. And no doubt my understanding of words was helped by the little Latin I had in school."[1]

I could not immediately understand, for Latin in our country begins in the ninth year of schooling, and I felt a little bewildered. "Where did you study Latin?" I asked. "In England," he replied, and then I remembered that Latin is included in the curriculum very early in that country. He went on to explain this, and then described his constant efforts to educate himself.

My father and I had quite a little library in New Mexico which included most of the poets. Shakespeare, Burns, Longfellow, and Bryant were my favorites. I read those so often that I could almost repeat from memory any part of their words that interested me most. That was where I gained some of my education. Another way I learned a good deal was by the dictionary. I always owned a dictionary, and a word I did not understand I would look up, and get its definition and pronunciation from there. The dictionary was my most highly prized book. Shakespeare was another of my favorites, and I believe Burns came next after the dictionary. Oh, you can get quite an education by even small pieces if you recognize and pick them up when you see them.

In newspapers I would read everything, even the advertisements, and I always picked up and read every scrap of newspaper I got a chance to. I seemed to have a craving for reading, and was frequently laughed at by the boys, both on the range and elsewhere, for putting in so much of my time that way.

There was a newspaper published in Trinidad, Colorado, in the 70s half in Mexican and half in English. It carried the same items in both languages, a column of English next to a corresponding column of Mexican. It was a four-page paper, and I would read it all. First I would read the Spanish item and try to interpret it into English. Then I would turn to the corresponding English item and see how near right I was. In that manner I got so I could read and write the Spanish almost as easily as I could English.

In the old days on the range our supply of literature was not the most highly elevating in the world but elevating or not, I read 'em all. The *Police Gazette, Pinkerton's, Diamond Dick,* and so forth, were the most commonly found reading matter at that time in that country, and of course, I would read and digest every one of them. In this way, I established a fairly good vocabulary, even as a boy, although it was still limited compared to what it later became after I went to Emporia. I found out that there were lots of words I could spell and define that I was mispronouncing. I corrected this by paying strict attention to educated people when they talked, also by getting well acquainted with several prominent lawyers in Emporia. Sam Spencer was one of them [and some others were] Owen Samuel, Billy Roberts, Judge [Wilburn Winstone] Parker, and Lon McCarty.

Lon McCarty and I were really close friends, from the time he was first making the race for County Attorney until his death. He served three terms as district judge after he was County Attorney, and was serving the fourth, I believe, when he died.

I first met Lon [in 1914] when he made his race for County Attorney the first time. We met on a street corner, and he paused and introduced himself to me. As we talked, I perceived that he was depressed, and when I questioned him he said that he thought he had lost the race. His opponent's father was an old railroad man, and his ward was the Third Ward. This was in the district composed almost exclusively of railroad men, in fact they called it the "railroad ward." It was also mine, and I had quite a little political influence there, so as I had taken quite a liking to Lon, and he was making absolutely no headway there, I told him to forget the Third Ward. I would take care of it, while he worked the rest of the county. So I worked for Lon in that ward, and he got about half of it, which gave him the election. Had I not done so, he would have lost.

Naturally Lon was grateful for my help, and we became the best of friends, and were until his death. It was through my contact with Lon that I learned many things which furthered my education. While I was Chief Clerk on the Santa Fe, I was elected to the City Council, and it came about as follows: Chris Tweedy,[2] who was one of the leading men in the labor union, came to me and asked me to run for City

Councilman from the Third Ward. Chris was the street overseer and we were well acquainted. He knew me thoroughly. Naturally I had never had any ideas along this line at all, but after considering it, I decided to run, as if I should be elected my education would be added to along another line. So I agreed to run, and was elected by a margin, as I remember, of six votes.

The eight City Councilmen elected by their votes, at their first meeting after election, a President of the Council. To my great surprise, after the next election (when I was serving my second year), they elected me to the presidency. Thus [in 1908] I became the first President of the Council that had been elected from the Third Ward for twenty years. All the rest of the Councilmen were business men, professors from the college, and so forth, and I was so astonished when they elected me without a dissenting word to be their President for a year, I even forgot to thank them for it.

Of course, in absence of [Frank McCain], the Mayor from the city, this made me acting Mayor, and when the Mayor took his fifteen-day vacation the following summer, I assumed his duties in his absence. And was I puffed up! I tried not to show it, but I was really proud of the honor which had been done me.

When I came up for re-election, I did not ask anybody for a vote, yet I had very few votes against me, so I served another term of two years. At the end of that term, a city commission form of government was voted in by the citizens of Emporia, so that I was one of the last Councilmen of Emporia.

A few years after I had moved away, I returned to Emporia on a visit, and of course, went down and chatted with my old friends on the Fire Department and others at the city building. There I met a man who had been a common laborer at the time of the change of city government, who was now one of the City Commissioners. I had known him well in the old days, and he invited me to ride around with him and see the improvements in Emporia which had come about since I left. He was riding in a fine car and I remarked, "The city must be doing you pretty proud, giving you a car like this to ride around in!" He laughed. "This ain't a city car, Frank," he told me, "it's mine!"

He told me that he had acquired considerable property and was living comfortably now. I never could get it through my head where the city bettered itself financially by making a change. None of the old councilmen that I knew were able to acquire much property, as we served without any pay what-ever. All we got while I was on the council was our lights and water free, as the city owned both plants at that time.

This reminds me of the only thing that I did while I was on the council, to take advantage of my position in order to better myself. I owned close to a half acre in city lots where I lived, and it was extra good land. I always liked to raise plenty of garden and could afford to water it freely while I was on the council. One year I had the Fire Department boys haul all the stable cleanings onto my place and pile it up. Also, I got the street commissioner to haul the street sweepings out there (this was still in the "horse and buggy" days). It was a very wet Spring, and my potatoes were knee high and grown up to weeds higher than the potatoes, and I could not get in to hoe them for the wet, so I took my wheelbarrow and hauled the fertilizer in and smothered the weeds between the rows, practically mulching them. It was getting warm weather and we still had a pile of fertilizer between my house and the alley, and it was becoming a nuisance. Neighbors began to complain of the fragrance, so I spread it all over my ground about a foot deep. I scraped away places to reach the ground and set out tomatoes and pepper plants packing the mulching back around them. I remember I planted my tomatoes eight feet apart each way, gave them plenty of water all summer, and did not have to use a hoe at all that year.

Mit Wilhite came out to look at it one Sunday and he and I counted over one hundred tomatoes on one vine (of the Earliana variety) that were as large as pigeon eggs. Later when they ripened, one of my Ponderosa tomatoes weighed 32½ ounces. I had to dig a cellar under my house that Fall to store my garden truck in.

One other way in which I used my influence as City Councilman for my own betterment was to get the electricity department to extend their line a quarter of a mile to reach my house which was on the edge of the city, so that I had my lights free, but the city was repaid for this by getting a lot of new customers. During the entire four years I was on the council, I was chairman of the Ordinance committee and also of the Fire Department committee. I had many interesting experiences in those committees and on the council as a whole, but it would take too much space to recount them.

It was after my experience [on] the City Council that I lost my job as Chief Clerk for the Santa Fe. One day, shortly before that, County Attorney Owen Samuel,[3] who was an old acquaintance of mine and whom I had befriended and aided while he was yet in college, called me up and asked me to come down and interpret a case in court which they had on hand against a Mexican, (if I could talk the language well enough). I told him I could handle the language all right, and would come down and interpret the case for five dollars. He said that he didn't see how he could pay that much as the deputy Sheriff allowance was only three dollars a day, and he'd have to pay me through the Sheriff if I handled it. He argued a while, but I wouldn't give in. I had a grin on my face but none in my voice, and he finally agreed to give me two days' pay as deputy Sheriff, which suited me all right. As I was then Chief Clerk, I could get away from my office two or three hours at any time, so I went on down and handled the case for them. I think there were at least a dozen lawyers craning their necks in through the door and listening to me handling the case. That really was the starting point of my getting the job of interpreter for all the courts of Emporia. After I lost my job with the Santa Fe, Lon McCarty, who had succeeded Owen Samuel as County Attorney, had Sheriff Walt Davis[4] appoint me a special deputy Sheriff and turned all Mexican trouble over to me. I remember one day while district court was in session (I had been appointed court bailiff for the session) I was called up on the phone before I had hardly eaten my breakfast. The caller said he was a lawyer from Topeka, defending a Mexican case that came up in court that day. He asked me to meet him downtown about an hour before court would open and do some interpreting for him. When I got downtown to meet him, I found he was a Negro lawyer, and that he was having trouble with his Mexican prisoner's friends about his fee. He was to turn the prisoner loose a free man for $150. When we had talked it over for a few minutes, as neither the lawyer nor the Mexican's friends would trust one another, it was arranged for the Mexican to deposit the money with a groceryman, to be paid over to the lawyer if and when he had fulfilled his part of the agreement. This was done, and I went up and opened court, but before the middle of the forenoon, I was called to the Justice of the Peace's office to interpret a case there.

The sheriff took my place as bailiff while I did this, and on my return to the court the Mexican's case came up and I interpreted that, in the district court, of course, getting my usual fee for that, in addition to that of bailiff.

When the Mexican's case came up, he pleaded guilty as he had been induced to do, and was at once sentenced to a year in the penitentiary, but was immediately paroled to his lawyer. Then the lawyer had me take him down and turn him loose on the street and collected his $150 fee. The lawyer gave me $10 for my services as interpreter, regretting that he could not make it more, as his expenses on the case, he said, had been quite high. He didn't come right out and say what they were, but from the way he stammered and hedged he might as well have.

It was during this time that I established a little grocery store in part of my house, and many of the Mexicans bought all their groceries from me. The store itself, though very small, more than made my living and with the extra money I took in, in connection with my job as deputy Sheriff, I was able to pay off the mortgage on my house, a thing I had not been able to do while I worked at a regular salary.

Another way that I picked up some cash was this: there were several Mexicans who would save their money until they had accumulated a hundred dollars "American money," and then bring it to me and ask me to get it changed into Mexican bills of a certain year and denomination. I would take the money to the bank, instruct the cashier what to do with it, and when the Mexican money arrived he would turn it over to me and divide the bank fee for handling it with me. I never charged the Mexicans themselves anything for doing this.

For another thing, I picked up quite a lot of money working with the Mexicans' favorite doctor. He was afraid of them for some reason, which only showed that he was ignorant of them. But he would not go into their "houses" (which were usually box-cars which had been discarded and then fixed up by the Mexicans for domiciles) without me. He could not understand their language, either, and had to have an interpreter. Then he would generally split his fee with me. I have assisted him in all sorts of cases, including childbirth.

One afternoon I was loafing at home, and my youngest son phoned me from downtown. "Dad," he said, "there's a couple of young fellers down here who rode in together from western Kansas on a Harley-Davidson motorcycle, and they're tryin' to sell it for fifty dollars. It's easy worth from a hundred to a hundred and a quarter. Maybe you ought to come down and investigate them and see if they've stolen it."

It was then about five o'clock, so I phoned Lon McCarty (then County Attorney) at his house, and arranged a meeting place with him. I told my boy to keep the fellows interested, advising him to say that he had a buyer on the string who would be down after a while, and told him where to have them waiting for us. So we all met on a certain corner.

Lon questioned them pretty thoroughly, and they told him where they had bought the wheels, and from whom. They said that the only reason they were offering it so cheaply was that they were stony broke and couldn't buy any more gasoline or even their suppers. Lon told them that he would furnish them a night's lodging's free if they cared to take it and that they would have to be under surveillance anyway. So why not let the Sheriff keep them overnight, not in the jail, but in his own apartments? They appeared to be grateful for the offer and Sheriff Walt Davis took care of them.

Lon at once went to his office and talked with the man who had sold the motorcycle to the boys, using the long-distance telephone. He found out that the boys' story was true, and that they had a perfect right to sell it. The next morning I proposed to Lon that we buy the motorcycle from them in partnership as an investment, which we did, and I put it in the Fire Department building, aiming to ride it home at noon. I had ridden a bicycle a couple of miles once, and that's all I knew about that kind of transportation, the Fire Department boys, knowing what I was aiming to do, were all standing around watching when I got ready to start home.

Well, I got the engine to running and climbed on and started out on Fifth Avenue, but I guess I was wobbling around even more than I realized I was. There was an old Welsh lady going east on Fifth Avenue on the sidewalk, and my steed must have been headed for her, for she let out a little yip and broke into a run. Of course, I had my eyes on her all the time, and I guess that's all I did see, for I kept closing in on her till I hit the curbing, and she was really running then. The fire boys were killing themselves laughing, so I quietly dismounted and pushed the thing back to the fire house and gave a colored boy a half-a-dollar to take it out to my house.

I had it there about ten days, letting a neighbor boy ride it for advertising purposes. I furnished the gasoline, of course, and our advertising soon paid off. A young farmer boy came in and paid me $75.00 cash for it. Both Lon and I were well pleased with our investment, as neither of us wanted to keep the wheels.

I had a number of experiences while I was deputy Sheriff which were really interesting, but which would take too long to describe. However, one was rather exciting above the average. I was walking one day with my wife down to the street-car line, intending to go downtown, and I saw a crowd gathered around a house between us and a Santa Fe roundhouse. So I told my wife to go on and do her shopping alone, I'd better go over to see what was going on. I thought they might need me, as I knew a Mexican family lived in the house. It was not the usual box-car type that the Mexicans used so much, but a little frame house. When I got there I was told by deputy Sheriff

Gibson that Eli Raymond, the Santa Fe [Railroad] Police special agent, had run a Mexican in there trying to arrest him, and the Mexican had shot Eli in the hip and then had broke and run down towards the Cottonwood River. Gibson told me to "go get him." I had no gun on me at the time, so Gibson tossed one to me over the heads of the crowd and said, "Here's Eli's. Take it!"

I started off for the river, and was joined by Roy Harlan, one of my former clerks at the roundhouse, and we followed his tracks to the bank of the river. Seeing that the Mexican had turned up the river from there I told Harlan and Chandler (another Santa Fe Police agent who had joined us by that time) to follow the river timber up around the bend and I would cut across the cornfield and get to the bridge at the upper end of it and head him off there. When I got to the bridge I "cut sign" on the embankment on the bridge approach, and saw that no one had climbed up it. Then I knew we had him between us. By that time two or three cars had come from town and they drove up onto the bridge approach. I told them the situation. One of them was the City Marshal's son. While we were talking the City Marshal himself reached there and he and I started down through the edge of the timber which skirted the river.

Before we had gone more than a hundred yards we heard shouting, and knew that the Mex had been sprung. There was a faint wagon trail between the edge of the timber and the cornfield, and we soon saw the Mexican running up this road towards us with his six-shooter in his hand. When he got close enough so he could hear me, I said, "Halt!" but he replied, "Get out of my way, I'm comin' on through!"

Of course, I still didn't know what damage had been done by the shooting we had heard, so I stepped out of the road and leaned against a tree and waited for him. The Marshal started back towards the bridge. He said afterwards that his gun had tangled in his clothes and he thought he'd better get back to where the other boys were. When the Mex got fairly close I opened fire on him and missed him all five shots. For the sixth one I ran out in the road behind him but was in line with the Marshal who was ahead and so I was afraid to shoot. However the Marshal's son gave him a load of birdshot when he got close to the embankment, and I guess that Mexican thought he was shot all to pieces as he dropped his gun and surrendered. While we were talking there, Chandler came limping up, shot through the calf of his leg, so we put him in one car and the Mexican in another at Chandler's request, and took them back to town. Eli had to spend two or three months in the Santa Fe hospital before he was able to be around again.

No book concerning Emporia would be complete without mention of the town's two renowned characters, Walt Mason[5] and [William Allen] "Old Bill" White.[6] I knew very little about either of them personally, although I came into little contact with them. I remember when Walt Mason first came to Emporia [in 1907]. I didn't see him come in, but they told me that he and his wife came there in a horse and buggy, and he went to White's office to find work. He was just a tramp printer then, and wouldn't stay any place. He drank up all he got, and was considered worthless, I guess.

When he asked White for a job, White asked, "Can you make copy?" Mason answered, "Yep," and stepped over to the typewriter and typed off a prose verse. White took him on and when he found out what Walt could do, White copyrighted Walt's prose poems and featured them. I understand Walt was making around a thousand dollars a week at one time.

White also broke him of the drinking habit and made a real man

of him. Walt Mason was very deaf and had a little old-fashioned pho-
nograph with ear-phones that he'd sit out on his front porch and listen
to. I've seen him do that many a time when I was driving by. I never
was really acquainted with William Allen White but I was driving a
draw for Holloway when he bought the *Emporia News* [*sic*, *Gazette*]
from Colonel Heskridge [in 1895], and I helped move his stuff into his
office. I heard that he began by firing all the old office force and hiring
men of his own. I heard at the time several old "cits" laughing about
this and saying that Bill White wouldn't last six months, but he fooled
'em all. I lived in the Third Ward, which polled about 1200 votes at
that time if the people were really interested, and the Third Ward
invariably voted against anything which "Old Bill" White strongly
advocated. The railroad ward was "south of the tracks," and there was
considerable friction between "south of the tracks" and "north of the
tracks." Naturally, the publisher, living "north of the tracks," pulled
for things which the Third Ward did not consider to be particularly
to their advantage, but rather for the "north" side. But when the City
Commissioner form of government went into effect in Emporia, the
people "north of the tracks" had very little trouble in gaining their
ends politically, for the Third Ward was no longer represented.

White gave my wife a nice write-up in his paper when she cured a
Mexican baby that the doctors had given up for dead. I kept the clip-
ping for a long time, together with my "obituary," but in some manner
they were lost.

Emporia was a beautiful little city, and I greatly enjoyed my life
there. When I arrived, it was much less extensive than it grew to be
even while I was there, and no doubt it has expanded a great deal
more now. I haven't been back there for many years.

I have mentioned a good many names in this book, but my best friends, and most of my family, I have left out, because I considered that my companionship with them, although highly interesting and satisfactory to me, would not be of interest to the general public. There were three couples who were, I consider, the best of all my friends in Emporia. We had many good times together, and helped each other out many a time. I could tell a great deal about our experiences together, but will only say this, that of all the people I ever knew, Dory (T. D.) and Effie Little were the only people I ever knew who professed religion and really lived up to it every minute. I am not a religious man myself, but I respect such a belief as that.

All of those people, however, were sinners and true to what they did believe, and loyal friends wherever their friendship was bestowed. In fact, I had many friends in Emporia, and it seems to me that wherever my path might lead, some friendly hand was sure to be held out to me.

CHAPTER EIGHTEEN

Mexican Experiences at Emporia

🌿 *"People in Emporia," said Mr. Wallace, "did not understand the Mexicans, and consequently did not like them. It was apparently the attitude that most people outside of the Southwest had toward our dark-skinned neighbors. Their language and manners and habits, even their food, was so different from all that the settled and respectable whites were used to, that the latter both feared and disliked the Mexicans.*

"I did not share this attitude. I had lived among them for so long in my youth, I understood and liked them well. Because I understood them and their language, I was put in charge of their affairs when I was deputy Sheriff there, and because I liked them they trusted me implicitly, and were my friends in return. Many interesting things happened during my work among them, some of which were really outstanding."

In the early 1900's the Santa Fe was using Mexican labor on section work in large numbers, and as many of these men had brought their families with them, there was a large Mexican population in Emporia. They lived for the most part in box cars and small houses constructed of railroad ties, on railroad land surrounded by a high board fence.

Very few could speak any English, and I was the only white man there at that time that could talk their language, which explains my activity as an interpreter. Many of them came to me for assistance in their problems, and many came to my wife for advice as to how to keep well and doctor themselves for minor ailments, for she was a natural nurse and just loved to help out in cases of sickness. "Old Bill" White even gave her a write-up about it when she cured the baby who was believed past saving. This helped me out, too, as I was given charge of the Mexican end of law enforcement in Lyon County when I was appointed deputy Sheriff.

I seldom arrested one of them, though. I preferred to talk things over and get them to settle everything they could out of court. One time in an elopement case, the father of the girl swore he was going to kill the Romeo on sight, but as the pair had married and had broken no law so far as I knew, I saw no reason to disturb them. Although I knew where they were all the time, I kept it to myself until the old man got over his mad, and was ready to be friends again. It took a lot of talking to him first though. I even wrote love letters for one Mexican whose girl lived in another place.

Their homes were occasionally raided by Railroad Special Agents for firearms, and the Sheriff's office also raided them, but I always managed so the "good" Mexicans never lost a gun, although I knew their hideout places. But the unruly ones' knives and guns were taken. One Mexican had a German Luger automatic he liked to play with, shooting it off repeatedly at night. It took me a month to locate it, and as he would not listen to me, I confiscated it one Sunday morning. I kept that gun for my own use, and had it yet when I went to Arkansas. I even talked his lawyer out of it when he threatened to replevin it.

I would eat occasionally at their houses, especially if they were going to have an old-time Mexican dish served. Mostly the women kept their houses clean as a pin, and were good at cooking their old-time foods. Chicken *tamales, chile con carne, tortillas*, I really enjoyed these meals with them but never could get my wife to go along. The women though, would frequently bring her a dish of some particular kind to try out, and if she liked it she would find out how it was made and make it herself. She was an excellent cook.

She didn't understand the Mexicans at all and had the usual attitude of that place and day towards them. She resented my friendliness toward them, as they were so looked down on in those days by white citizens. One day I was walking downtown with her, when we met a Mexican who was a stranger to me. It was in Rumboldt [sic, Humboldt] Park, and I stopped for a few words with him. We chatted for several minutes, my wife insisting that we go on. As we parted he said he wanted to ask me a question, and I said, "Go ahead."

"Señor," said he earnestly, "did you learn to talk American after you came to the United States, or before?" He would hardly believe that I was not a Mexican, or at least of Spanish descent. I went on laughing about this as it amused me highly, but my wife was very indignant at him for mistaking me for a Mexican, and at me for taking it so lightly, she "combed my hair" all the rest of the way.

In spite of the fact that she distrusted the Mexicans and didn't approve of my intimacy with them, my wife always helped them out when they came to her for advice or "doctoring." She was a very capable nurse, and as we lived near the Mexican settlement, it was a common thing for a Mexican woman to bring her ailing child over after I was home in the evening and get her to "doctor" it up.

One day I came home to dinner at noon, and found a young Mexican woman there waiting, holding a baby girl in her lap. The child, six or seven months old, was little more than skin and bones, and seemed to be at the point of death. My wife could not speak any Spanish at all, and had to wait for me to interpret to find out what Juanita wanted. When I got around to interpreting, the mother said she wanted my wife to try and save the child's life, as she had done all she could and failed. My wife said she would have to take the child to a doctor first, and it was agreed that she should do it, and the mother should stay at our house until my wife got back.

The doctor told my wife, after looking the baby over, that she would be lucky if she got the child back to the mother alive, that it was dying right then. But my wife insisted the doctor do what he could for it, so they gave it a tonic of some sort, and she made it back home with the baby still breathing. The mother was on her knees praying all this time, I was told.

My wife on arriving home put the child in warm water at once, and used some of her "old granny" restoratives, and to the astonishment of all the child revived, and the next morning seemed to be stronger. It was kept at our house for a week, my wife and oldest daughter, Mary, doing for it. At the end of that time the baby was improved enough so its mother took it back home, and only came in with it every day or so for my wife to look it over. The child improved fast, and got fat and sassy, and Juanita's gratitude knew no bounds.

Her name was Juanita Villaflores [Valleflores?] which means ("valley of flowers") and one day she and one of her Mexican friends had their pictures taken and Juanita brought one over and showed it to me. Both the women in the picture were standing up, over-dressed, and as rigid as statues. They even had cotton gloves on. I "hoorawed" Juanita about its not looking the least bit like her, and she then asked me if I wouldn't take her down and have a good picture taken of her and the baby. I managed to side-track the "take her down," but told her if she would be at Stevenson's shop at ten o'clock the next morning, I would meet her there and get the picture taken for her.

I made it a point to get down to Stevenson's ahead of her, and told him exactly what I wanted him to do. He was well-pleased that I was there, as he couldn't talk Mexican and she couldn't talk English, so he agreed to do as I said.

When she came in, he set her in a chair, cattie-cornered across the room from where I was sitting. He rigged up his camera and got all ready to take her picture, then went to fussing around at this and that, waiting for the right moment, as Juanita and I chatted with one another, then, when he caught her off guard, he snapped her picture.

Both Juanita and her husband were very much elated over this picture as the baby's was also very good. Several other Mexican women, after seeing this picture, wanted me to take them down and have their pictures taken, too, and I had to use considerable diplomacy with them to get out of it, as I didn't want to be "ragged" to death by my white acquaintances for walking down the street with Mexican women.

One evening as I was finishing supper at home a Mexican came running in and told me that Cuco, a young Mexican boy of about nineteen, had been stabbed and was bleeding to death. Of course, I went right over and found Cuco lying beside his car with his cheek slashed to the bone, but it was not bleeding profusely enough to prevent their getting him to the hospital before he bled to death. But he looked white and weak, and I told them to give him a drink of whiskey, if they had any, to tone him up. While they were getting it, I opened his shirt and examined him more closely, and found another knife wound, a hole near his heart. That meant he really was dying right then. He was unconscious, and when they brought the whiskey he was almost gone. So I said, "He won't need that now. Gimme a draw at it. I do!"

We could never find out who did it. They declared they didn't see anyone. They said they had just heard Cuco and some one else quarreling beside the car, but that it was too dusky for them to see. Even I couldn't find out any more than that, not even from Juanita. She sometimes told me things that the others wouldn't tell, which helped me out often, but she was always scared to death when she did, and in the case of Cuco she absolutely refused to say a word.

The old Mexican *peons* had a queer custom. They would marry a woman and if they got dissatisfied with her for any reason after a few months, or even a year or two, they would simply take her home and turn her over to her parents again. They considered this a divorce, and that each was free. They couldn't see the necessity for going through a long process of court when the other was so simple. This also complicated matters among the Mexicans when they came to the United States. They didn't understand so many things. I remember one time when Juanita Villaflores had appendicitis.

Doctor Annie Ellsworth[1] and Frank Ecdall [*sic*, Eckdall][2] told her she would have to have an operation, and that nearly scared her to death. She hid out, and Dr. Ellsworth called me up and said that the woman would die without an operation, and it was free, so wouldn't I see if I couldn't find her and persuade her to come.

I had a hard time locating her, and a harder time talking her into it, and in the end only gained her consent by promising her that I would be present at the operation. Of course, I knew I couldn't be, but I had to get her to consent someway, so I said I would. I told Annie Ellsworth that when Juanita woke up from the ether to tell her I'd been there and I knew that would be all right with her. She lived, and the last I heard of her she'd gone to live at Kansas City. She had implicit faith in my wife and me. She believed we could do *anything*.

My wife knew and used certain old "charms" in her doctoring. One of these was the old "blood-charm," which is an old charm for stopping blood. One day I was over at my son-in-law's house, helping to clean out his well, and as my wife couldn't talk Mexican and had to have correct answers to certain questions before she could use the charm, she brought some Mexicans over to where we were working. Joe Elliot and Tom Francis, both close friends of ours and fellow-lodge-members of mine, were there helping also. Tom and Joe and I had always ragged her plentifully about such foolishness, so of course, we were much interested in watching her work her charm on the Mexican patient. The boy had been splitting kindling, and had struck himself on the base of the thumb, and severed an artery, and the blood was spurting out. I got the information from him that my wife needed, and repeated it to her, and we saw the pulsations getting weaker and weaker until it had entirely stopped. Then my wife took the boy back to our house and treated him in the usual way. She never charged anyone for her services of course, and the boy didn't even go to a doctor. We never ragged her about her blood charm any more, as we had seen it work and were convinced.

She also learned the fire charm successfully. I learned this one, and while I always thought it was silly even while I was using it, it never has failed to work yet.

An old remedy that I use for burns was dry calomel. I used it because when I was on the plains, it was the only thing that you could use to cure a sore on a horse's back and ride him at the same time. It always worked, and it works for burns.

The same Mexican woman who brought the boy to my wife,

brought over her three-year-old girl one Sunday. The little girl had been playing in the wood-pile and she fell and ran a sliver as big as a woman's little finger into her leg. It had broken off, leaving the sliver embedded in. The mother (aunt to the boy) said she wanted me to take it out. I told her to go to a doctor and have him do it. No, sir, I had to do it. So I took my pocket-knife and sharpened the little blade some more, cut in till I could grip the sliver with a pair of pliers and yanked it out of there. Then my wife doctored the sore, and it got well without any further treatment. If some of the doctors at Emporia had known this, I expect they'd have made me sweat for it, but I was not afraid of the Mexicans giving me away. And they would often neglect something rather than go to a doctor, if I wouldn't do it, so I always tried to accommodate them and so did my wife. And we found that they always appreciated it, as it saved them money and trouble, and they had such absolute faith in us.

Taking it all in all, I think I have enjoyed my experience with the Mexicans as much as anything I have ever done. And those at Emporia did not form the least of it.

CHAPTER NINETEEN

Arkansas

"When my wife's failing health caused me to leave Emporia," said Mr. Wallace, "I again entered a new world. My life has been both varied and interesting—interesting, that is, to me—and this phase of it intrigued me as much as any. Especially the trip we made from Emporia to our destination, Little Rock, Arkansas. We made a wonderful and fearful procession, I am sure, on that memorable trip!"

In the summer of 1916 I bought a team and a lumber-wagon with bows and sheet, and decided to drive through and see the country as I went. My oldest daughter's husband [Frank Morris] and my second daughter (Kate) and her husband [Otto Janzen] had already gone to Arkansas and were living in Little Rock, so that's where I headed for. My oldest daughter, Mary, and her children were with her mother and me; our youngest daughter, Shirley [Dorothy], was with her family in Kansas; and my oldest son [John Roy Wallace] lived in Oklahoma City. We were to be rather scattered apart, but that is to be expected when a family grows up and starts building worlds of their own.

One of my horses, a large black, was full of life, and for the first week or two of the trip, tried to pull his share of the load with his mouth. My oldest daughter drove a single wagon behind me, pulling a little roan Indian pony. I bought the outfit she handled, from a Mexican in Emporia for $55.00. That sure was one fancy little mare! Quick as a cat and pretty and trim. My wife sold the mare alone for $55.00 afterwards, when I was working in Camp Pike.*

The wagon Mary drove was loaded with chickens and a few ducks. My wife even took her canary bird along, but we soon found out that we could not properly take care of these on a camping trip, and we expressed the canaries on ahead from a little town close to Fort Scott, Kansas. It had been a *very* dry season. I remember I was driving along beside a field of corn of above fifty acres not far from Fort Scott, and I observed that this was all burnt up and they told me at a farmhouse where I went for water that that particular field had just been sold to a cattle man for fifty cents an acre. And it looked to me like that was all it was worth.

Down by Joplin [Missouri] and along to Siloam Springs [Arkansas], the country was not so badly burnt up. I could graze my horses there, but all the rest of the trip I had to buy hay and corn.

I routed myself through Waldron, Arkansas, as I had corresponded with a man there about trading my Emporia property for a farm and I wanted to see what he had to offer. To reach Waldron I had to go through Rogers and Fayetteville. When I saw what the Waldron man had to offer I wanted none of it, and drove on. After going through Fayetteville, we followed the White River down for a few miles, then had to cross the Boston mountains.

There was no paved highway then. An old hillbilly that I asked for directions kinda grinned and said, "When you get to the Boston Mountains, well, you just got to go ovah them!" I figured it would

*Camp Pike was a World War I training camp for the 87th Division (National Army), which occupied the cantonment from August 1917 to June 1918.

be pretty bad driving crossing those mountains, and I was absolutely correct in that, as it was the roughest riding I ever saw.

When we got across and down to the first little town, I was glad to see a blacksmith shop, as I'd had to lock my hind wheels on the light spring wagon coming down the mountain in order to get down. The spokes were broken and turning the wheel over would have ruined them.

The blacksmith refused to work on my light spring wagon and told me that he wouldn't know how to go about it, but I was at liberty to use his tools and fix it myself. So I did just that, paying him for the use of his tools and fuel (coal, as wood did not make a hot enough fire for welding). I had to shrink the tire and weld it, put it back on, drive in three or four spokes, and otherwise make it good enough to go on. It might not have been a very good-looking job, but it lasted me to Little Rock. Coming through the Boston Mountains I saw my first muscadine grapes, and we didn't know if they were fit to eat or not. My wife thought they might be poison, so I fed them to the chickens. As it didn't hurt them I ate one myself. As it didn't hurt me, we all turned loose on 'em. This was Fall, and there were many hazelnuts in the mountains, and we gathered them as we went along.

When we got to Ozark, a little town still in the mountains but on the banks of the Arkansas River, I found a ferry there which deposited my outfit on the south bank of the river for $2.50. I headed on down, and struck Dardanelle, where they charged me three dollars for taking us across to the eastern bank (the river having changed its course toward a southerly direction). The land in Arkansas had looked good to me up to this time, but after I crossed to the eastern bank of the Arkansas, and headed down through Russelville [sic, Russellville], it didn't look so good, and when I had passed through

Atkins and struck an old white dusty road I didn't like it at all. It was very dry that Fall, and the drouth had extended there also, so that white dust all but choked us. However, I was headed for Little Rock, and kept on going until I reached there.

We must have been an interesting sight, driving down Main Street in Little Rock. My outfit looked pretty well, for it was fairly new; although the black horse was so played out that I had been only able to drive a few miles a day. But Mary's [wagon] was a sorry-looking sight, with the wheels patched up and the chickens and ducks squawking constantly, and the old Dominecker rooster crowing lustily, as he did at every opportunity (and he usually made his own opportunities). In fact, what with being travel-worn and covered with that white dust, with all the rest, we looked in such a state that at Conway, where we had camped overnight, some folks came up to us and asked us to tell their fortunes! They thought we were a gypsy gang.

Poor Mary was so ashamed she could hardly stand it to drive down Main Street like that, but we managed to make it, and finally came to where the boys were, over by Bruce's Mill, at what was then called the "Red Row." This was a string of half-a-dozen houses all on one street, and all painted red. Bruce's Mill had burned shortly before this, and the contractor for the new building had just started work, and as both the boys were working for the contractor I went over the next morning and "struck 'em" for a job for myself.

They put me on at once in the labor gang, which was a mixture of whites and Negroes. I worked at that my first day. In the late afternoon the contractor asked me if I knew how to file a saw. I had never filed a saw for anyone else, but I had always filed my own, so I said, "Sure! Been filin' saws for twenty-five years!" He told me to take charge of the tool-room the next day. He said he had a lot of saws on hand which were in pretty bad condition from use on the last job, so next day I took the tool-room and found out to my astonishment that the saws, of which he had fourteen, were all cross-cut saws! And I had never put a file on one in my life. However, I wouldn't back out, as I was making more than I would in the laboring gang, and it would be easier work, so I went to work on them. It took some figuring, but I managed to discover how to file the cross-cut saw, and kept them in workable order, but before I got them absolutely correct, I had an interesting experience concerning them.

To people who know nothing of tools, filing a saw must seem perfectly simple—if they have ever thought of it at all. The little hand saw is comparatively simple. In this the teeth are all the same depth, and are filed so that the beveled edge is on opposite sides on each alternate tooth.

When the teeth are filed, an automatic set is used to set the teeth. It sets each tooth a hair's breadth and no more. But the cross-cut saw is a different proposition. Its teeth are so arranged that there are four teeth the same height and then a "drag tooth." Of the four single teeth, each alternate one is filed on opposite sides as in the hand saw, then the drag-tooth is filed flat, and its points tapped with a hammer *very lightly* to set them.

Now I thought I had figured this all out pretty well, but there were two carpenters who worked together sawing big timbers and they kept complaining to me about the conditions of their saws. Something was always wrong, and they'd say they couldn't cut with their saws. When they'd bring the saws back for retouching I'd give them another saw, as I tried to have four or five saws on hand all the time.

The contractor noticed what was going on, and one morning he made it a point to come in as they were bringing a saw back to me. He asked them what was wrong with the saw and they commenced to tell him this and that, so he said, "Come on back out here, I want to try that saw myself." He took one end of it and one of them the other end, and they sawed a timber in two, then he told them the saw was all right, for them to go ahead, or if they couldn't use it he could find plenty of men that could. They didn't send any more saws back to me for re-touching as long as I worked on that job.

When the superintendent came back to the tool-room he said to me, "Dad, the drag-tooth was je-est a trifle too long on them fellers' saw, but I wouldn't tell them that. All you got to do is use your gauge a leetle closer."

I was not expected to file handsaws used by the carpenters, and was not furnished files to do it with, but I always managed to have spare time enough to file a saw for any of them, and would do so providing they brought me a new file to file it with. I could really do a good job of filing a handsaw in those days, as my eyes were then good, and it takes good eyes. I never charged the carpenters anything for sharpening their sharpening their handsaws.

I worked at this job from the time I landed in Little Rock until the forepart of January. And believe it or not, that contractor even begged me to stay on the job and not quit when I did. But I had closed a deal to rent a farm for the coming season, and I wanted to move onto it. I don't know why it is, but every railroad man yearns to try farming at some time in his life. He thinks if he can get "a little piece of land," and move on to it, he will have an easy life, and a lot of fun. So I had my yearning for a farm, and thought that here was a chance to fulfill it, despite the fact that I knew almost nothing about farming in Arkansas. Perhaps I should say because of that fact.

This venture was a dismal failure, as I found that the railroad man's conception of farming was distinctly short of the actual facts, and it was really impossible to raise anything on a hill farm in Arkansas.

Now the advent of our entering the World War in 1917 brought another change in my mode of livelihood. Camp Pike (Camp Robinson [as] it is now) was only about five miles from where my farm was located, and when they advertised for time-keepers I drove over to apply, but I didn't even find the chief time-keeper's office. Everybody was flapping around like chickens with their heads off, and didn't have any time to talk with an old "rough neck" like me, and I got disgusted and went home. However, I knew that was where I belonged. So next day I went back and persisted till I found the building I was looking for. There was a slide window on one side of the little shack, and I hammered on it till I got it opened. It was opened by a man on the inside. He was a Jew and had a thick accent. He looked at me as though I was something the cat had drug up, and said, "Vell, vot de hell do you vant?"

I replied, "You advertised for time-keepers, didn't you?"

"Vot de hell do you know about time-keeping?" he snapped.

I was getting a little warm under the collar myself by then, so I looked him straight in the eye and said, "Fella, I guess I know as much about it as you do and maybe more!"

He said, "The hell you do! Come around to the door and I'll let you in. We'll find out!" When I got in, he pointed to a little rough board home-made table, and said, "Sit down there! Let me see your hand-writin'!"

That was right up my alley, as one of the things I had always persisted in doing was improving my hand-writing, so I started in:

"Now is the time for all good men—" I got that far when he stopped me and said, "That's enough. That's your desk over there. I'll bring you some stuff to work on."

There was a clerk sitting across the table which he indicated, and while the Jew was getting me my stuff I passed a few words with the clerk. I found they had over eighteen thousand men working there and were way behind on their pay roll. They kept me in this main office for four or five days. By that time they had hired several other time-keepers and they moved me out into a little booth and gave me a regular bunch of men to keep time for.

There was three of us company time-keepers in that little booth besides the Government time-keepers who attended to the issuing of the brass number checks—"work checks," we called them.

One of the company time-keepers was a young doctor. The other was an ex-bank cashier. They both seemed to feel that they were socially superior to me. The doctor especially disliked me and was always trying to belittle me, but after about two weeks I concluded I'd taken about enough of him, and one day he sprung something really insulting and I saw a good opening to turn it back onto him. Which I did, expecting to have to fight him for what I said, but he didn't seem to want any fighting, so he dried up.

However I was pretty well disgusted and concluded I had had enough, so I went over to the main time office and asked for a discharge check. Mr. Peck, the chief time-keeper was surprised and asked me why I wanted to quit. I told him we were too crowded up in that little booth, and anyhow two men could do the work as well as three, and I thought I'd get out and get a little fresh air.

"Well," he said, "who can you spare the easiest? You know you are in charge of that booth!" Which was a complete surprise to me. Of course, I told him that I could get along nicely without "Doc," so he told me to tell Doc to come over when I went back to the booth. So I did, and that was the end of Doc on that job. If I remember rightly, they put Doc on the carpenter's list, then a few days later they gave the ex-bank cashier a booth of his own, which left only the Government time-keeper and me in that booth. Rogers was a fine man, and we got along well together from then on until the completion of the original quarter of a million dollar contract.

At the wind-up Mr. Peck gave me a very nice letter of recommendation, which got me a job at Lonoke aviation field, which they were just starting up, and I worked until that job was finished.

Then I went to Tulsa to visit with my daughter Shirley for a while. Not wanting to be idle, skirmishing around one day and looking for something, I got over to the Frisco shops and found out there that they wanted a store-keeper. So I went over to the store-house and convinced Mr. Reed (who was holding the job down till they found a man) that I was the man they were waiting for. In fact, in fifteen minutes after I went into his office he was getting ready to take the next train out. I had a good crew there and there was very little to do. It was about the easiest job I ever had in my life.

However, one day I was pretty nearly struck. They had routed a gasoline car to the different store-houses allotting a certain amount to each one. They told me to take out down to eight hundred gallons and ship the car on to Enid [Oklahoma]. Now to find out when the gasoline was down to eight hundred gallons was a problem, as we had no chart to go by. My stenographer-clerk, a fine young lady, and very smart, and I "rastled" around with it for over an hour. Then she looked up and asked me what company car it was. I looked at the bill and told her and she commenced to laugh. I asked her what tickled her. She said, "Why, that company is right over here at Sand Springs!"

Sand Springs was about four miles from Tulsa. I said, "Push that telephone over to me!" and I called up the oil company and asked for the Chief Clerk, and told him my problem. He asked for the number of the car, and told me to hold the line, and in a few minutes told me exactly how many inches of gasoline to leave in the car. So I did just that and shipped the car on to Enid. Now West Tulsa was not at that time the main division point, and the Frisco at Sapulpa had the railroad company tied up so they had to keep at least nominally the division point, and maintain a storehouse there. The store-keeper at Sapulpa who was of course directly over me afterwards tried to get me to explain to him how I figured that out, as he said Enid got exactly the eight hundred gallons they asked for. But I just let him think I'd figured it and never did give him the truth of it. It was just like finding a piece of money in the street.

I worked there for something over three months, then got a wire from my old chief time-keeper at Lonoke that the same company had the contract to double the capacity of Camp Pike, and offering me sixty dollars a month more than I was getting in the store house, if I would come back to him. So I quit the Frisco as it was about time to get my wife back to the southern climate again anyway, and I was at Camp Pike when the Armistice was signed.

After that, as my wife's health was very much improved, we decided to go back to Emporia and try the Kansas climate again. The next Spring I was appointed assessor for the Third Ward, and that in itself would fill a chapter, but I'll just say that the next year I was written to from Little Rock, and urged to return and take the job again, for my wife did not thrive in Kansas, and I had to return.

So I went back down to Little Rock and bought a hundred and

sixty acres for myself which proved a bad investment, as I knew little about farming and had not much to farm on in that place.

In the meantime, my daughter Kate's husband, Otto Janzen, had been bitten by the farming bug and had bought himself a farm which he later traded off for a hill farm. So I let my place go back to the former owner and started to clear up his farm for him. He took a railroad job to keep up the expenses meanwhile. I had mules, teams, and farming implements, and I stayed and made a pretty nice place for him, even if it was in the hills, for a part of the land lay quite level. One forty is as level as the floor and not a rock on it. The rest is full of rocks. One forty has on it an old soap-stone hill. Even this farm was not good enough to have made a family a good living by farming alone, so Otto kept his railroad job and bought a home [at 220 East 119th Street] in North Little Rock.

When I came to Emporia, I started in to obey the Biblical injunction to multiply and replenish the earth. Today I have twenty-eight direct descendants living, and more in prospect, and I wish there were enough to make it thirty. I guess I wouldn't be satisfied then, for children are like dollars—the more you get, the more you want.

In the spring of '33 my wife came down with her last sickness [and died on May 21 of that year]. Since then I've made my home with Otto and Kate in North Little Rock, only waiting for the shadows.

NOTES

CHAPTER 1

1. When the Wightmans came to Cimarron in 1871, the Maxwell mansion was being leased to Henry Lambert as a hotel while he was building his St. James Hotel across the street. "Two-storied, wide-veranda'ed, with adobe walls nearly four feet thick," the house—or more accurately, the complex, for it was as large as a city block—was not only Maxwell's home, but also a place of business that included gambling rooms, a saloon, a dance hall, a billiard parlor, and a designated area for women of "special virtue."

The residential rooms were said to have had high, molded ceilings, deeply piled carpets, velvet drapes, paintings in gold frames, and four pianos—two for each floor. "There was silver, and crystal, and fine china. One room was set aside as a museum . . . There were hundreds of stuffed birds—rare species from remote corners of the world [and] two royal Indian tigers that guarded the foot of the grand staircase which led from the entrance hall."

The mansion burned down in 1922, and nothing remains of it today.

Sources: Chuck Hornung, personal correspondence with author, April–May 2009; Agnes Morley Cleaveland, *No Life for a Lady* (Boston: Houghton Mifflin, 1941).

2. Pennsylvania-born Joseph Holbrook (listed in the 1870 census for Colfax County as Joseph *Holbroke*, age thirty-five) was never sheriff of Colfax County. A former sergeant in the 1st Regular Colorado Cavalry, he was a carpenter by trade who served for a time as Cimarron's postmaster, justice of the peace, probate judge, and, briefly in 1876, special deputy sheriff. His ranch east of Cimarron with its bridge across the river was a popular overnight stopping place for travelers between Fort Union and Trinidad. He was later a leader in local politics. See also chapter 2, note 1.

3. Lucien Bonaparte Maxwell was born on September 14, 1818, in Kaskaskia, Illinois. On June 2, 1844, he married Ana Maria de la Luz Beaubien. Clifford mistakenly calls her family Beaubien y Quintana; correctly it would

be Beaubien y Lovato, but there seem to be very few references to the family in that style. Among the Maxwell children were Pierre (Peter) Menard Maxwell, in whose bedroom Pat Garrett killed Billy the Kid, and Paula Maxwell, whom both history and legend have conspired to label the Kid's sweetheart. Their ancestry was a mixture of Irish, French, and Spanish.

In 1872 Maxwell bought the buildings and fixtures (but not the land) of the abandoned Fort Sumner, where he converted the old officers' quarters building into a home and began running cattle and sheep. He died on July 25, 1875.

SOURCES: Lawrence R. Murphy, *Lucien Bonaparte Maxwell: Napoleon of the Southwest* (Norman: University of Oklahoma Press, 1983); Jim Berry Pearson, *The Maxwell Land Grant* (Norman: University of Oklahoma Press, 1961).

4. English-born Henry Pascoe and his Kentuckian wife, Elizabeth, who lived a few miles east of Elizabethtown, indeed had a lot of daughters, although not ten; they were Alice (b. 1844), Louisa (b. 1854), Ellen (b. 1858), Hepzibah (b. 1861), and Jennie (b. 1864)—all born in Missouri—and the twins Celina and Elizabeth (Libbie)—born in 1866 in Colorado.

SOURCE: U.S. Bureau of the Census, Colfax County, New Mexico, federal census (Washington, D.C., 1870).

5. The complexities of the sale of the Maxwell Land Grant are amply covered in a number of historical studies; the deal was consummated in the summer of 1870 and the price was $1.7 million, an enormous sum in those days. The name the new owners chose was "The Maxwell Land Grand & Railway Company."

SOURCES: Full histories of the grant are Pearson, *The Maxwell Land Grant;* William A. Keleher, *Maxwell Land Grant: A New Mexico Item* (Santa Fe: Rydal Press, 1942); F. Stanley, *The Grant that Maxwell Bought* (Denver: World Press, 1948).

6. The Red River stage station was better known as the Clifton House, a two-story adobe building with a raised half-story basement built by Tennessee-born cattleman Thomas L. Stockton in 1867, using furniture, glass, and shingles brought overland from Dodge City, Kansas. It boasted a large parlor, sleeping rooms with fireplaces, and a high-ceilinged dining room. A veranda supported by Doric posts ran around the front and sides of the building, creating a promenade balcony on the second floor. Later it became a stop on the Barlow and Sanderson stage line, and featured a trading post, a blacksmith shop, and a post office. For a brief period, Clifton House was the headquarters of the Maxwell Land Grant and Railway Co. but was abandoned in 1879

when the railway arrived. It later burned down, and nothing remains now but its graveyard. There is a historic marker near the site about six miles south of Raton, New Mexico.

Sources: Robert Julyan, *The Place Names of New Mexico* (Albuquerque: University of New Mexico Press, 1996); David Pike, *Roadside New Mexico: A Guide to Historic Markers* (Albuquerque: University of New Mexico Press, 2004).

7. The two men who came to kill James Wightman must have been Joe McCurdy (McIntyre in some accounts) and John (sometimes Frank) Stewart, the killers of Coal Oil Jimmy Buckley (a.k.a. Buckner/Burns) and his partner Tom Taylor (alias Baker/Barber), a recent escapee from the Cimarron jail, where he had been awaiting trial for murder.

Buckley, Taylor, and Frank Jones had robbed the Elizabethtown–Cimarron stage on October 9, 1871, and got away with about $500. Eight days later, Buckley and Taylor stopped another stagecoach, but due to their own incompetence their pickings were negligible (one of the passengers was carrying about $15,000 in notes and drafts, but the thieves searched no one). When the grant company posted a reward of $600 for each of them, a posse tracked the robbers to a cabin owned by a man named Jack Booth, but, using Booth as a human shield, the two men escaped.

On October 23, acting governor Henry Wetter offered a further reward of $1500 for their capture. McCurdy and Stewart, who knew the outlaws, offered to join forces with them, and a meeting was arranged at Collier's ranch, about six miles from Fort Union. There, on October 31, McCurdy and Stewart cold-bloodedly shot the two outlaws and brought their bodies to Cimarron in a wagon. Why they might have wanted to kill James Wightman is unclear.

Sources: *Santa Fe Daily New Mexican*, October 12 and November 14, 1871; Howard Bryan, *Robbers, Rogues, and Ruffians* (Santa Fe: Clear Light, 1991), 12ff.

8. James Temple Wightman, who died after a short illness in September of 1874, is indeed buried in the cemetery at Cimarron; the grave is no longer marked. Next to him is the grave of his five-month-old grandson, John Frederick Walters, who died on August 6, 1876, perhaps during the smallpox epidemic of that year. John's mother, Marianne Isabella Wightman, had accompanied her father to New Mexico in 1871 and had married John Walters on June 2, 1875, at the Colfax County home of her brother, Sinclair (or St. Clair) Walker Wightman; the officiating clergyman was Rev. F. J. Tolby.

Other than that he died sometime after 1880 and is also buried in the

Cimarron cemetery, the date and circumstances of Sinclair Wightman's death are not known.

Sources: Wightman/Wallace family research by Michael Winter, Beebe, Arkansas; Nancy Robertson, Raton New Mexico; and Richard Roynon, Talywain, Monmouthshire.

CHAPTER 2

1. As previously noted, Joseph Holbrook, "a fiery little Indian scout who had served with Kit Carson," was not sheriff during any of the events described. The sequence of sheriffs seems to have been John C. Turner (1874–75), Orson K. Chittenden (1875–76), Isaiah Rinehart (1876–77), and Peter Burleson (1877–80).

By beginning with the murder of Reverend Tolby, Clifford renders his chronology confusing, making it seem as if Clay Allison's killing of Chunk Colbert happened after Tolby's death, when in fact it took place a year before, and interpolating the matter of Allison's foot wound (if it happened then) between the death of Griego (1875) and the Crockett-Heffernon shootout (1876). He likewise confuses his sheriffs; at the time of the Tolby murder, John C. Turner was sheriff. When Griego was killed, Orson K. Chittenden was the incumbent. Following the *Cimarron News and Press* incident, Chittenden was fired by Governor Axtell and Isaiah (not Jack) Rinehart was appointed. It was not until November 1877, a month after the demise of Crockett and Heffernon, that Burleson (who had served as a deputy to all his predecessors) was elected sheriff. Perhaps also it is apposite to again add the caveat that at the time of these events, the author was only a lad—albeit a strapping six footer of a lad—of fourteen or fifteen.

2. Kentucky-born Isaiah Rinehart came to Cimarron in 1864 to operate a new grist mill for Maxwell. He appears in the 1870 census as a thirty-year-old miller, living with his wife, Sarah, twenty-eight; daughter, Elizabeth, eight, both born in Pennsylvania; and a son, Irwin J., four, born in Virginia. Sarah, born August 2, 1842, in Shrewsbury, Pennsylvania, contracted tuberculosis and died May 24, 1874. Her infant son, Melvin W., died on September 17 of the same year.

Rinehart, a close personal friend of Lucien B. Maxwell, was appointed sheriff of Colfax County by Governor Samuel Axtell on March 8, 1876, to complete the term of incumbent Orson K. Chittenden, who had been removed from office. The timing could hardly have been worse. On March 24, Crockett and his pals killed three black troopers and got away with it; thereafter, they ran Rinehart ragged, until he and his deputies confronted them in September and killed them (see also note 14).

Rinehart's last appearance in Cimarron was on August 31, 1877, when he sold his "dwelling house . . . near the grist mill" for $250. He bought forty-one acres of land in Tascosa, Texas, on which he and Jules Howard built a general store. He remained in Tascosa until the 1890s; when a stroke left him partially paralyzed, he moved to Texline, in the Texas Panhandle, and is thereafter lost to history.

SOURCES: Hornung, personal correspondence with author, April–May 2009; Frederick Nolan, *Tascosa: Its Life and Gaudy Times* (Lubbock: Texas Tech University Press, 2007).

3. Benjamin Franklin Tolby, born in Eel River Township, Hendricks County, Indiana, in 1840, was the sixth of the eight children (two born in Kentucky, the rest in Indiana) of North Carolinian Thomas and Kentuckian Nancy Tolby. Somewhere between there and his arrival in New Mexico, Tolby decided to be known by the name that is on his tombstone. It is often mistakenly said that he was murdered because he published a denunciation of the Santa Fe Ring in the *New York Sun* on August 16, 1875. Why it should have been attributed to him when it was signed by S. H. Newman is not clear. A more probable motive for murder was Tolby's July 14 testimony before a grand jury that "Pancho" Griego had been responsible for the murder of three soldiers at Cimarron on May 30, 1875 (see note 11) and his statement that he, Tolby, would seek an indictment.

At the time of his death, Tolby was married and had two daughters, five-year-old Rachel and two-year-old Grace; it is said that another child was born after his death. He died with personal property worth only $65.55 and debts of almost $500. Another source suggests that soon after Tolby's death Clay Allison raised a purse and paid Mary Tolby a visit; shortly thereafter she and her children left New Mexico forever. Tolby's grave was not marked until 1913.

SOURCES: U.S. Bureau of the Census, Hendricks County, Indiana, federal census (Washington, D.C., 1850); J. S. Peters, Charles Norman Parsons, and Marianne Elizabeth Hall-Little, *Mace Bowman: Texas Feudist, Western Lawman* (Yorktown, Tex.: Hartmann Heritage Productions, 1996).

4. Cruz Vega, only recently elected constable of Cimarron's third precinct, was a nephew of "Pancho" Griego and had been raised by the Griego family; he and his cousin Manuel Cardinas were well-known troublemakers. Both men

had been seen in the canyon on the day Tolby was killed. Finding himself unable to persuade Sheriff Rinehart to take action, Oscar P. McMains, now the anti-Ring leader, put the matter in the hands of Clay Allison.

The unsuspecting Vega was captured on the night of October 30–31. The mob beat him mercilessly, put a rope round his neck, and yanked him up and down a telegraph pole between questions about the murder (McMains, doubtless seeing the way the wind was blowing, quickly absented himself from the proceedings). Hardly surprisingly, Vega confessed, identifying Cardinas as the murderer, whereupon he was dragged by the feet behind a running horse and finally shot dead.

When "Pancho" Griego took the body to the cemetery for burial, however, Clay Allison and his men would not allow him to bury Vega either there or within the city limits. The grave was finally dug on the open prairie about a half mile west of Cimarron.

SOURCES: Peters, Parsons, and Hall-Little, *Mace Bowman*; Philip J. Rasch, "Taking a Closer Look at Cimarron Murders," *National Association of Outlaw and Lawman Quarterly* 3, no. 3 (Winter 1977–78); Rasch, "Sudden Death in Cimarron," *National Association of Outlaw and Lawman Quarterly* 10, no. 4 (Spring 1986); Cleaveland, *No Life for a Lady*; Cimarron (N. Mex.) *News and Press*, August 30, 1877.

5. Manuel Cardinas—sometimes spelled Cardenas—was arrested at Elizabethtown on November 5, 1875, and in short order made an affidavit that implicated Griego, Florencio Donoghue, local doctor J. H. Longwill, and attorney Melvin W. Mills, the last three of whom were known pro-Ring supporters, in the Tolby murder. On November 10, Cardinas was committed to jail to await action of the grand jury but was shot through the head while being taken there. With racial reprisal looming, Sheriff Chittenden and deputy Burleson spirited Allison away to a ranch twenty miles south of Springer and kept him there until things quietened down.

SOURCES: *Santa Fe Daily New Mexican*, November 11, 1875; J. S. Peters, "Riders for the Grant," *WOLA Journal* 11, no. 2 (Summer 2002); Rasch, "Sudden Death."

6. Robert Clay Allison, the third child of Jeremiah Scotland and Maria (Brown) Allison, was born in Wayne County, Tennessee, on September 2, 1841. During the Civil War, he served under Nathan Bedford Forrest and others, occasionally as a scout or spy. He was captured during the Battle of Shiloh and escaped, but ended up in May 1865 as a prisoner of war in Alabama. After he was paroled, he went to Texas, where he worked for Texas Panhandle cattle-

men Louis G. Coleman and Irvin Lacy; somewhere along the trail, Allison dropped his first name.

At the beginning of the decade, the Allison brothers established their own ranch at the junction of the Red and Vermejo rivers, probably as squatters; Allison is said to have led an Elizabethtown mob, which on October 7, 1870, lynched Charles Kennedy, on trial for murdering patrons of his hotel. On April 30 of the following year, he was involved in the theft of twelve U.S. Army mules at Crow Creek, north of Cimarron; on a similar mission in the fall, he accidentally shot himself in the foot. This would appear to be the wound to which Clifford refers.

On January 7, 1874, Allison killed John "Chunk" Colbert at the Clifton House and probably also an Englishman named Charles Cooper who had witnessed the shooting. In addition to his Cimarron vigilante activities, he killed "Pancho" Griego on November 1, 1875; and in 1877 he killed a constable, Charles Faber, at Las Animas, Colorado. In 1880, he moved on to land northeast of Mobeetie, Texas, where on February 15, 1881, he married Medora (Dora) McCullough. In 1883, they moved to a two-room rock house near Pope's Crossing on the New Mexico-Texas border; a daughter, Patti Dora, was born August 9, 1885. On July 3, 1887, Allison fell from a wagon, which ran over and killed him.

SOURCES: Sharon Cunningham, "The Allison Clan—A Visit," *WOLA Journal* 11, no. 4 (Winter 2003); Chuck Parsons, *Clay Allison, Portrait of a Shootist* (Seagraves, Tex.: Pioneer Book Publishers, 1983); Dan L. Thrapp, *Encyclopedia of Frontier Biography* (Spokane, Wash.: Arthur H. Clark, 1990).

7. The citizen Clifford was reluctant to name—leaving us wondering why—was Dr. James H. Longwill. It seems that Clay Allison became furious when the details of Cardinas's confession reached town. Longwill, justifiably apprehensive, decided to make a run for the safety of Fort Union, with Allison, his brother John, and deputy Pete Burleson in hot but unsuccessful pursuit. Back in Cimarron, Mills and Donoghue were arrested and jailed; a detachment of soldiers from Fort Union arrived on Sunday November 7, and martial law was immediately imposed. Dr. Longwill was never heard from again.

SOURCES: Rasch, "Sudden Death"; Peters, "Riders."

8. Around midnight on January 19, 1876, Allison and others (some historians believe Allison had only one helper) broke into the building that housed the *Cimarron (N. Mex.) News and Press*. After setting off a charge of black powder on the printing press, they dumped it, the type, and other equipment into

the Cimarron River. The following morning Allison repented when he found Ada Morley, the pregnant wife of one of the newspaper's backers, weeping in the office; he gave her money to buy a replacement press and told her, "I don't fight women." (Could this have been the moment he renounced his ties with the grant and the Santa Fe Ring?) Apparently, the sabotage was sloppily done; type was strewn along the riverbanks, local children were employed to collect and return it to the newspaper office, and editor Will Dawson got out a four-page special a week later.

SOURCES: Cleaveland, *No Life for a Lady*, 12; Peters, Parsons, and Hall-Little, *Mace Bowman*; Peters, "Riders"; Pearce S. Grove, Becky J. Barnett, and Sandra J. Hansen, eds., *New Mexico Newspapers: A Comprehensive Guide to Bibliographical Entries and Locations* (Albuquerque: University of New Mexico Press, 1975), 97–100.

9. The suspension of the courts, which rendered Colfax County unable to hold its own grand and petit jury proceedings, was effected on January 14, 1876, by Governor Samuel B. Axtell. This arbitrary act was seen as just another means of assuring the political and financial dominance of the Santa Fe Ring. Such were the protests that the next session of the legislature reestablished the courts in Colfax County. Axtell's actions eventually led to his ignominious removal from the office of governor.

SOURCES: Peters, Parsons, and Hall-Little, *Mace Bowman*; Peters, "Riders"; Parsons, *Clay Allison*.

10. Whether the Clifton House had crockery strong enough to divert a .45 caliber bullet fired at close range we may take leave to doubt; the most common version of the story has it that Colbert and Allison both had their guns in their laps as they ate their oysters and chili, and that Colbert made the first move but as he brought his gun up to fire, the barrel hit the underside of the table and spoiled his aim; Allison made no such error. Charles Cooper, a young Englishman who witnessed the shooting, was never seen again, and it was not unnaturally assumed that Allison killed him.

SOURCES: Peters, Parsons, and Hall-Little, *Mace Bowman*; Peters, "Riders"; Parsons, *Clay Allison*.

11. Thirty-eight-year-old Griego, a gambler, was said to have killed "many Americans." At about 10:00 P.M. on the night of May 30, 1875, he was dealing monte in Lambert's saloon; several troopers of the 6th Cavalry were at the table. Somehow a dispute arose, and Griego pulled a gun and a "dirk knife" and started shooting, killing Private Benjamin Sheahan and wounding teamster

Patrick Gaitly, who was just entering the building. Private Michael Carral, trying to get out of the room, was stabbed in the back. Other soldiers present went
back to their camp to arm themselves, but by the time they returned Griego had
fled. Sheahan's body was taken back to camp and buried there; Carral recov-
ered, but Gaitly died of his wounds on June 28.

Griego turned himself in on July 14. In his examination before justice of
the peace Harry A. Simpson, he was defended by pro-Ring attorney Melvin
W. Mills and bound over in the sum of $1,000 to await action by the next grand
jury. It did not go unnoticed that this judgment came following an hour-long
consultation between Simpson (who was a clerk in Mills's practice), Mills himself, and probate judge Dr. Longwill—all good friends of the Santa Fe Ring.
It was as a direct result of this "fix" that the Reverend Tolby testified against
Griego (see note 3).

Sources: Peters, Parsons, and Hall-Little, *Mace Bowman*; Peters, "Riders"; Rasch,
"Sudden Death"; Rasch, "Closer Look"; *Santa Fe Daily New Mexican*, June 7, 1875.

12. Clifford's account of Griego's death is clearly based on hearsay. In view
of the events of the preceding day and the morning that followed, it is a certainty that Griego was "on the prod," and Allison knew it. On the night of November 1, they met—unexpectedly—in the street. Griego was wearing a revolver
and carrying a rifle, and two friends he had with him were similarly armed.
Allison backed off, hand on pistol, but after a brief conversation Griego handed
his Winchester to one of his friends, and he and Allison proceeded together to
the St. James Hotel. The bar was deserted; Lambert served them drinks and
returned to the kitchen. After a while, he heard shots, but when he cautiously
looked in, the bar was empty, so he turned out the lamps and closed down.
It was not until next morning that Griego's corpse was discovered behind the
billiard table. To this day no one knows exactly what happened; perhaps the
author's version is as good as anyone's.

Once again racial strife looked probable, but at around noon that day Allison and a dozen of his pals rode in and took over the town in the approved
Tejano fashion. Two days later they repeated the exercise, this time threatening
News and Press editor Will Dawson with firearms and knives. The following
night Allison rode in yet again, this time to perform a bizarre dance on the spot
where Griego had died.

Sources: *Santa Fe Daily New Mexican*, November 5, 1875; Peters, Parsons, and Hall-
Little, *Mace Bowman*; Peters, "Riders"; Rasch, "Sudden Death"; Rasch, "Closer Look."

13. Some accounts of his life state that Allison shot himself in the foot accidentally while trying to steal some U.S. Army mules in the Fort Union area, but there is some doubt whether it happened. Perhaps Clifford was referring to the events of December 21, 1876, when, after delivering some cattle to Las Animas, Colorado, Clay Allison and his brother John were braced by constable Charles Faber for carrying firearms but refused to surrender their weapons. They all repaired to the Olympic Dance Hall, where they had some drinks and danced. As the Allisons became more and more obnoxious, Faber slipped out, returning around midnight carrying a shotgun and accompanied by two deputies. Apparently mistaking John Allison for Clay, Faber fired, hitting John in the chest and shoulder and knocking him off his feet. Almost simultaneously, Clay Allison drew and fired, fatally wounding the constable, but as he fell Faber fired again, this time hitting the fallen John Allison in the legs. The two deputies scuttled out the door, closely followed by Clay Allison, who fired a couple of ineffective shots. He then came back into the dance hall and dragged Faber's body over to where his brother lay, beating the dead man over the head with his pistol and shouting, "John, here's the man who shot you, I killed the sonofabitch!" Sheriff John Spiers arrested both the Allisons, and at a hearing next morning they were charged with murder, but no further action was taken. As far as anyone has been able to ascertain, Clay Allison never used a gun in anger again for the rest of his life.

SOURCES: *Las Animas (Colo.) Leader,* December 22, 1876, January 9, 1877, and January 12, 1877; Peters, "Riders"; Kenneth C. Jessen, "Clay Allison's Last Gunfight," *National Association of Outlaw and Lawman Newsletter* 16, no. 3 (July–September, 1992).

14. It would appear that the "humiliation" happened when Rinehart took Allison to Taos (but "with a strong escort" and not alone as related) to face charges dealing with the murder of Manuel Cardinas.

15. About nine o'clock on Monday March 24, 1876, three local bad boys, Davy Crockett, Gus Heffernon, and Henry Goodman, who were drinking at the St. James Hotel, got into a fracas with three black 9th Cavalry troopers, George Small, Anthony Harvey, and John Hanson, members of a thirty-man detachment from Fort Union acting as militia. Although they knew all bars were off limits to the military, the soldiers loudly persisted in trying to get the bartender to fill their canteens with liquor. As Crockett got involved in the argument and Heffernon egged him on, Henry Goodman slid out and hid himself behind a lumber pile. Inside the hotel, shooting started. Crockett is said to have

killed two of the troopers at the bar and the third as he ran for the door.

Capt. Francis Moore, Scottish-born commander of the detachment, reported that he was unable to make an arrest because even though he knew "it was Davy Crockett and Gus Heffron that did the shooting," he was able to find only one witness who would admit to having seen Crockett use his pistol; this was probably Henry Lambert, who wrote in his journal, "Crockett is a bad man. Killed 3 negro soldiers. Murder! Sheriff made search. Can not find. Soldiers patrol town. *Canaille* [scum]." At the September term of court in Taos, Crockett was fined one hundred dollars for "carrying arms." Having gotten away with murder, he and Heffernon began "hoorawing" the town on a regular basis. Rinehart, as sheriff, seems to have been powerless to restrain them; one tale has it that Crockett forced him at gunpoint to consume drink after drink until he became helplessly drunk.

SOURCES: *Santa Fe Daily New Mexican,* March 25, 1876; Chuck Hornung, "The Forgotten Davy Crockett, Bad Boy of Cimarron, New Mexico," *National Association of Outlaw and Lawman Quarterly* 13, no.1 (Summer 1988) and no. 2 (Fall 1988); J. S. Peters, "Davy Crockett of Cimarron," *WOLA Journal* 16, no. 2 (Summer 2007); Philip J. Rasch, "Bad Days at Cimarron," *New York Westerners Brand Book* 18, no. 1 (1971): 12–13.

16. David Crockett was born in Erath County, Texas, on February 4, 1853, the son of Andrew Jackson and Mary (Danley) Crockett. Davy's father was the son of Wilson Crockett, brother of the more famous Davy. He probably came to New Mexico with one of the Lacy and Coleman cattle drives on which Clay Allison was trail boss. On December 9, 1872, he was convicted in DeWitt County of stealing a gelding and was sentenced to five years imprisonment, but seems to have escaped serving time.

Six months later he and Heffernon decided to go on another spree. When Sheriff Ike Rinehart (not Burleson) tried to cool them down, they told him that "they intended to run the town and would kill him if he interfered with their simple pleasures." At about nine P.M. on Saturday September 30, Rinehart—backed by special deputies John B. McCullough and Joseph Holbrook—hid near a well behind Schwenk's barn and waited for the duo to leave town. As they came into sight, Rinehart stepped out and demanded their surrender. "Instead of throwing away their arms, Crockett and Heffron at once placed themselves on the defensive when the Sheriff's party fired one volley, and as the horsemen started off toward the river on the run, let loose the other barrel of shotguns. Crockett was found dead on the other side of the river, and Heffron [*sic*] was arrested, having been shot in the wrist and the head." Heffernon escaped from jail on October 31, 1876, and lived out the rest of his life in Colorado. SOURCES: Hornung, "Forgotten Davy Crockett"; Peters, "Davy Crockett of Cimarron"; Rasch, "Bad Days."

CHAPTER 3

1. SOURCES: United States Army, Military Division of the Missouri, *Record of Engagements with Hostile Indians within the Military Division of the Missouri from 1868 to 1882* (Washington, D.C.: Government Printing Office, 1882), 92.

CHAPTER 5

1. Born to a poor family in Kingston, Ontario, Canada, in 1833, Wilson Waddingham joined the gold rush to California and wound up tending bar in a San Francisco saloon. By the 1860s, having abandoned his wife, Emma, and two daughters, he was promoting gold and silver mines in Idaho. In that same decade, he established the New York Waddingham Gold and Silver Mining Company, shuttling from the East Coast to the West Coast and even to England to make his deals. A shamelessly ostentatious entrepreneur who preferred to pretend he was English, he made his living by always keeping one step ahead of his creditors, wheeling and dealing in cattle, railroads, real estate, mines, saloons, and other profit-bearing activities of the day. In 1871, when in partnership with Jerome B. Chaffee and David H. Moffatt, Waddingham is said to have bought the Maxwell Land Grant from Lucien B. Maxwell for a reported $750,000 and six months later sold the property to an English company for $1,350,000.

Operating out of the old, abandoned Fort Bascom, Waddingham first brought cattle onto what was to become the Bell Ranch in 1872, and registered the famous Bell brand in 1874. The area encompassing the ranch had originally been granted to Pablo Montoya in 1824 by Mexico and remained in his lineage until 1867, when John S. Watts gained ownership; just three years later Waddingham bought the land, on which he proceeded to establish what became the Bell Ranch, organized under several different holding companies: the United States Agricultural Society, the Fort Bascom Cattle Company, Red River Land and Cattle, and finally the Bell Ranch Company, this title first bestowed in 1889.

A massive, pushy, arrogant, high-living 240-pounder, Waddingham lent much to the stereotype of the cattle barons of the Gilded Age, but in 1894, over-stretched and desperate, he lost the Bell Ranch to New York financiers John H. Greenough and James Brown Potter. Despite numerous attempts, Waddingham was never to regain ownership. He was still trying when, on May 16, 1899, after a 4.00 A.M. rise and a 6.00 A.M. business breakfast, he died of apoplexy as he scurried upstairs for some papers relating to his Bell Ranch holdings.

SOURCES: An excellent and comprehensive history of the ranch is David Remley, *Bell Ranch: Cattle Ranching in the Southwest, 1824–1947* (Albuquerque: University of New Mexico Press, 1993). Also of interest is John H. Culley, *Cattle, Horses and Men of the Western Range* (Tucson: University of Arizona Press, 1984).

2. Michael Slattery was born in New York City in August of 1843 and headed west when he was sixteen. For some ten years, he worked in freighting in Utah, Idaho, and Montana. Having met Wilson Waddingham, Slattery came with him to New Mexico in 1869 and started up the ranching operation that eventually developed into the Bell Ranch. He was an imposing figure in the cattle industry, an incorrigible bachelor who enjoyed the niceties of the drawing room equally as much as he relished being the dauntless ranch manager. In an 1885 account of his life, he recorded that his parents were dead, his two brothers John and James had been living in Chile since 1859 (the same year he himself left home), and his two sisters, both married, were in New York. When Greenough and Potter took over the Bell Ranch in 1894, they let Slattery go. For five years, Waddingham kept trying to regain control and reinstate him, but he died before he could carry out his plan, and Slattery never returned to the Bell.

SOURCES: Michael Slattery, dictated statement, July 18, 1885. Reel 4, PE 27. The Bancroft Library Collections Pertaining to New Mexico and New Spain (Mexico) on Microfilm (1581–1904) (Center for Southwest Research, University of New Mexico); Remley, *Bell Ranch*.

3. SOURCES: Remley, *Bell Ranch*.

4. La Cinta (meaning "the Strip") was a settlement at the junction of La Cinta Creek and the Canadian River near present-day Conchas Lake, some miles west of Fort Bascom and about eight miles above San Hilario. It boasted a ferry and a store run by the widow Yetta Kohn and her sons, Howard, George, and Charles, and a general merchandise store operated by Reuther and Nahm. This is the same area recorded in the 1880 Census as "District 38," which somehow included San Lorenzo. San Hilario, which, like La Cinta, had a post office, also had two general stores that traded in horses, mules, sheep, cattle, hides,

and pelts. It, too, was located near Conchas Dam and is now a ghost town.

SOURCES: Census research by Gregory Scott Smith, Jemez, New Mexico; Julyan, *Place Names of New Mexico*.

5. Louis/Luis Hommel, born 1832 in Saxony, Germany, an immigrant who had taught himself Spanish and English, was the editor of the newspaper *Red River Chronicle* and its companion, Spanish weekly *La Cronica del Rio Colorado*, which began publication in June 1880. His wife was Mary Ann (née Skinner) Dorsett, the widow of local rancher John W. Dorsett who died at Springer, Colfax County, in 1877; she had married Dorsett in Texas in 1858. Three other Dorsett brothers, Charles, James, and Willis, ranched in the area. Mary Ann, "a jolly young woman with a round, red face," had given birth to Axtell Hommel (her first child with Louis/Luis) in July 1880, so they probably married (if they married at all) in 1879. Mary Ann already had six children by Dorsett: Willis Arnold, age twenty-one in 1880; James, nineteen; Mary, seventeen (who must have been the object of Clifford's affections); Henry, fifteen; Lee K., eleven; and Elice, five. All were still using the Dorsett surname in 1880, but might have changed it to Hommel later. In August 1881, the newspaper moved from La Cinta to nearby San Lorenzo, and to San Hilario in 1882, where the Dorsett brothers were the publishers and Mary Dorsett did the composing.

SOURCES: Census research by Gregory Scott Smith, Jemez, New Mexico; U.S. Bureau of the Census, San Miguel County, New Mexico, federal census (Washington, D.C., 1880).

6. Which of the Dorsett boys tried to brain Clifford remains a mystery; it was probably Willis, the oldest.

CHAPTER 6

1. Caleb Berg Willingham was born in Georgia around 1850. At the start of the Civil War, his father enlisted and took his son with him into the army; they fought side by side until it ended. After two years in school, Willingham headed west for Texas where he broke broncos on a Brown County ranch for $20 a month. In the spring of 1873, he took a herd to Colorado, where he hired out to Charles Goodnight. In 1878 Goodnight brought him to the Panhandle, and a year later he signed on for the LX Ranch, owned by Lee & Reynolds. In 1880 he took charge of the Star Route U.S. Mail line from Fort Elliott (Mobeetie) to Las Vegas, New Mexico (a.k.a the "Lightning Express").

When Oldham County was organized in 1882, Willingham became its first sheriff; during his term of office, he killed Fred Leigh, a Texas cowboy. When he stepped down, the Hansford Land & Cattle Company, owners of the Turkey Track Ranch, made him its superintendent, and he held that post for twenty years. During his incumbency, he was involved (as a deputy to G. W. "Cap" Arrington) in the 1886 killing of two Leverton brothers. In 1903 he moved to El Paso and went into business as a cattle dealer. He died at Ajo, Arizona, on January 20, 1925.

For fuller biographical details see Nolan, *Tascosa*, 128–36.

2. Tee Sillman worked on the LX Ranch near Tascosa at the time its foreman was William C. "Outlaw Bill" Moore; honest men had no hesitation in calling him one of Moore's team of rustlers. He appears in some accounts—and not in others—of the formation of the Panhandle posse. The E-Cross-E Ranch was at the mouth of Blue Creek, which ran into the Canadian River some forty-five miles down from the LX. It was probably Sillman's hideaway ranch for mavericked LX stock: it is not difficult to see how LX could become EXE.

SOURCES: Nolan, *Tascosa*, 108.

3. Although Clifford mistakenly sticks to calling it the "Canadian Cattleman's Association," it was actually the Panhandle Stockmen's Association, formed in 1880 on the initiative of Charles Goodnight., who became its first president, with H. H. "Hank" Creswell (of the CC Bar Ranch) as vice president, and Thomas Bugbee (Quarter Circle T), Robert Moody (PO), and John F. Evans (Spade) making up the executive committee.

SOURCES: Nolan, *Tascosa*, 78–79.

4. Charles Angelo Siringo was born in Matagorda County, Texas, on February 7, 1855, and died in Altadena, California, on October 19, 1928.

A comprehensive biography is Howard R. Lamar, *Charlie Siringo's West: An Interpretive Biography* (Albuquerque: University of New Mexico Press, 2005).

5. Alonzo Chambers ("a great single-handed talker," according to Charlie Siringo) was born in Texas in 1849; his parents were from Missouri. He represented the LS on both of the expeditions sent from the Panhandle into New Mexico to recover cattle, the first in the fall of 1880 led by Frank Stewart and consisting of Chambers, Garrett "Kid" Dobbs, Lee Hall, and Charlie Reasoner. On September 29, 1883, he was one of four men—the other three were Mack Dean, Harry Doneley, and Jim Looney—who tried to hold up a westbound train at Coolidge, Kansas. During the course of the abortive robbery, the en-

gineer, John Hilton, was killed in cold blood, and the fireman, George Fadel, was badly wounded. The four train robbers were speedily arrested by a posse led by deputy Sheriff "Mysterious Dave" Mather. The case came to trial almost immediately but was dismissed on Monday October 8 for lack of evidence.

Chambers returned to the Panhandle, where he served as one of Pat Garrett's Home Rangers between May 1884 and the disbandment of the group in the spring of 1885. He is last heard of on December 16, 1890, when, age fifty-one, he married Elizabeth Halsbird in Oldham County, Texas.

SOURCES: Dodge City Times, October 4, 1883; Ford County (Kans.) Globe, October 9, 1883; Nyle H. Miller and Joseph W. Snell, Why the West Was Wild: A Contemporary Look at the Antics of Some Highly Publicized Kansas Cowtown Personalities (Topeka: Kansas State Historical Society, 1963); Nolan, Tascosa.

6. Lee Hall is another mystery man. Jim East said his real name was Lee Hall Smith (Cal Polk often refers to him as Lee Smith), and he had been raised in Caldwell County, Texas, which is where Polk came from. Hall is confused in some accounts with Jesse Leigh "Lee" Hall (1849–1911), the almost-legendary Texas Ranger who served on Capt. L. H. McNelly's Special Force, helped break up the Sutton-Taylor feud, and arrested King Fisher, but in fact they were two completely different men. Lee Hall Smith was gored to death in the summer of 1882 when a wild longhorn he had roped pulled his horse over; his spur got caught in the saddle cinch, and he could not free himself in time.

SOURCES: Harry Ingerton, interview by J. Evetts Haley, June 5, 1939, Haley History Center, Midland, Texas (hereafter HHC); Charles A. Siringo, A Lone Star Cowboy (Santa Fe: n.p., 1919), 115.

7. Calvin Warnell Polk was born near Prairie Lea in Caldwell County, Texas, on January 8, 1863. By age seventeen, he had already made two cattle drives to Dodge City. He was working at the LX Ranch when the second Panhandle posse was formed. He married Ann Hampton, who was also from the Prairie Lea area, and they moved to Holdenville, Oklahoma, in the Creek Nation, where he served as a deputy U.S. marshal and later as city marshal. He wrote his own free-wheeling account of the Panhandle expedition in 1896, with some further material added in 1901. Cal Polk died in 1904 from a wound accidentally inflicted by his own gun.

For Polk's account of the posse's antics, see James H. Earle, ed., The Capture of Billy the Kid (College Station, Tex.: Creative Publishing, 1988).

8. Apart from the fact that his real name was William T. Hughes, "Tender-

foot Bob" Roberson (or "Robertson" or "Robinson") also remains something of a mystery; he apparently changed his name after killing a man at Huntsville, Texas. He told Lucius Dills it was an unintentional murder; perhaps he meant "justifiable." After the LIT sold out, Roberson was "put in as manager of the Prairie Cattle Company." Later, according to D. J. "Dick" Miller, Roberson and Jesse Jenkins "established quite a ranch out of the offspring of the LIT cows in there right below Kenton [Cimarron County, Oklahoma]. . . . He got to be very wealthy and died at Clayton [New Mexico]."

Sources: D. J. "Dick" Miller, interview by J. Evetts Haley, June 23, 1937, HHC; Lucius Dills, interview by J. Evetts Haley, August 5, 1937, HHC; Nolan, *Tascosa*.

9. According to one contemporary, Tom Emory was "a little scrawny red-headed strawberry roan of a fellow." After delivering Billy the Kid to Santa Fe with Garrett, Emory returned to the Panhandle. He "worked for the LIT until they sold out to an English syndicate and he could not get used to their ways, he got in the habit of wintering in Tascosa and trying his luck at gambling." Later, after a few years at Las Vegas, he located in Roswell, where, believing he was dying, he confessed to Pat Garrett that his real name was William Arnim and that he was wanted in central Texas. He surrendered to the authorities, and on June 16, 1896, he was granted a pardon by the governor of Texas. William Oscar Arnim (Tom Emory), born January 2, 1854, in Moulton, Texas, died on May 26, 1914.

Sources: Nolan, *Tascosa*; documentary records from Texas Secretary of State, Clemency Proclamations, file 4010, June 15, 1896, Texas State Archives and Information Services Division, Texas State Library and Archives Commission, Austin; Arnim/Emory biographical data from Fayette Heritage Museum and Library, La Grange, Texas; U.S. Bureau of the Census, Fayette County, Texas, federal census (Washington, D.C., 1870); J. R. Jenkins, interview; and W. H. Ingerton, interview, both September 16, 1937, Vandale Collection, Center for American History, University of Texas, Austin, Texas.

10. James Henry East was born on August 30, 1853, on a farm near Kaskaskia, Illinois. He died at Douglas, Arizona, on May 14, 1930, aged seventy-seven.

For a fuller biography, see Nolan, *Tascosa*; and J. Evetts Haley, "Jim East— Trail Hand and Cowboy," *Panhandle-Plains Historical Review* 4 (1931): 39–61.

11. Louis Philip Bousman, a.k.a "The Animal," was born in Kanawha County, Virginia (now West Virginia), on January 4, 1857, and died in Waurika, Oklahoma, on Friday January 2, 1942. It is believed he got his nickname because he had the ability to smell water.

For fuller biographical details, see Nolan, *Tascosa*; *Waurika (Okla.) News Democrat*, January 9, 1942; Louis P. Bousman, interview by J. Evetts Haley, Wichita Falls, Texas, September 7, 1934, HHC; Louis Bousman, interview by J. Evetts Haley, 1934, HHC.

12. "Mr. Wallace" was being less than honest with his amanuensis, but having lived most of his life under that name, he could hardly confess that he had been born John Menham Wightman. Even his own wife and family did not know his real name.

13. Sammy Tise's encyclopedic *Texas County Sheriffs* (Halletsville, Tex.: privately published, 1989) makes no mention of any Lee Hall serving as sheriff in Oldham County or anywhere else in Texas.

14. Patrick Floyd Jarvis Garrett, the oldest son of John Lumpkin and Elizabeth Ann (Jarvis) Garrett, was born near Homer, Chambers County, Alabama, on June 5, 1840. He was shot to death on February 29, 1908, while traveling by buggy to Las Cruces with Carl Adamson and Jesse Wayne Brazel; although Brazel confessed to the murder and was acquitted on grounds of self-defense, conspiracy theorists are still arguing over who killed Garrett and why.

Two fine biographies are Mark Lee Gardner, *To Hell on a Fast Horse: Billy the Kid, Pat Garrett, and the Epic Chase to Justice in the Old West* (New York: William Morrow, 2010), and Leon C. Metz, *Pat Garrett: The Story of a Western Lawman* (Norman: University of Oklahoma Press, 1974).

15. Cattle detective "Frank Stewart" was born John W. Green in New York City on October 23, 1852. He died at Raton, New Mexico, on May 11, 1935.

For fuller biographical details, see John L. McCarty and Mel Armstrong, "Interview with Garrett 'Kid' Dobbs," September 12, 1942, Amarillo Public Library; *Amarillo News-Globe*, November 30 and December 22, 1930; and death certificate, New Mexico Bureau of Public Health.

16. In the summer of 1879, placer miners hit gold on a flat of rocky ground about forty miles by road northwest of Lincoln, New Mexico, and a boomtown sprouted up about a mile from the diggings. White Oaks, named for the heavy white oak trees bordering two large springs further up the valley, was soon a thriving frontier town with a population of over one thousand souls. The main street, White Oaks Avenue, ran roughly east-west. It was half a mile in length and a hundred feet wide, with substantial dwellings and stores on both sides. North of it was Jicarillo Street, south of it Livingston and Harrison streets,

then Lincoln Avenue with its large family homes. Cross streets in the center of town were Chloride, Carizo, Placer, and Washington. When its mines played out and it was bypassed by the railroad at the turn of the century, it soon became a ghost town.

Although Clifford says the Kid and his pals did not shoot up towns, they had certainly done something remarkably like it. Just a few weeks before Clifford's arrival at White Oaks, they took potshots at Jim Redman outside Hudgens's saloon and were tracked by a posse of townsmen to the Greathouse Ranch where, following a siege, deputy Jim Carlyle was killed and the outlaws escaped. Perhaps "Pinto Tom's" reaction was motivated by the fear that the outlaws had come back seeking revenge.

Sources: Frederick Nolan, ed., *Pat F. Garrett's "The Authentic Life of Billy, the Kid"* (Norman: University of Oklahoma Press, 2000), 117; Morris B. Parker, *Morris B. Parker's White Oaks: Life in a New Mexico Gold Camp, 1880–1900,* ed. C. L. Sonnichsen (Tucson: University of Arizona Press, 1971); F. Stanley, *The White Oaks (New Mexico) Story* (N.p., n.d.).

17. Thomas Christopher "Kip" ("Kit"?) McKinney was not Garrett's deputy at this time; more probably the deputy was Barney Mason. Clifford is the only participant who said Garrett had five men with him. He did not.

18. David Rudabaugh was born on born July 14, 1854, in Fulton County, Illinois. On February 18, 1886, during a fracas in a Parral cantina, a man said to have been Rudabaugh killed two men and wounded another before being himself decapitated by an angry mob. His severed head was then paraded around the plaza on a pole.

For fuller biographical details, see Stuart N. Lake, *Wyatt Earp, Frontier Marshal* (Boston: Houghton Mifflin, 1931); Robert K. DeArment, *Bat Masterson: The Man and the Legend* (Norman: University of Oklahoma Press, 1979); Miller and Snell, *Why the West Was Wild; Las Vegas (N. Mex.) Gazette,* November 4, 1879; and Frederick Nolan, *The Lincoln County War: A Documentary History,* rev. ed. (Santa Fe: Sunstone Press, 2009).

19. Charles Bowdre was born late 1848 or early 1849 in Wilkes County, Georgia, the firstborn of Albert and Lucy Bowdre. He and Josiah G. "Doc" Scurlock arrived in Lincoln, New Mexico, around 1875 and shared a Ruidoso valley farm. In September 1878, Bowdre with his wife Manuela moved to Fort Sumner, where he worked first for Pete Maxwell and later Tom Yerby. He was killed by Pat Garrett's posse at Stinking Spring on December 23, 1880.

For fuller biographical details, see *Santa Fe Weekly New Mexican*, May 25, 1878; *Albuquerque Daily Review*, August 16, 1882; and Nolan, *The Lincoln County War*.

20. We are still a long way from knowing anything much about the teenager who has gone into the history books as Tom O'Folliard. To begin with, the only official document that gives any biographical information renders his name as Thomas Folliard. Philip J. Rasch concluded that "Big Foot Tom," born at Uvalde, Texas ca. 1854, (Thrapp says 1858) was the son of Tom and Sarah (Cook) O'Folliard, but since the 1870 census gives his age as nine, both dates are clearly wrong. The family is said to have moved to Monclova, Coahuila, Mexico, where Tom's parents died of smallpox, and Sarah's brother John Cook went to Mexico and brought the orphan back to Uvalde, where he lived with his aunt, Margaret Jane Cook, until 1873, when she married Pat Dolan.

Once again, the census contradicts all this, for in 1870 Tom was living with South Carolina–born farmer and stock raiser David Cook, fifty-nine, and Cook's second wife, Eliza Jane "Elija" (McKinney), forty-one, born in Mississippi. Living in the same household were Cook's thirty-three-year-old son from his first marriage (to Salona McNatt), John Enoch Cook, and children twenty-three-year-old James C. (both born in Alabama); eighteen-year-old Margaret and fifteen-year-old Robert (both born Arkansas); and twelve-year-old Thalis T., nine-year-old Polly C., and six-year-old Edna E. (these last two names are partially illegible) (all three born in Texas).

Rasch says after 1873, Tom lived with his uncle John, but this again is incorrect because John Enoch Cook (1837–1905) married Elizabeth Francis McKinney (1854–1940), a cousin of Kip McKinney, on April 4, 1875, by which time Tom was in the care of his grandmother, Mrs. James Cook, mother (we again assume) of David. There are some hints that Folliard had been involved in a killing and left Texas for New Mexico, turning up in Lincoln in the summer of 1878. What is abundantly clear is that a lot more work needs to be done before we have anything remotely like an acceptable biography.

SOURCES: Philip J. Rasch, "The Short Life of Tom O'Folliard," *Potomac Westerners Corral Dust* 6 (May 1961); Jack Shipman, "Brief Career of Tom O'Folliard, Billy the Kid's Partner," *Voice of the Mexican Border* 1 (January 1934); Mrs. O. L. Shipman, *Letters Past and Present to My Nephews and Nieces* (N.p., n.d.); Thrapp, *Encyclopedia*; Cook, Dolan, and McKinney family genealogical research by Jim McKinney.

21. Most authorities agree that Billy Wilson was born in Trumbull County,

Ohio, on November 23, 1861, making him but nineteen and perhaps almost exactly the same age as the Kid when he rode with him. When and why he left home so young is not known. He worked as a cowboy, drifting from Tascosa and Las Vegas to Lincoln County, where he bought a share in a livery stable at White Oaks; this he in turn sold to W. H. West, who paid him in counterfeit money which Wilson unwittingly passed, committing a federal offense. On the run, he teamed up with the Kid and rode with him until captured by Pat Garrett in December 1880. On February 18, 1882, he was found guilty of robbing the U.S. mail and passing counterfeit money and was sentenced to seven years imprisonment.

Wilson escaped from the Santa Fe jail with three other felons on September 9, 1882. He went to Texas and changed his name [back?] to David L. Anderson. In 1889 he married Maggie Fitzmorris at Bracketville, and they had one child and adopted another. "Doc," as he was known, served as an official of the U.S. Customs Service from 1891 to 1894. Through the intercession of Pat Garrett and George Curry, his former attorney William Thornton, now governor of New Mexico, filed a petition for a presidential pardon, which was granted conditionally August 25, 1896.

In 1915, Wilson became sheriff of Terrell County, Texas, and was killed at Sanderson, Texas, on June 14, 1918, while attempting to arrest a drunken cowboy.

SOURCES: William A. Keleher, *Violence in Lincoln County, 1869–1881* (Albuquerque: University of New Mexico Press, 1957), 323–24; Thrapp, *Encyclopedia*, 1581; *Santa Fe New Mexican Review*, January 11 and 13, 1884.

22. The prisoners were taken first to Las Vegas and from there to Santa Fe. It was not until the following April that the Kid was taken to La Mesilla to stand trial.

23. Rudabaugh tried to free his pal John J. Webb from the Las Vegas jail on April 30, 1880, which would mean he appeared at the Bell Ranch on May 1. Since Las Vegas was something over sixty miles away as the crow flies, the narrator may have been a day or two out in his recollection. Billy Wilson was not involved in the Las Vegas rescue attempt; Rudabaugh's helper that day was John Llewellyn, a pint-sized carpenter and house painter from Georgia known as "Little Allen." It was he, not Rudabaugh, who shot the jailer, Antonio Lino Valdez.

NOTES TO PAGES 91–94

CHAPTER 7

1. Charlie Siringo said they camped "out in the open with the snow nearly two feet deep; then we rented a building to live in. Two of the leading merchants, Mr. Whiteman and Mr. Sweet, gave us unlimited credit for grub and horsefeed. . . . White Oaks was only a year old, but she contained over a thousand population, mostly venturesome men from all parts of the land." Sources: Siringo, *Lone Star Cowboy*, 136.

2. Ellen (Ella) Bolton was the daughter of John R. and Ellen Doyle Bolton, both born in Ireland. The family tradition had it that John Bolton was forced to flee Ireland in 1865 because of Fenian sympathies, leaving behind his wife, Ellen; a son Thomas, born in 1857 (and who died before the family was reunited in the United States); and two daughters, Amelia, born in Wexford, Ireland, on July 3, 1862, and Ellen ("Ella"), who was born two years later. Ellen married Cyrus H. Davidson, who died in November 1919, after which she operated a boarding house at her home in Roswell for many years. As the two sisters neared advanced age, Ella moved in with Amelia and lived there until her (Ella's) death in April 1951.

Amelia, now Mrs. Church, became a Roswell society and civic leader and was instrumental in bringing about the founding of the Roswell Museum, and the Historical Society for Southeast New Mexico. She died on March 22, 1957. Sources: Elvis E. Fleming, "Amelia Bolton Church: Remarkable Frontier Woman," in *Treasures of History IV* (Roswell: Historical Society of Southeast New Mexico, 2007).

3. Known to everyone as "Uncle Jack," John V. Winters was born in Tennessee of German parentage in 1826. A veteran placer miner, he was one of a group working around the Jicarilla mining area when, legend has it, an outlaw named George Wilson happened by, stopped to eat with Winters and his partner John Wilson, wandered up Baxter mountain to check the lay of the land, and struck gold. Anxious to move on before the law arrived, he sold his share in the strike for nine dollars and a pistol. Winters and Wilson staked out a standard 1500 × 600 ft. mining claim called the Homestake, later divided into two parts, North and South. It turned out to be a bonanza, and, at once, the gold rush was on.

Siringo said that just before he arrived in White Oaks, Winters and Wilson sold their Homestake mines to a St. Louis company, each receiving $300,000. At about the same time, on December 23, 1879, Winters conveyed half of his half claim to Carolina (Fritz) Dolan, wife of James J. Dolan; they on the same day conveyed half of their interest to Joseph A. LaRue, probably to fund Dolan's purchase or lease from LaRue of what had been the Tunstall store.

"The sudden fortune was too much for poor old Winters," Siringo said. "Whiskey killed him within a year." The old man also gave "a young lady—Miss B" (Wilson's residence in the Bolton home confirms this can only have been Ellen Bolton) $20,000 to care for him until he died. That event occurred on Sunday March 6, 1881; according to the *White Oaks Golden Era*, Winters passed away "at an early hour, and on Tuesday afternoon, the remains were laid in the earth of the little burying ground about a mile south of town." The glass-eating episode is a hoary legend that still persists in ghost town White Oaks.

SOURCES: *White Oaks (N. Mex.) Golden Era*, March 10, 1881; Walter N. Jones, *Tree Branches* (Greenbank, Wash.: n.p., 1994); Siringo, *Lone Star Cowboy*, 139.

4. Siringo offers an alternative—and significantly different—version of the Shelton (he calls him Sheldon) incident and its aftermath. Clifford, he says, was summoned to appear before justice of the peace Frank Houston Lea (a brother of the "father of Roswell" Lea) on a charge of attempted murder. "We all mounted and rode downtown," he continues. "I employed lawyer John Y. Hewett . . . to defend 'Big-foot.' There were five of us in the crowd, and we wore our six-shooters and bowie-knives into the court room. 'Pinto Tom' [Longworth], the town marshall [*sic*, constable] demanded that we take off our firearms while court was in session. This request was refused, then he called on Judge Lea to make us put up the guns.

"Now I called 'Pinto Tom' to step outside with me, which he did. There I told him that he was committing suicide, as the boys were ready to fill him full of holes if he persisted any further. This settled the matter, and the case proceeded. 'Big-foot' was cleared of the charge.

Sheldon was never arrested for his part in the shooting scrape—possibly because he did such poor shooting, which convinced Judge Lea that he was harmless."

SOURCES: Siringo, *Lone Star Cowboy*, 154–55.

5. Here—perhaps understandably—Clifford tiptoes carefully around his own connection with the matter of Shelton's demise. According to Siringo, "Big Foot" and Ethan Allen (possibly a member of the White Oaks Allen family) had robbed a store in Los Lunas. Pursued by officers of the law, Clifford got

away by swimming "the raging Rio Grande river, amidst a shower of bullets" and headed for Mexico. Allen, however, was captured and thrown into jail, where his fellow prisoners were Shelton (jailed overnight for drunkenness), and a black man, sins unknown. Toward morning, "a mob of Mexicans broke into the jail and liberated the black man, hanging young Allen and the White Oaks school-master to a nearby tree. This was done to spite the 'Gringoes' (Americans) for hanging the Baca brothers a short time previously." (This appears to refer to the lynching at Los Lunas on October 6, 1881, of three men, but none of them was called Baca.) If he was indeed involved, not a hint of this appears in Clifford's memoir.

The facts are more than somewhat different: there were a series of lynchings at Los Lunas beginning on Sunday March 5, 1882, when the victim was a man identified only as "Allen." The following Tuesday a mob hanged three more men who were in the jail for various offenses: Charles Shelton, charged with the murder of a railroad section foreman named Woodruff; Johnnie Redmond, who had killed one James McDermott at Gallup; and Harry French (alias Simpson), charged with having been a member of a gang of outlaws who shot to death deputy sheriff Jones in Albuquerque. Having hanged the trio, the mob then set upon two black men, flogged them, then turned them loose, warning them never to come back to Los Lunas. During the proceedings, J. W. Bargoin, a former telegraph operator at Grants who was in jail for embezzling Wells Fargo funds, made his escape. Five other prisoners were not harmed.

SOURCES: Siringo, *Lone Star Cowboy*, 155–56; *Albuquerque Morning Journal*, March 8, 1882.

6. Patrick Coghlan was born in Clonakilty, County Cork, Ireland, on March 14, 1822. He emigrated to the United States in 1845 and enlisted in the U.S. Army. He ended his service in Texas in 1852 and farmed in Mason County for three years before moving to the town of Mason, where he kept a store and ran cattle. In 1862 he married Irish-born Anna A. Crosby, and they settled on a farm in Menard County. In 1873 he moved west to the Tularosa valley in New Mexico (driving before him, according to one witness, a herd of cattle belonging to his father-in-law) and began buying town lots, so many that people began calling him the King of Tularosa. He also established a store, a saloon, and a wagon yard and acquired a ranch and stock.

In April 1880, he won the contract to supply beef to the Mescalero Reservation at Fort Stanton and soon linked himself to rustlers like Billy the Kid, whose inroads into the herds of the Panhandle ranchers had brought Siringo and his group to New Mexico. On February 18, 1881, Siringo found the hides of five LX steers at the Fort Stanton slaughterhouse owned by Coghlan and operated by former sheriff George Peppin. On August 16, the grand jury indicted Coghlan on eleven counts of "illegally purchasing cattle." He took a change of venue to Doña Ana County, where, in March 1882, he pleaded guilty to one count and paid a fine of $250; the other charges were dropped.

The preceding September, Coghlan employee George Nesmith; his wife, Lucy (Clifford calls them "Nesbitt"); and their adopted four-year-old daughter had been found murdered; it was not until March 1885 that two suspects, Ruperto Lara and Maximo Apodaca, were arrested. Lara confessed that Coghlan had offered him $1,000, a wagon, and a pair of horses to kill the Nesmiths. Coghlan was arrested for complicity in the murders, but when Apodaca contested Lara's statement and said no offer of money had been made, and when Lara was unable to identify Coghlan in a lineup of twenty-five men, Coghlan was released.

By 1886, Coghlan was in financial trouble; he sold off most of his cattle and mortgaged his properties, seemingly unaware that the interest rates he was paying could wipe him out. Wipe him out they did; on January 16, 1906, he signed a warranty deed to Albert B. Fall, who had bought up his notes, leaving Coghlan in straitened circumstances. His wife (some said Pat had divorced his first wife, Anna, and this was her sister) died in 1903; Coghlan himself, now frail and palsied, died January 27, 1911.

SOURCES: *Santa Fe Daily New Mexican,* April 22, 1880; *Tularosa Valley (N. Mex.) Tribune,* January 28, 1911; C. L. Sonnichsen, *Tularosa: Last of the Frontier West* (New York: Devin-Adair, 1960), 247–58.

7. The Kid was not imprisoned from December to June. Following his capture at Stinking Springs, he was jailed at Santa Fe, where he remained until March 28, 1881. On that day, he and Billy Wilson were taken by train to Rincon, and from there to La Mesilla, a two-day journey. He was in jail there during his trial and until April 16, when he was sent by road to Lincoln to be hanged, arriving there on April 21. He escaped on Thursday April 28.

CHAPTER 8

1. Joseph Calloway Lea was born in Cleveland, Tennessee, on November 8, 1841, and died suddenly at Roswell, New Mexico, on February 4, 1904.

A comprehensive biography is Elvis E. Fleming, *Captain Joseph C. Lea: From Confederate Guerilla to New Mexico Patriarch* (Las Cruces, New Mexico: Yucca Tree Press, 2002).

2. The location given for the "creek" suggests it might have been the Hondo River, or perhaps Rocky Arroyo (not the one where the Jones family lived near Seven Rivers), which runs to the south and west of the town.

3. The Corn family, Roswell's other dynasty, was headed by Martin V. Corn (1841–1913), who brought his clan to Roswell in 1877 and settled on a 364-acre homestead north of John Chisum's twelve-room adobe ranch house on the South Spring River. Corn and his wife, Mary Jane Nicholas Hampton (1838–1883), produced six sons and four daughters (one, Zilpha, died in infancy), and subsequent to his wife's demise, Corn married again and produced a further eight boys and three girls. He died in 1915.

The "Corn girls" referred to were his oldest daughters, Mary Elizabeth (Molly), who was born March 3, 1868, and Arminta, born May 31, 1869. Molly would have been a few months past thirteen and her younger sister not quite twelve years old at the time of the dance. In 1884 sixteen-year-old Molly married Edward Hudson; in 1888 her sister Arminta married Charles Littlepage Ballard, who figured notably in local law enforcement and was one of Teddy Roosevelt's Rough Riders.

Sources: Elvis E. Fleming and Minor S. Huffman, eds., *Roundup on the Pecos* (Roswell: Chaves County Historical Society, 1978), 182–88.

4. This all took place in April, not June. Billy the Kid was scheduled to be hanged on Friday May 13, 1881. He broke out of jail in Lincoln on Thursday April 28.

5. Note that later, Clifford avers he has read three books by Charles A. Siringo, all of which give fairly detailed accounts of the Kid's escape and the deaths of Olinger and Bell.

6. The family name was originally Ohlinger (with a hard "g"), and Bob was the son of William C[harles?] Olinger, who married Rebecca Robinson (born Ohio, ca. 1826–1828). There were three children: John Wallace, born at Delphi, Carroll County, on May 3, 1849; Robert, born April 1850; and Rosa Anna, date of birth not known. According to one family genealogist, Bob was shown in the Carroll County census for 1850, and his age was listed as four months. On legal papers executed by his mother, his name is Ameridith Robert B. Olinger.

In 1858 the family relocated in Mound City, Linn County, Kansas, where

William Olinger died in 1861. The family settled for a while in the Indian Territory, and Bob joined his brother at Seven Rivers in 1876, bringing along their mother, who had by then become Mrs. Stafford; 1878 tax assessments show Olinger in partnership with his brother and Charles Kruling. He is described as having been 6' 3" tall, weighing around 240 pounds, and having a red complexion, dark eyes, and long hair. As well as John Jones, he is said to have killed several men, including Juan Chavez at Seven Rivers, and one Frank Hill, but details are sketchy. He was killed on April 28, 1881, by Billy the Kid.

SOURCES: Lily Klasner, *My Girlhood among Outlaws*, ed. Eve Ball (Tucson: University of Arizona Press, 1972); *Cimarron (N. Mex.) News and Press*, March 11, 1880; Rasch, Philip J., "They Fought for the House," in *Portraits in Gunsmoke*, ed. Jeff Burton (London: English Westerners' Society, 1971); *Las Vegas (N. Mex.) Gazette*, May 3, 1881.

7. If the census of 1880 is to be trusted, James W. Bell was born in Georgia in 1853; the fact that he named one of his placer mines in the Jicarilla Mountains "The Georgia" might be considered supporting evidence. Described as being "of medium height, soft-spoken, with a knife scar across his left cheek from mouth to ear," and "a cool and daring man," he became Garrett's deputy—actually a "special constable"—on or about February 3, 1881. Just a few days later he and his mining partner R. D. Lypard "struck it big" hitting "galena [lead] ore in an immense body" and were deemed to have "a fine prospect in the Jicarillas." Two months later Bell was killed by Billy the Kid. There is still some uncertainty over where Bell was buried, but a monument has been placed at a gravesite believed to be his in White Oaks.

SOURCES: Keleher, *Violence*, op cit. 332; Leon C. Metz, *The Encyclopedia of Lawmen, Outlaws, and Gunfighters* (New York: Checkmark Books, 2003), 20; Thrapp, *Encyclopedia*, 91; Bill Reynolds, *Trouble in New Mexico: The Outlaws, Gunmen, Desperados, Murderers, and Lawmen for Fifty Turbulent Years* (Bakersfield, Calif.: privately printed, 1994), 158–59; Nolan, *The West of Billy the Kid*, 233–36; Parker, *Morris B. Parker's White Oaks*, 16–18; *White Oaks (N. Mex.) Golden Era*, February 3 and March 10, 1881; White Oaks research by Roberta Haldane.

8. The Kid's escape has been told and retold in a thousand books and more; there is no point in examining this one for inaccuracies, but it is safe to state that the Kid's killing Olinger most certainly had nothing to do with a lady named Dolores.

9. As noted earlier, Olinger's mother was now known as Mrs. Rebecca Stafford, which suggests she may have married (and been widowed) again. Rather more interestingly, she appears in the 1880 census keeping house in the same

residence as Billy biographer Ash Upson.

10. Clifford is wearing the hat that belonged to the Kid in the photograph on page 117.

11. According to reports made in October 1880 by Secret Service operative Azariah F. Wild, the former Chisum Ranch at Bosque Redondo was being used as a staging post for stolen cattle and counterfeit money by Dan and Mose Dedrick, W. H. "Harvey" West, and others. Perhaps they spooked it up to keep away unwelcome visitors.

Sources: Azariah F. Wild, "Reports of Azariah F. Wild," New Orleans District, Records of Secret Service Agents, 1875–1930, U.S. Treasury Department, Secret Service Division, Microfilm T915, Roll 308, RG 87, National Archives (Washington, D.C.).

12. Fort Sumner *bailes* were usually held in the building adjacent to and south of the Maxwell house.

13. This observation might be taken as confirmation that just a couple of months before he was killed, the Kid's romance with Pablita Maxwell was common knowledge.

14. As with his escape, the story of the death of Billy the Kid has been told many times, yet Clifford oddly decides not to tell it. For the record, and only that, Sheriff Pat Garrett shot the Kid dead in Peter Maxwell's bedroom around midnight on Thursday July 14, 1881. That event has given rise to almost as many theories as the escape that happened seventy-seven days earlier.

CHAPTER 9

1. Clifford has the story of the Lincoln County War so wrong that it is difficult to know how to correct it—or even whether to bother. Perhaps its real value lies in showing us how much, just a couple of years after the events themselves, the facts had already become garbled, and how additional faulty memories such as Clifford's garbled them still further. It probably does not need saying that Clifford not only has what he says wrong but also evinces no appreciation of the causes and events of the Lincoln County troubles, nor of how long they went on.

John Tunstall, the young Englishman whose arrival in Lincoln County was the spark that lit the fire, arrived in Placita (Lincoln)—a place he called "about the 'toughest' little spot in America, which means the most lawless"—in November 1876. By the beginning of the following year, he had enlisted the support (both moral and financial) of cattle king John Chisum and had formed a business partnership with attorney Alexander McSween, a Scot or of Scottish descent, with the aim of overthrowing and replacing the existing political and mercantile monopoly of the firm of L. G. Murphy & Co., which had dominated the economy of Lincoln County for more than a decade.

As Tunstall—with loans from Chisum given against expected finances from Tunstall's well-off father in London—set up a mercantile store, filed on ranch land, and purchased cattle and horses with which to begin ranching, his opponents took steps to thwart his ambitions. With friends (and backers) in high places, and the law and territorial authority backing them, Tunstall's adversaries first targeted McSween, who was embroiled in a long-standing dispute with the heirs of one of the original partners of L. G. Murphy & Co. over the proceeds of a will that McSween had collected but refused to turn over.

James J. Dolan, leader of the opposing party, saw to it that a writ of attachment was served on McSween and—the real purpose of the legal ploy—on Tunstall as his partner. Tunstall reacted by accusing L. G. Murphy & Co. of illegally appropriating taxes he had paid for their own use. By the turn of the year 1878, the situation had become confrontational, and on February 18 Tunstall was killed—having fired on a sheriff's posse sent to arrest him (according to those in the Murphy camp) or murdered in cold blood by hired guns paid by the Murphy machine (according to supporters of the Tunstall-McSween faction).

Open warfare ensued, with further fatal collisions on the ground that included a number of ambushes and murders, notably that of Lincoln County sheriff William Brady and one of his deputies. The "war" culminated in a five-day battle in Lincoln that resulted in the McSween home being destroyed by fire and the violent death of five men, one of them the lawyer. All of this was accompanied by bewildered and largely futile interventions at territorial, military, and federal levels and even—albeit later—on an international level.

Of course, although the Kid did indeed escape from the blazing McSween house in that final gun battle, he did not do so alone nor did he shoot any soldiers. The military had become involved—in spite of an act of Congress that forbade it to do so—ostensibly to protect civilians, but in fact because the officer commanding the troops favored the Murphy faction and considered their opponents common criminals.

Investigations, inquiries, and even a military court of inquiry followed, none of which solved anything, but which together paradoxically created an unparalleled documentary record of who did what, who said what, and why they did or said it. The result has been to make the Lincoln County War one of the most studied of all such Western conflicts, and to turn the life story of the young outlaw who called himself William H. Bonney into one of the most potent of all American legends.

Recommended for further reading: Nolan, *The Lincoln County War*; Robert M. Utley, *High Noon in Lincoln* (Albuquerque: University of New Mexico Press, 1987); Robert N. Mullin, ed., *Maurice Garland Fulton's History of the Lincoln County War* (Tucson: University of Arizona Press, 1968).

2. This folktale has appeared in many guises and has been set in many locations (although always in the home of some humble New Mexican family). It may even contain a kernel of truth, but, of course, its purpose is not so much to document Billy the Kid's adventures as to demonstrate how the ordinary people loved and protected him, a theme that persists right up to the events of the final night of his life.

3. Although Clifford states that he was present during the events related here, the story itself has the faint aroma of tall tale-telling. While it may be true the Kid and Charlie Siringo had a similar outlook on life, the proposition that they looked alike is not borne out by the photographs we have of them.

4. The details of how Pat Garrett killed of the Kid are well known, and it is not necessary to repeat them here. The idea that the Kid would have been carrying a knife as a weapon is, as the writer says, unbelievable, and for those who have seen the actual knife, not just unbelievable but downright ridiculous.

CHAPTER 10

1. No documentary record of how many cattle the White Oaks group drove back to the Panhandle has ever been found, so we have a choice of accepting this yarn at face value or of considering the general practice of driving cattle in the 1880s. Three thousand head of cattle was about the upper limit for trail driving any distance; such a herd when reaching water would occupy a frontage of about a mile. As a result, the rough rule of thumb for a large herd was one puncher for every 350 cattle (a figure reduced to 250 if the drive had to pass through dangerous country), suggesting a minimum complement of 8, not including a foreman, a cook, and a "cavvy man" to handle the remuda. So it is safe say that the drive described here would have been quite an achievement for two men and two part-time helpers.

CHAPTER 11

1. This incident took place in Tascosa on or about August 8, 1881, soon after the Panhandle men got back from New Mexico. Fred Leigh, an English-born cowboy who came in with a herd from Texas, got drunk and decided to take potshots at some ducks foraging on the street. When challenged, he refused to hand over his gun to Sheriff Cape Willingham, who feigned to let it go because he knew even if he killed Leigh, the cowboy's pals would probably kill him. As the group turned away laughing, however, Willingham got a shotgun, slipped out through the back of the Howard & McMasters store, and caught the cowboys flat-footed. Leigh foolishly went for his gun, and Willingham shot him dead.

For fuller details, see Nolan, *Tascosa*, 102–4.

2. Cattle frequently headed for water—if there was no river near, a lake or pond would do—to escape the attention of heel flies, summer pests that clustered on and bit their heels painfully. In doing so they frequently got bogged down in the mud and had to be hauled out by brute force. Cowboys called this unpleasant, repetitive, and wrenchingly hard work "bog riding."

CHAPTER 13

1. An ancient Spanish settlement in the Texas Panhandle converted to a trading post in 1843 by the firm of Bent, St. Vrain & Company, Adobe Walls was the scene of two famous Indian battles—the first in November 1864 between troops led by Kit Carson, and the better-known second fight between buffalo hunters and Comanches a decade later. At the time of this narrative, the post was part of the Turkey Track Ranch. In 1978, the remains of the old trading post were added to the National Register of Historic Places and recognized as a Texas state archaeological landmark.

CHAPTER 16

1. Clifford's gloomy remarks—he was only twenty-three—and his aside that in all the United States he had "no one of his own," might be read as confirmation that his brother Sinclair was already dead; no doubt he also knew his sister and her family had already returned to England. His seventeen-year-old bride was Sarah Frances Timmons, the daughter of Charles and Melissa (Sherwood) Timmons; she was born on October 28, 1866, in Indiana. With justice of the peace F. P. Payne officiating, the marriage took place on October 13, 1883, at

the residence of the bride's parents on Sixth Avenue, Emporia, suggesting that Clifford's tale of his mother-in-law's disapproval was pure invention.

Although "John Francis Wallace," as he now identified himself, mentions them only fleetingly, there were to be seven children, all born in Emporia: Mary Elizabeth (b. August 9, 1885); Melissa Isabel (b. December 2, 1886); John Roy Francis (b. September 6, 1888); Kate Esther (b. June 3, 1890); Laura Sherwood (b. October 17, 1892); Dorothy Ethel (b. January 12, 1895); and John Walter Otto (b. July 10, 1897). Between 1887 and 1896, the family lived at various addresses on Mulberry Street in Emporia.

SOURCES: Emporia, Kansas, city directories, 1887–1916, Lyon County Historical Society, Emporia, Kansas; *Emporia (Kans.) News*, October 18, 1883, p. 3, col. 7; Wallace family genealogical research by Michael E. Winter.

2. No clues exist to tell us what exactly a "dragman" was. It might have been a railroad worker—certain railroad carriages were called "drags"—or even a cowboy used to riding drag, i.e., at the rear of the herd, although they were usually referred to as "drag riders."

3. Dorothy Ethel Wallace died June 26, 1896; she was a little over eighteen months old. At the time of her death, the family was living at 116 Mulberry Street.

4. No such death notice has been found in the *Emporia (Kans.) Daily Gazette*.

5. Because of the social stigma associated with the disease, the location and dates of smallpox outbreaks at this time—and not just in Emporia—were often hushed up, and the names of victims were not published. Although it does not appear to be the one Wallace mentions, a newspaper report, fraught with reproach, mentions an 1889 outbreak at Bushong (a small railroad community about fifteen miles north of Emporia, now a ghost town) that involved twenty-one patients, one of whom died. "There are a number of others likely to take down with the dread disease," ran the story. "Dr. Burke went up to make an investigation with regard to turning the patients of the pest house out. The nurses were turned out, but the patients will probably be kept in till Friday . . . There is really no danger as far as is known . . . It is to be hoped that the cases already known of may be the last and that no other family in the neighborhood has been so utterly low-lived and villainous as to keep the disease a secret and expose a community to it as has been the case with some individuals there."

SOURCES: *Emporia (Kans.) Weekly Republican*, March 7, 1889.

6. Dr. J. M. Poindexter was born in Sellersburg, Indiana, in 1856. He attended the Louisville University in Kentucky and received his medical education at the Kentucky School of Medicine in Lexington. He opened his practice in Emporia about 1885 and became president and secretary of the Lyon County Medical Society and chairman of the board of health. Suffering from ill health, he moved to Kansas City in 1903, where he died at age sixty-five on May 13, 1921. He was survived by his wife, Ada, and two daughters.

SOURCES: *Emporia (Kans.) Daily Gazette,* May 14, 1921, p. 8 col. 2.

7. William D. Deveny was born in Topeka, Kansas, on October 18, 1874. Educated in public schools there, he entered the Atchison, Topeka & Santa Fe Railroad shops as an apprentice in 1890. He was made roundhouse foreman at Topeka in 1903 and transferred to Emporia as division foreman in 1907. Promoted to general foreman at Newton in 1910, he went on to La Junta, Colorado, as master mechanic, and from there to Amarillo, Texas, as mechanical superintendent. He returned to Topeka as superintendent of the shops on January 1, 1921.

He was killed in a bizarre accident on August 22, 1922, when, while he was cranking his Nash sedan outside his home on West Seventh Street, Topeka, the engine started and the car ran over him, fracturing his skull; he died within fifteen minutes.

SOURCES: *Emporia (Kans.) Daily Gazette,* August 23, 1922.

8. Alonzo C. McCarty was born in a sod house in Decatur County, Kansas, on October 21, 1881. Soon after their marriage in 1879, his parents had come to farm in Kansas from Green County, Illinois, but after enduring years of adverse conditions, they moved to Reading Township in Lyon County. After attending district school near his home, Lon McCarty attended Kansas State Normal school in Emporia and in 1907 entered Washburn College in Topeka. In 1911, after graduating from law school at Washburn, he hung out his shingle in Emporia. On December 20 of that year, he married Mamie Noggle in Topeka. He was appointed justice of the peace by Governor George H. Hodges in 1913 and the following year was elected county attorney. After three terms in office, he returned to private practice. In 1928, he ran successfully for the office of district judge, and was reelected in 1932 and 1936. He died of pneumonia on January 30, 1937.

SOURCES: *Emporia (Kans.) Daily Gazette,* January 30 and February 3, 1937.

CHAPTER 17

1. "Mr. Wallace" may have again been in a quandary here, for had he revealed where he went to school, he would also have had to spill the beans about his secret self. In his original incarnation, John Menham Wightman had been sent by his father to St. Saviour's, a famous boarding school founded in 1858 in the English seaside town of Shoreham, West Sussex. It was one of the three schools (the others were Lancing and Hurstpierpoint) established in that area by the Reverend Nathaniel Woodard (1811–1891), who believed fervently in the importance of religion in education. St. Saviour's was built especially to cater for the "lower middle classes," and the fees were very low. When the school started in Shoreham, the annual fee was thirteen guineas (approximately $68.00 at that time).

Building started on what is now Ardingly (pronounced Arding-*lie*) College at Chichester, Sussex, in 1864, and the first boys moved into the school in the autumn of 1870, though there was no lighting or heating and in some areas no running water. Most pupils were the sons of "tradesmen, small farmers, mechanics and others of limited means," and the new school was intended "under God's blessing to be a home where the sons of persons of very small means may be boarded and thoroughly educated and instructed in the subjects necessary for their station in life at an expense little more than the cost of food." The curriculum included "Reading, Writing and Arithmetic, Vocal Music, English and Latin Grammar, Mathematics (Euclid, Algebra and Mensuration), Book-Keeping, Geography, Linear Drawing, English and General History." There were two vacations of about four weeks in the year.

Most boys left the school at a comparatively early age, some after only one term. By 1880, over 3,500 boys had passed through the school, among them eleven-year-old Sinclair Walker Wightman, born April 3, 1856, and his brother, seven-year-old John Menham Wightman, who were registered at St. Saviour's School as pupils 1363 and 1364 in the year 1868. They were attending the new Ardingly College in Chichester (and Sinclair had become a prefect) when the UK census of 1871 was taken, so it may be safely assumed that they remained at the school until their father decided to take them with him to the United States.

SOURCES: Research in Ardingly College archives by Andrea King, Archivist; National Census of the United Kingdom, 1871, National Archives, Kew, London.

2. Christopher H. Tweedy was born September 27, 1857, in Springfield, Illinois, and had come to Kansas in 1878; Emporia was his home for the rest of

his life. On August 17, 1881, he married Nancy C. Finnell, and they had seven children. He died June 29, 1928, at the age of seventy.

SOURCES: *Emporia (Kans.) Daily Gazette,* June 30, 1928.

3. "Widely known over Kansas," Owen S. Samuel, "dean of Emporia attorneys," was born October 1, 1882, in Arvonia, Virginia, the son of William R. and Lillie (Williams) Samuel. At age eighteen, he joined the Santa Fe Railroad as a section hand, and was later a locomotive "wiper." He graduated from the Kansas School of Law in 1903 and hung out his shingle in Emporia. At the same time, he became a member of the Emporia Masonic Lodge, serving as its Master in 1912; he also became a patron of the Order of Eastern Star and exalted ruler of the Elks Lodge. A member of the State and Lyon County bar, he practiced before the U.S. Supreme Court, served two terms as Lyon County district attorney, and sixteen years as judge of Emporia Police Court. He married Ruth R. Ellis in September, 1906; they had three children—Owen, Jr., Oliver, and Virginia. On March 4, 1919, two years after the death of his wife Ruth, he married Mamie Varnar. In later years, he was a member of the board of directors of the Newman Memorial County Hospital. He died at Emporia following a heart attack on Monday June 9, 1966.

SOURCES: *Emporia (Kans.) Daily Gazette,* June 14, 1966.

4. Born in Chase County, Kansas, in 1872, Walter Davis spent his early years on his father's farm and came to Lyon County in 1896, settling six miles east of Emporia. Following his marriage to Tina Searcy shortly after his arrival, he served as county assessor from 1913–14. In the latter year, following his election as sheriff, he moved to Emporia. On August 16, 1916, soon after the death of his wife, Davis himself was shot and killed by one William Hickey in the messy aftermath of an alleged robbery.

At about 9.00 P.M. on Wednesday August 16, Ernest Mellen of Fredonia was "held and robbed of $8" by two men near the Emporia high school. City policeman Andy Armstead told Sheriff Davis, who was sitting in his car outside the jail with his friend Idris Jones, that he had seen two men he thought "suspicious characters" nearby, and they drove over to Fourth Avenue and Union, where they stopped the two men. As one of them—who had given his name as William Earl Smith—was being searched, the other ran away. Sheriff Davis fired three shots after the man as Idris Jones chased the fugitive toward Third Avenue. He brought the man down with a flying tackle, but the man pulled a gun and shot him in the neck, then broke away and headed east on Third Avenue across the Santa Fe tracks. By this time, Davis was on the scene, and they were no more than ten feet behind the fugitive, Davis on the south and Jones the north side of the street. Without warning, the fugitive turned and fired, and Davis fell, saying to Jones, "Welshman, I'm gone." Jones tried to get Davis's gun, but the sheriff gasped, "No use—bullets all gone." He died a few moments later.

The alarm was spread by ringing the fire bell, but the fugitive had disappeared. An angry crowd of perhaps two hundred citizens had gathered outside the city jail where the other prisoner, Smith, had been taken; Santa Fe officer Eli Raymond and deputy sheriff Wallace Jones were detailed to transfer him to the county jail for his own safety.

Soon a call came in that there had been a fight with the killer on the Santa Fe tracks near Wiggam. Five citizens—Frank Totsche, J. L. Boggs, J. R. Keeler, Art Gwinner, and a man named Haslee—saw a man coming down the tracks but were afraid to fire without being sure of his identity. The killer had no such inhibitions and started shooting. One bullet splintered the bones in Boggs's leg, a second hit Totsche in the calf, and a third wounded Haslee in the foot. Gwinner fired his shotgun at the fugitive and thought he hit him, as the man stumbled and fell twice as he fled. The five men decided to await the arrival of help before pursuing him further.

At around 3.00 A.M., bloodhounds were brought to the scene, and the posse—which now consisted of a large band of citizens—was divided into two groups for the pursuit; however, before it could begin, someone accidentally fired a shot, whereupon a further thirty or so more were fired, one of which wounded a man named Jones in the hand. No one had any idea where the wanted man could have gone, and the bloodhounds were unable to find a trail.

Later, the prisoner Smith told law enforcement officers he was from Salt Lake City and had been planning to go into the barbershop business with the killer, who had told him that his name was William Hickey and that he had robbed a store in Wagon Mound, New Mexico, but was planning to return the money as soon as he got himself straightened out. By this time, the rabble—something like a hundred automobiles were involved—had abandoned the chase, and, although the Lyon County commissioners and Kansas governor Arthur Capper each posted a $100 reward, it appears that "Hickey" was never apprehended.

SOURCES: *Emporia (Kans.) Daily Gazette,* August 17, 1916.

5. Walt Mason, familiarly known as "Uncle Walt," was the Emporia poet whose inimitable wit brought him national reputation. William Allen White, editor of the *Emporia Gazette*, called him the "poet laureate of American democracy." Born at Columbus, Ontario, May 4, 1862, the fifth of six sons, Mason was born to poor parents. Left an orphan at fifteen, he worked in a Port Hope, Ontario, hardware store for a year and a half, "drawing the princely salary of two and a half dollars a week . . . I was not a success in a hardware store, and when I told my employer I was going to leave he said it was the proudest and happiest moment of his life."

For the next three or four years, Mason bummed around the country, ending up in St. Louis, where he got a job in a print shop. "There was a humorous weekly called the *Hornet*," and I sent some stuff to it," he recalled. "The *Hornet* printed it, and the editor . . . offered me five dollars a week to go to work in the office, writing gems of thought, reading proofs, sweeping the floors, and otherwise making myself useful. I took the job." When the paper went broke, he went to Kansas and got a job on the *Leavenworth Times*.

In 1884 Mason was hired by the *Atchison (Kans.) Globe*, and from there was hired in a dozen cities until he was laid off by a Washington, D.C., newspaper in the depression of the 1890s. After spending some years in an alcoholic haze, he returned to Kansas to work for William Allen White's *Emporia Gazette*, turning out dozens of stories, rhymes, and poems week in and week out. In spite of his popularity, Mason never enjoyed his celebrity. He left Kansas in 1929 and moved to California, where he died in 1939.

SOURCES: Dave Webb, "Distinguished Alumnus," in *399 Kansas Characters* (Dodge City: Kansas Heritage Center, 1993), 176.

6. Legendary journalist William Allen White (known as "Old Bill" to distinguish him from his son, William Lindsay White, "Young Bill") was born on February 10, 1868, in Emporia. Though he never received a degree from the University of Kansas, White got a job with the El Dorado newspaper and in 1892 went to work for the *Kansas City Star* as an editorial writer. Then, on June 1, 1895, he borrowed $3,000 to purchase the *Emporia Gazette*, which he ran and edited for the remainder of his life.

He became nationally known in 1896, when he wrote a sarcastic editorial, "What's the Matter with Kansas," a piece born after White (a staunch Republican) got into an argument about the McKinley-Bryan presidential campaign with a local populist while waiting for a train. In the midst of the argument,

White remembered he had some editorials to write, dashed to the office, and, still "boiling mad," sat down and wrote a scathing piece, flaying the Democratic leaders. Although he did not publish the editorial, it was somehow seen by "Boss" Mark Hanna, the Republican national chairman, who liked it and had it distributed throughout the country. When White returned home from his vacation in Colorado, he found himself famous.

On April 27, 1893, White was married to Miss Sallie Lindsay of Kansas City. The couple had two children, Mary and William Lindsay White. After McKinley's election in 1896, White made many national contacts, which kept him in touch with leaders and current affairs; he was a close friend of President Theodore Roosevelt until Roosevelt's death in 1919.

The last quarter century of White's life was spent as an unofficial national spokesman for Middle America; he was fondly known as the "Sage of Emporia." Such was his popularity that President Roosevelt asked him to help generate public support for the Allies before America's entrance into World War II. He continued to write editorials for the *Gazette* until his death in 1944. His autobiography, published posthumously, won a 1946 Pulitzer Prize.

SOURCES: The abundant works on White include Sally Foreman Griffith, *Home Town News: William Allen White and the* Emporia Gazette (New York: Oxford University Press, 1989), and William Allen White, *The Autobiography of William Allen White*, ed. Sally Foreman Griffith (Lawrence: University Press of Kansas, 1990).

CHAPTER 18

1. Dr. Anna Elizabeth Ellsworth was born in Kansas in 1866. A graduate of Kansas City Homeopathic Medical College, she was licensed to practice in 1901 and died at Wichita, Kansas, on February 14, 1941.

SOURCES: *Emporia (Kans.) Daily Gazette*, February 18, 1941.

2. Frank Albert Eckdall, the second son of Swedish-born building contractor Jonas Magnus and Eva Mary (Landstrum) Eckdall, was born at Emporia on November 20, 1872. He studied pharmacy while working at Emporia drugstores and passed the state pharmacy examinations in 1894. After eight years as a druggist, he entered the Louisville, Kentucky, Medical School, transferring from there to Bush Medical School in Chicago, where he received his M.D. degree in 1901. The same year, he returned to Emporia and set up in practice with Dr. L. D. Jacobs. On May 28, 1904, he married Ella Funston at Carlyle, and

they had three children—Lida, Frank, Jr., and Funston. From 1904 to 1945—apart from his service as a captain in the army medical corps during World War I—Eckdall was the Emporia physician for the Santa Fe Railroad, during which period he also served as chief of staff of St. Mary's Hospital and of Newman Hospital, as well as president of the Lyon County Medical Society and vice president of the American Association of Railway Surgeons of North America. He died at Emporia on Friday July 31, 1959.

SOURCES: *Emporia (Kans.) Daily Gazette*, August 1 and 3, 1959.

REFERENCES

This bibliography lists only works and records referred to by the editor or cited directly; it does not include many of the hundreds of books written about Billy the Kid and the Lincoln County War or, for that matter, the history of the Colfax County troubles and the Santa Fe Ring.

ARCHIVES

Baptismal and Burial Records. Parish Church of St. Cadocs. Trevethin, Wales.

Clemency Proclamations. File 4010. June 15, 1896. Texas Secretary of State. Texas State Archives and Information Services Division. Texas State Library and Archives Commission, Austin.

Colfax County Criminal Records. New Mexico State Records Center and Archives, Santa Fe.

Colfax County Probate Court Proceedings. Record A 63–64. Colfax County Courthouse, Raton, New Mexico.

Elder, Ethel V. Interviews. June 17, 1937. Indian Pioneer History Project for Oklahoma, vol. 16, 38–43, 104, and 127–130. Oklahoma Historical Society, Oklahoma City.

Emporia, Kansas, city directories, 1887–1916. Lyon County Historical Society, Emporia.

Fayette Heritage Museum and Library, La Grange, Texas.

J. Evetts Haley Collection. Haley History Center, Midland, Texas.

National Census of the United Kingdom, 1851, 1861, 1871, 1881, 1891, 1901. National Archives, Kew, London.

School Register, 1868. Ardingly College. Haywards Heath, West Sussex, England.

Slattery, Michael. Dictated statement. July 18, 1885. Reel 4, PE 27. The Bancroft Library Collections Pertaining to New Mexico and New Spain (Mexico) on Microfilm (1581–1904). Center for Southwest Research, University of New Mexico.

U.S. Bureau of the Census. Colfax County, New Mexico. Washington, D.C., 1870.

———. Fayette County, Texas. Washington, D.C., 1870.

———. Hemphill County, Texas. Washington, D.C., 1880.

———. Hendricks County, Indiana. Washington, D.C., 1850.

———. Lincoln County, New Mexico. Washington, D.C., 1880.

———. San Miguel County, New Mexico. Washington, D.C., 1880.

———. Tippecanoe County, Indiana. Washington, D.C., 1860.

———. Wayne County, Tennessee. Washington, D.C., 1860.

Vandale Collection. Center for American History. University of Texas, Austin.

Wild, Azariah F. "Reports of Azariah F. Wild." New Orleans District. Records of Secret Service Agents, 1875–1930. U.S. Treasury Department, Secret Service Division: Microfilm T915, Roll 308, RG 87. National Archives. Washington, D.C.

NEWSPAPERS

Albuquerque Daily Review, August 16, 1882.

Albuquerque Morning Journal, March 2 and March 8, 1882.

Amarillo News-Globe, November 30 and December 22, 1930.

Cimarron (N. Mex.) News, May 30 and September 19, 1874.

Cimarron (N. Mex.) News & and Press, August 30, 1877; March 11, 1880; March 4, 1882.

Dodge City Times, September 1, 1877; October 4, 1883.

Emporia (Kans.) Daily Gazette, August 17, 1916; May 14, 1921; August 23, 1922; June 30, 1928; January 30 and February 3, 1937; February 18, 1941; August 1 and August 3, 1959; June 14, 1966.

Emporia (Kans.) News, October 18, 1883.

Emporia (Kans.) Weekly Republican, March 7, 1889.

Ford County (Kans.) Globe, October 9, 1883.

Las Animas (Colo.) Leader, December 22, 1876; January 9 and January 12, 1877.

Las Cruces (N. Mex.) Thirty-Four, February 5, 1879.

Las Vegas (N. Mex.) Gazette, October 7, 1876; November 4, 1879; May 3, 1881.

Santa Fe Daily New Mexican, October 13 and October 18, 1870; October 12
    and November 14, 1871; December 30 and December 31, 1873; January 7,
    January 13, and January 20, 1874; June 7, July 19, September 18, October 8,
    November 5, November 10, and November 11, 1875; January 22, January 25,
    March 25, April 13, May 9, and October 17, 1876; March 5, 1877; March 25,
    1876; April 22, 1880.

Santa Fe New Mexican Review, January 11 and January 13, 1884.

Santa Fe Weekly New Mexican, September 18, October 12, November 9, and
    November 16, 1875; March 26 and October 17, 1876; May 25, 1878.

Tularosa Valley (N. Mex.) Tribune, April 22, 1880; January 28, 1911.

Waurika (Okla.) News Democrat, January 9, 1942.

White Oaks (N. Mex.) Golden Era, February 3 and March 10, 1881.

BOOKS AND ARTICLES

Blair, Sheila. "Bob Olinger Family History." *BTKOG Gazette* 8, no. 1
    (December 1995): 6.

Bryan, Howard. *Robbers, Rogues, and Ruffians*. Santa Fe: Clear Light, 1991.

Cleaveland, Agnes Morley. *No Life for a Lady*. Boston: Houghton Mifflin, 1941.

Culley, John H. *Cattle, Horses and Men of the Western Range*. Tucson,
    University of Arizona Press, 1984.

Cunningham, Sharon. "The Allison Clan—A Visit." *Western Outlaw-Lawman
    History Association Journal* 11, no. 4 (Winter 2003): 3–24.

DeArment, Robert K. *Bat Masterson: The Man and the Legend*. Norman:
    University of Oklahoma Press, 1979.

Dobbs, Garrett "Kid." Interview by John L. McCarty and Mel Armstrong.
    September 12, 1942. Amarillo Public Library.

Earle, James H., ed. *The Capture of Billy the Kid*. College Station, Tex.: Creative Publishing, 1988.

Fleming, Elvis E. "Amelia Bolton Church: Remarkable Frontier Woman" in *Treasures of History IV*. Roswell: Historical Society for Southeast New Mexico, 2007.

———. *Captain Joseph C. Lea: From Confederate Guerilla to New Mexico Patriarch*. Las Cruces, New Mexico: Yucca Tree Press, 2002.

Fleming, Elvis E., and Minor S. Huffman, eds. *Roundup on the Pecos*. Roswell: Chaves County Historical Society, 1978.

French, Laura M. *History of Emporia and Lyon County, Kansas*. Emporia: Emporia Gazette Print, 1929.

Gardner, Mark Lee. *To Hell on a Fast Horse: Billy the Kid, Pat Garrett, and the Epic Chase to Justice in the Old West*. New York: William Morrow, 2010.

Grove, Pearce S., Becky J. Barnett, and Sandra J. Hansen, eds. *New Mexico Newspapers: A Comprehensive Guide to Bibliographical Entries and Locations*. Albuquerque: University of New Mexico Press, 1975.

Griffith, Sally Foreman. *Home Town News: William Allen White and the Emporia Gazette*. New York: Oxford University Press, 1989.

Haines, Helen. *History of New Mexico from the Spanish Conquest to the Present Time, 1530–1890*. New York: New Mexico Historical Publishing, 1891.

Haley, J. Evetts. "Jim East—Trail Hand and Cowboy," *Panhandle-Plains Historical Review* 4 (1931): 39–61.

Horn, Calvin. *New Mexico's Troubled Years*. Albuquerque, Horn & Wallace, 1963.

Hornung, Chuck. "The Forgotten Davy Crockett, Bad Boy of Cimarron, New Mexico," *National Association of Outlaw and Lawman Quarterly* 13, no. 1 (Summer 1988): 8–13, and no. 2 (Fall 1988): 14–15.

Jessen, Kenneth C. "Clay Allison's Last Gunfight" *National Association of Outlaw and Lawman Newsletter* 16, no. 3 (July–September, 1992): 1, 4.

Jones, Walter N. *Tree Branches*. Greenbank, Washington: n.p., 1994.

Julyan, Robert. *The Place Names of New Mexico*. Albuquerque, University of New Mexico Press, 1996.

Keleher, William A. *Maxwell Land Grant: A New Mexico Item*. Santa Fe: Rydal Press, 1942.

———. *Violence in Lincoln County, 1869–1881*. Albuquerque: University of New Mexico Press, 1957.

Klasner, Lily. *My Girlhood among Outlaws*. Edited by Eve Ball. Tucson: University of Arizona Press, 1972.

Lake, Stuart N. *Wyatt Earp, Frontier Marshal*. Boston: Houghton Mifflin, 1931.

Lamar, Howard R. *Charlie Siringo's West: An Interpretive Biography*. Albuquerque: University of New Mexico Press, 2005.

Metz, Leon C. *The Encylopedia of Lawmen, Outlaws, and Gunfighters*. New York: Checkmark Books, 2003.

———. *Pat Garrett: The Story of a Western Lawman*. Norman: University of Oklahoma Press, 1974.

Miller, Nyle H., and Joseph W. Snell. *Why the West Was Wild: A Contemporary Look at the Antics of Some Highly Publicized Kansas Cowtown Personalities*. Topeka: Kansas State Historical Society, 1963.

Mullin, Robert N., ed. *Maurice Garland Fulton's History of the Lincoln County War*. Tucson: University of Arizona Press, 1968.

Murphy, Larry. *Out in God's Country: A History of Colfax County, New Mexico*. Springer, New Mexico: Springer Publishing, 1969.

Murphy, Lawrence R. *Lucien Bonaparte Maxwell: Napoleon of the Southwest*. Norman: University of Oklahoma Press, 1983.

Nolan, Frederick. *The Lincoln County War: A Documentary History*. Rev. ed. Santa Fe: Sunstone Press, 2009.

———, ed. *Pat F. Garrett's "The Authentic Life of Billy, the Kid."* Norman: University of Oklahoma Press, 2000.

———. *Tascosa: Its Life and Gaudy Times*. Lubbock: Texas Tech University Press, 2007.

———. *The West of Billy the Kid*. Norman: University of Oklahoma Press, 1998.

Parker, Morris B. *Morris B. Parker's White Oaks: Life in a New Mexico Gold Camp, 1880–1900*. Edited by C. L. Sonnichsen. Tucson: University of Arizona Press, 1971.

Parsons, Chuck. *Clay Allison, Portrait of a Shootist.* Seagraves, Tex.: Pioneer Book Publishers, 1983.

Pearson, Jim Berry. *The Maxwell Land Grant.* Norman: University of Oklahoma Press, 1961.

Peters, J. S. "Davy Crockett of Cimarron." *Western Outlaw-Lawman History Association Journal* 16, no. 2 (Summer 2007): 42–49.

———. "Riders for the Grant." *Western Outlaw-Lawman History Association Journal* 11, no. 2 (Summer 2002): 15–42.

Peters, J. S., Charles Norman Parsons, and Marianne Elizabeth Hall-Little. *Mace Bowman: Texas Feudist, Western Lawman.* Yorktown, Tex.: Hartmann Heritage Productions, 1996.

Pike, David. *Roadside New Mexico: A Guide to Historic Markers.* Albuquerque: University of New Mexico Press, 2004.

Rasch, Philip J. "Bad Days at Cimarron." *New York Westerners Brand Book* 18, no. 1 (1971): 12–13.

———. "The Short Life of Tom O'Folliard." *Potomac Westerners Corral Dust* 6 (May 1961): 9–11, 14.

———. "Sudden Death in Cimarron," *National Association of Outlaw and Lawman Quarterly* 10, no. 4 (Spring 1986): 6–8.

———. "Taking a Closer Look at Cimarron Murders." *National Association of Outlaw and Lawman Quarterly* 3, no. 3 (Winter 1977–78): 8–9.

———. "They Fought for the House." In *Portraits in Gunsmoke,* edited by Jeff Burton, 34–64. London: English Westerners' Society, 1971.

Remley, David. *Bell Ranch: Cattle Ranching in the Southwest, 1824–1947.* Albuquerque: University of New Mexico Press, 1993.

Reynolds, William. *Trouble in New Mexico: The Outlaws, Gunmen, Desperados, Murderers, and Lawmen for Fifty Turbulent Years, the B's.* Bakersfield, Calif.: privately printed, 1994.

Shipman, Jack. "Brief Career of Tom O'Folliard, Billy the Kid's Partner." *Voice of the Mexican Border* 1 (January 1934): 216–19.

Shipman, Mrs. O. L. *Letters Past and Present to My Nephews and Nieces.* N.p., n.d.

Siringo, Charles A. *A Lone Star Cowboy.* Santa Fe: n.p., 1919.

Sonnichsen, C. L. *Tularosa: Last of the Frontier West.* New York: Devin-Adair, 1960.

Stanley, F. *The Grant that Maxwell Bought.* Denver: World Press, 1948.

———. *The White Oaks (New Mexico) Story.* N.p., n.d.

Thrapp, Dan. *Encyclopedia of Frontier Biography.* 3 vols. Spokane, Wash.: Arthur H. Clark, 1990.

Tise, Sammy. *Texas County Sheriffs.* Halletsville, Tex.: privately published, 1989.

United States Army, Military Division of the Missouri. *Record of Engagements with Hostile Indians within the Military Division of the Missouri from 1868 to 1882.* Washington, D.C.: Government Printing Office, 1882.

Utley, Robert M. *High Noon in Lincoln.* Albuquerque: University of New Mexico Press, 1987.

Webb, Dave. "Distinguished Alumnus." In *399 Kansas Characters.* Dodge City: Kansas Heritage Center, 1993.

White, William Allen. *The Autobiography of William Allen White.* Edited by Sally Foreman Griffith. Lawrence: University Press of Kansas, 1990.

Williams, O. W. *Pioneer Surveyor/Frontier Lawyer: The Personal Narrative of Judge O. W. Williams, 1877–1902.* Edited by S. D. Myres. El Paso: Texas Western Press, 1968.

Younger, Cole. *The Story of Cole Younger by Himself.* Chicago: Press of Henneberry, 1903.

INDEX

* 9 7 8 0 8 0 6 1 6 5 0 6 6 *